CALCULATED CHAOS

Institutional Threats to Peace and Human Survival

Butler D. Shaffer

Llumina Press

The author also acknowledges the editing assistance of Paul Bateman.

ABOUT THE AUTHOR

For more than two decades, the author has been both a student and observer of the attitudes and institutional arrangements by which human society functions, with particular emphasis upon the nature and causes of conflict. He received his J.D. from the University of Chicago Law School, and has written articles for scholarly journals, as well as a weekly editorial page column that appears in a number of newspapers across the country. One of his law review articles, "Violence As a Product of Imposed Order," was reprinted in Ken Templeton, ed., *The Politicization of Society,* and he has written a forthcoming book *In Restraint of Trade: Business Attitudes Toward Competition and Regulation, 1918-1938.*

He is presently professor at Southwestern University School of Law in Los Angeles, where he teaches in the SCALE program (Southwestern's Conceptual Approach to Legal Education), which offers an alternative approach to traditional methods of legal education.

DEDICATION

To Dorothy's dog, Toto, whose natural irreverence and skepticism exposed to the awestruck the human purposes at work behind the screen.

TABLE OF CONTENTS

1

OUR

WELL-ORGANIZED

CONFLICTS

Man is born free; and everywhere he is in chains.
—Jean Jacques Rousseau[1]

Should institutionalized society ever experience a decline and fall, its undoing may prove to have been the work *not* of radical anarchists or a modern-day neo-Luddite, neo-Jacobin, neo-populist coalition, but of a small, four-legged folk hero with the unassuming name of "Toto." Most of us became acquainted with Toto as we followed L. Frank Baum's Dorothy on her trip to visit "The Wonderful Wizard of Oz." Along the way, we met those lovable but insecure additions to American folk culture: the Scarecrow, the Tin Woodman, and the Cowardly Lion. We were able to discover something of ourselves in these characters, for each of us had experienced, at one time, some inadequacy of courage, or understanding, or emotional expression.

We also shared with these uncertain pilgrims that uniquely human quality of reverence and awe for institutional authority. With the same unquestioning faith we had in the adults around us, these wayfarers in a world of fantasy set out, undaunted by threats of death and other hardships, to seek the fulfillment of their characters and souls in institutional certification. They knew what each one of us was learning through our school, our church, and our parents, namely, that only in obedience to constituted authority can we transcend our personal inadequacies; that those who possess power can protect us from the menace of witches, falling houses, and wrong turns in the road. But their search—whether for self-perfection or a return to the loving certainty of home—was not without experiencing the manipulation, fear- and guilt-peddling, and other discomforts associated with satisfying institutional expectations.

To Toto fell the task of exposing the humbuggery that manipulated both the institutional machinery and followers. Because he did not share his companions' trembling reverence for established wizardry, this free-spirited, tagalong mutt was able to approach the screen that separated the leaders from the followers. In knocking over that screen, however, Toto did far more than simply reveal the systematic bamboozlement of the Ozians. He also made it possible for his companions to discover that the personal qualities they had labored to earn as institutionally-bestowed rewards, were qualities that had always been within themselves. In believing that the virtues they sought lay *outside* themselves, and that some institutional alchemy could convert their leaden instincts to golden conduct (to paraphrase Herbert Spencer)[2], they had set themselves up to be manipulated and exploited for the benefit of institutional interests.

With the same aweless innocence that energized Toto's curiosity, I propose that we, too, approach some of the sanctified screens that mask the institutional sorcery in our own lives. If we can marshal the courage to ask ourselves uncomfortable questions, we may discover how our systematic, organized behavior has had adverse and often disastrous consequences. We have been taught that institutions are necessary in order to provide for peace, order, and coordination in society; and yet our society is filled with much discord, agony, and violence. We are very much aware that institutions have failed to provide their promised harmony. What is not so familiar to us, however, is the central role institutions have played in actually *generating* the personal and social conflict that permeates our lives.

We are reminded, in so many ways, that our well-organized and highly productive world is not an altogether peaceful or happy one. We are paying an enormous price—in the form of personal conflict—for the benefits we receive from the highly-structured institutional environment in which we live. We could talk about that near constant state of psychological tension, confusion, fear, anger, frustration, guilt, anxiety, self-doubt, and shattered nerves so many of us experience; the drug use and alcoholism; the high suicide rates or other forms of self-abuse; or the emotionally debilitating sense of malaise; all of which seem to be so closely associated with the pressures of our organized society. We could count the guilt-laden human vessels that get beached on psychiatrists' couches; or measure the polluted environment into which continue to be dumped the unprofitable by-products of industrialization; or note the cancers, heart attacks, kidney and nervous disorders, strokes, tension headaches, emphysema, and other ailments which appear to have their origins in the ways we live. We are internally divided and confused. We have fragmented ourselves with conflicting wants and value systems. We distrust our own natures and believe that we must exercise self-control lest the darker side of our personalities emerge. We offset the pursuit of our well-being with notions of altruism, and temper our happiness with feelings of guilt. In the vernacular of pop psychology, we speak of being "self-alienated" people who have learned to reject our very selves. Whatever other advantages flow to us from our institutionalized world, the personal disadvantages carry a prohibitive price tag.

There is an even more significant cost associated with our highly-structured patterns of living. For reasons inextricably related to institutional behavior, conflict and violence have become a way of life for us. Group confrontations have become the norm, and we learn to adjust our social expectations to new thresholds of tolerable violence. Nation wars with nation; religious groups battle in the streets over their theological differences, as the followers of a multitude of "one true Gods" seek converts at the points of automatic rifles, and smite busloads of school aged infidels with plastic explosives; terrorist groups threaten, injure, or slaughter total strangers as "a matter of principle"; corporations compete with one another for shares of markets and for political influence to deprive others of their market advantages, often using the machinery of the State to precipitate millions of human beings into wars designed for no more noble purpose than to advance their economic interests; crime and violence have become synonymous with urban living; environmental, consumer, racial, sexual, political, ethnic, and social groups have made confrontation their ordinary responses to an ever increasing discovery of disputes; labor organizations and employers struggle for the right to manipulate and control employees; women's groups organize to demand their "fundamental human right" to exterminate their own unborn children, while self-styled "moralists" seek to invoke the power of the State to compel adherence to their inspired views; governments threaten and punish their own citizens, and insist upon an ever-growing share of their property and income as tribute; stockholder groups organize to fight the managements of their own corporations; untold numbers of persons compete for the control of governmental machinery in order to have their preferences enforced upon others; ideologies and lifestyles vie for supremacy, as true believers segregate themselves with their respective uniformities of dress, language, and behavior to man the bloodstained barricades of one cause or another; industries flourish, employing hundreds of thousands of persons, whose entire product lines consist of devices for controlling, punishing, or slaughtering people; cities are besieged by rioters, airlines by terrorists, inner-city residents by muggers and gun-happy policemen, bank offices by hostage-takers, politicians and celebrities by assassins, and universities by demonstrators; while some religious leaders have even taken to terrorizing, assaulting, or annihilating their own followers. So bloody have our practices become that, in this century alone, we humans have managed to intentionally kill between 100 and 200 million members of our own species.

It may already be clear that this is not one of those polite pieces of social criticism that only address *symptoms* instead of *causes*, or that talk around the edges of problems while carefully avoiding the sacred ground at the center. It has always been fashionable and safe to maintain that the disorder, corruption, oppression and conflict we associate with formally organized society is the fault of those who control institutions, or of imperfections in organizational design. We take as established truth that war, competition, and crime are natural and inevitable expressions of the human character, but that through effective institutional leadership such conditions can at least be tempered and made sufferable. Human suffering is simply "the way things are," we tell ourselves, and we must do what we can to "make the best" of our sorry human condition. We delude ourselves with beliefs that the established order suffers only from policy or style defects, and that new leadership or new legislation or organizational reforms are sufficient to overcome any problems. We can *tinker* with the machinery, but dare not think of doing without it. We may be willing to believe that the *emperor* is naked, but certainly not the *empire* itself. We accept the institutional scheme of things without much question, and regard the resulting confusion as only a temporary failure to fine-tune the machinery to prevent "excesses" and "abuses."

By contrast, I propose that we be so bold as to enter the institutional holy of holies buried deep within our minds; that we explore the consecrated burial grounds that contain the fossilized bones of our ancestral social premises. If we are to understand the causes of social conflict in time to reverse the practices that threaten the destruction of us all, we must be prepared to ask ourselves the uncomfortable questions that challenge many of our basic assumptions. In so doing, we will discover that our major social problems are not the fault of malevolent, greedy, or shortsighted leaders, but are inherent in institutions themselves.

Briefly stated, the basic theme of this book is that *institutions are the principal means by which conflict is produced and managed in society. Peace is incompatible with institutional activity.* Stated another way, *the success of institutions depends upon the creation of those conditions in which personal and social conflict will flourish.* We experience so much conflict in our lives because we have permitted ourselves to be organized into self-perpetuating, self-justifying organizations with which we have identified our personalities and to whom we look for direction. We have allowed our lives to be taken over and monopolized by a variety of political, religious, educational, economic, and social agencies over which we have little, if any, influence. These entities have helped us construct the barriers that not only restrain *us*, but keep us separated from one another and serve as the boundary lines for the intergroup struggles of which we are a part. Through these groupings, we have helped to institutionalize conflict, to make it a seemingly permanent and necessary feature of human society. Such conflict has not resulted from mere accident or inadvertence, nor has it been the product of vicious or depraved minds. Rather, for reasons to be developed herein, conflict is a condition upon which the health and well-being of institutions is absolutely dependent. We have made an industry of human suffering and violence, the members of which have been institutions under the management of generally good and well-intentioned people. Through a variety of forms, we have put together very sophisticated organizational machinery for human manipulation, control, and inflicted pain.

We have systematized conflict and discontent, have spilled the blood of hundreds of millions of our fellows, and tortured and oppressed hundreds of millions more. We have formalized practices that violate even our most relaxed standards of decent and responsible human conduct, and have loosed upon human society a nearly universal spirit of fear, distrust, and animosity toward one another.

Every institution is a racket. Whether we are considering political, religious, economic, ideological, or educational institutions, each is a formal, elaborate system designed for one purpose: *to control people.* Each seeks to persuade or compel individuals to divert their energies from the pursuit of private, personal objectives, and to dedicate themselves to organizational purposes.

A major contributing factor to the conflict, misery, and disorder existing among people throughout the world has been our willingness to allow institutions to dominate our lives, to control and direct almost every facet of human activity, including our relationships with other people. We live our lives in unquestioning subservience to the demands of institutions, allowing them to preempt our own purposes and decision making in favor of their self-serving priorities. We have, far more than we care to admit, turned ourselves into emotional cripples who are so grateful to those who have provided us with the crutches that help us to maintain our dependency. We have made ourselves weak in order that institutions may become powerful; we have been willing to doubt and deny ourselves, but express increased faith in our leaders; we have denigrated ourselves as we have aggrandized the power and the glory of the State, the Church, or some other organized racket. We have suspended the reality of our own lives, preferring to believe that meaning and purpose, as well as security, is only to be found in those agencies for whom we have trained ourselves to be dependent. We have, like the person who has suffered from pain all of his life, come to believe that no other way of living is possible. It may prove to be the fate of all of us to suffer the ultimate, destructive consequences of our undoubting faith in institutionalized authority.

What I have said thus far should not be taken as a denial of the benefits we all derive from organized activity. Each of us is an individual, but we are also social beings with needs to associate with one another and to organize to accomplish mutually beneficial objectives. Though many of us have, at some time, dreamed of retreating to a personal hermitage, few of us could manage without some form of human contact. We are born into and become part of a family, we live in neighborhoods, enjoy play groups, benefit from divisions of labor that permit us to produce and exchange with one another, and help one another in times of need. It is our nature to live in society, to cooperate with and assist one another, to love and comfort one another, to communicate and share our experiences with one another: in short, to realize with one another the full meaning of being human. Though our egoistic minds prefer to think of ourselves as separate and distinct individuals, in truth we share a common biological, emotional, and intellectual makeup. There is even abundant evidence for the presence of a collective unconscious that provides our subconscious minds with a great deal of inherent knowledge, the content of which transcends all races and cultures and is independent of our individual experiences.

Without some degree of organization, then, neither you nor I would have survived: newborn infants are not renowned for their self-sufficiency. Our daily lives are better *because* we have learned to cooperate with one another. Even the allegedly self-sufficient Thoreau depended on others to produce the paper on which he wrote, the tools with which he worked, and the clothes he wore. Isolating ourselves from others in an effort to go it alone would deprive us of tremendous social and material benefits. For these reasons, human beings—from the most primitive to the most industrialized—have been characterized by social organization. Part of the explanation for our easy seduction by institutions is, no doubt, that we have believed they would help us satisfy our social needs. Our problem—if we wish to put an end to the organized turmoil and violence in our lives—is *not* how to dismantle all forms of social organization and learn to live in self-sufficient seclusion from one another, but how to live and work together without those institutionalized systems that foster conflict.

Since the word "institution" has a variety of usages, I must tell you how I will be using it. By "institution," I mean to refer to *any permanent social organization with purposes of its own, having formalized and structured machinery for pursuing those purposes, and making and enforcing rules of conduct in order to control those within it.* An institution is an independent, self-justifying, self-perpetuating organization that is, for all practical purposes, no longer accountable to nor under the control of its members. The verb "to institutionalize" has particular meaning for our efforts to understand the impact of organizational behavior upon our lives. Dictionaries often refer to persons learning to "adapt" to the expectations of particular institutions. One offers a definition of "institutionalize" as it relates to the legal confinement of individuals: "to accustom (a person) so firmly to the care and supervised routine of an institution as to make incapable of managing a life outside."[3] How appropriate for our inquiry. Perhaps there is an intuitive understanding of the nature of all institutions that underlies the popular usage of that verb as an involuntary commitment of an individual to a prison or mental facility, within which that person will be subject to the absolute authority of others.

As we can see, not all forms of organized human activity fall within this definition of an institution. There is a major distinction between *institutional* and *noninstitutional* forms of organization. The essence of that distinction has to do with the relationship between the organization and those of us who comprise it. In *noninstitutional* systems, the organization tends to be little more than a convenience, an informal tool of cooperation that helps each one of us to further our interests through the group. The organization has no independent purposes of its own, but represents only the composite of our personal objectives. The *organization* does not control *us*, for there is no division of purpose—and thus, no conflict—between personal and group purposes. The group is but a reflection of the interests of those within it: it has no independent identity or other organizational interests that could preempt our own. If the group has any leadership, it tends to be temporary and informal: the leaders do not set themselves or their purposes apart from the others, or perceive their functions as being policymakers or supervisors over the rest of the group. Such leaders are more likely to function as "player coaches," to borrow a phrase from team sports, than as manipulative, threatening, behavior controlling authorities.

In *institutionalized* systems, however, such harmony does not prevail. The institution is an organization that has taken on a purpose of its own, a purpose set apart from and superior to those of the individuals who comprise the organization. An institution is a permanent entity, with its own internal goals and interests, its own separate identity, and a leadership that differentiates itself from those who make up the organization. With individual and group interests thus divided, the institution must now endeavor to control those within it. The leaders—who have identified their interests with the institution—regard their functions as being to manipulate, threaten, induce, or coerce the group members into subordinating their personal interests and promoting organizational purposes. There is an energy force within any institution that helps to mold the behavior of people, including its leaders, channeling all that energy in the direction of satisfying the separate and transcendent interests of the institution itself.

Before offering examples of these differing organizational types, the reader is cautioned against attaching importance to being able to accurately label a given organization as "institutional" or "noninstitutional." Labeling is a poor substitute for understanding. Rather than looking for absolutes, it is far more important to become sensitive to the distinctive features and practices of each type of organization in order to become aware of the structuring and institutionalizing *tendencies* within most organizations. That informal groups may contain certain institutional features (and vice versa) is not to be denied. As we shall discover in subsequent chapters, the changes that transform a member-oriented group into an organizationally-centered institution are gradual. All that really matters is that one become aware of the significance of subtle and gradual transformations; to learn to read between the lines of resolutions and memos; to note the increase in organizational rules and their impact upon one's autonomy and purposes, as well as the emergence of organizational hierarchies and the increased importance of the organizational entity itself. One must learn to observe the increasing distinctions between the roles and authority of organizational leaders and others within the group, with decision making increasingly centralized; and to be sensitive to the increased importance attached to obedience, protocol, bureaucratic procedures, and the "greater good" of the group.

Some examples may help to clarify this distinction. Most families, for instance, would be described as noninstitutional organizations. I recall no more clearly enunciated purposes my wife and I had in getting married than to live together and raise children. The promises and responsibilities we undertook were to *each other* as a way of furthering our mutual interests. We did *not* marry for the purpose of creating some detached entity called a "family," for whose greater purposes we were promising to sacrifice our personal happiness and well-being. Each of us understood, at least implicitly, that if either of us became dissatisfied with the arrangement we could secure a divorce and put an end to what we had created. Even when our children were born, we thought of our family relationships as being supportive of one another. We have not looked upon our children as family resources to be employed, at our direction, in satisfaction of the interests of the family superorganism. On the contrary, we have regarded our function as being to help our children learn to be self-controlling, self-responsible people who could *leave* our family upon reaching adulthood and go out to pursue their own interests in life.

Contrast this with the highly institutionalized royal families of monarchical nations, or their American counterparts in families of long-established wealth. Such families—often referred to as "houses"—enjoy perpetual existences that go beyond the lives of their individual members. They are, in fact, virtually indistinguishable from large, corporate entities. Status and authority (over both family assets and members) are usually inherited; family members develop identities inseparable from the family name; children are expected to assume particular roles on behalf of the family entity, expectations that might even include—as Edward VIII of England discovered—subordinating one's personal preferences for a mate to the greater interests of the family itself. One may, in fact, find oneself labeled a "black sheep" and cut off from family ties by imprudent acts or attitudes that prove embarrassing to the family hierarchy.

Or contrast a small, family owned grocery store and the large chains operating in most states. The grocery stores with which my parents did business when I was a child were small operations that were virtually synonymous with the grocers who owned and ran them. The grocers and the clerks working at these stores were close acquaintances of ours, many of whose names I still recall. They knew us and we knew them as individuals, and we took a genuine interest in one another's joys and sorrows. The butchers knew how we liked meat cut without asking; the men who worked in the produce department would put aside fruits or vegetables that met our tastes. I ran into a man who had been a checkout clerk at one of these stores and, even though it had been some twenty years since I had shopped there, he and I were able to pick up the same personal tone of conversation I had known in my youth. To this day, I feel a greater closeness to this man than I do the faceless and interchangeable clerks and store managers who work at the neighborhood chain grocery where I have regularly shopped for the past five years.

Or compare the small partnerships engaged in the practice of law or medicine, with the large metropolitan law firms or clinics employing hundreds of lawyers or doctors. In the small organization, each member is accustomed to having personal and direct dealings both with one another and the clients and patients for whom they work. The organization is probably too small to afford the luxury of a full-time managing partner, meaning that each member is directly involved in doing the work of the group. The larger organization, on the other hand, is characterized by hierarchies of status and authority, as well as managing partners or other supervisory officials whose job is to direct and oversee the work of others within the organization. Contacts among group members tend to diminish as the size of the organization increases. Unlike the smaller organizations, the individual members of larger organizations tend to be interchangeable; with one's job title often having greater significance than one's character or other personal attributes. The depersonalized, group-oriented nature of such firms was reflected in an incident involving two men who saw each other periodically in the same New York City office building. One man finally turned to the other, noting that he had seen him frequently on the elevators, and asked for whom he worked. As it turned out, both men were attorneys employed in the same law firm.

We could also distinguish a traditional family farming operation from that conducted by subsidiaries of large industrial corporations, or a Wednesday night league-bowling team from a major league baseball team. In the small organizations, the purposes of the group are indistinguishable from the personal interests of the group members, while in the larger and more established groups the *organization* itself *is its own reason for being*: the members are looked upon as little more than employees hired to serve the group's interests.

Labor organizations provide further contrast between the two types of systems. A group of employees might join together for the common purpose of bargaining with their employer for better wages or working conditions, or to promote educational, recreational, or other social activities, or to provide insurance or funeral benefits for one another. Such associations have existed since the early days of the industrial revolution. As long as these groups are under the control of and responsive to the needs of the members they were designed to serve—instead of being dominated by international union officials—they could be characterized as noninstitutional organizations.

Contrast such a member-oriented association with the modern-day labor union with headquarters in such distant and power-centered places as Washington, D.C.—which reflects an institutional perception of where its interests lie—and often under the lifetime control and domination of leaders whose salaries range well into six figures. Most labor unions can scarcely be considered as member-controlled and member-oriented organizations. Far too often, in fact, members who have tried to assert any influence within the union contrary to that of the established leadership have met with threats, violence, and sometimes death itself. The modern labor union and its leadership has a purpose of its own, and its members are subject to regimentation, manipulation, and threat of discipline to compel their obedience and subordination.

Or consider the distinction between the more informal, unstructured systems of learning, and the overly-administered, overly-bureaucratized public school, college, and university systems that exist today. There was a time when school was little more than a setting in which scholars contracted with students to teach them a particular field of study. The administration of such schools had very limited supporting roles, often referred to in terms of "keeping the snow off the sidewalks." Even the word "principal" referred to the role of "principal *teacher*" in a school, *not* to certified career administrators. The emphasis was upon the learning relationship existing between the student and the teacher, and the school was generally small enough to permit a very personal involvement with each student. When my wife was a student at a small college in the mid-1950's, for instance, she received her grades from the college handwritten, often with personal comments written in by the registrar. This is contrasted by the impersonal, computerized grades one's social security number receives from colleges and universities today.

Today, however, schools, colleges, and universities have become top-heavy with administrators, to the detriment of both faculty and students and the learning that is any school's announced *raison d'etre*. One can go into the recent history of most schools, from primary through college and graduate schools, and discover that the rate of increase of administrators has far outstripped that of both students and faculty. A typical example of this occurred while I was teaching at a midwestern university. When I joined the faculty, our college had a dean and one secretary. One year later, the college had acquired a new dean, along with three associate deans, an assistant to the dean, and approximately four secretaries. This administrative explosion came about even though the size of the faculty remained substantially the same, and the number of students in the college had actually decreased.

This ever-expanding nature of institutions should be familiar to us all. Parkinson told us enough about organizational proliferation to permit us to observe how increasing the number of administrators in any organization leads to an increase in things to administer (i.e., rules, regulations, record keeping, new procedures for doing things, and systems to monitor and enforce compliance with all of this). In colleges and universities, for example, faculty and students alike begin to focus more of their energies upon organizational politics. Learning is preempted by such administrative priorities as uniform examination and grading standards, accreditation reports, the recording and enforcement of attendance, grant proposals for projects designed principally to channel more money into the institution, student evaluation forms, disciplinary due process, admissions criteria, cumulative grade point averages, tenure and promotion guidelines, student honor code violations, and campus parking. Is it so surprising to discover many thoughtful students and faculty members alike abandoning the structured environment of academia?

As I have already suggested, it is not my purpose to suggest dismantling all forms of social organization. Such an alternative could only be premised upon the assumption that there is an inherent antagonism between the interests of the *individual* and the *group*. While institutional success has been achieved through the suppression and exploitation of individuals, human sacrifice is not an inherent feature of all forms of social organization. To believe that we must choose between ego-centered individualism and selfless collectivism is to express the depth of our self-alienation: the former denies our needs for social cooperation and belonging, just as the latter squeezes out our personality and reduces us to part of an undifferentiated pulp. If we could see clearly, we would understand that we are neither the rugged individualist nor the self-effacing servant of the institutional ant hill, and that any group action against the individual cannibalizes the group itself.

My purpose, rather, is to examine the nature of organizational behavior in order to distinguish those member-oriented and member-controlled organizations (which afford mutual benefits and pose little or no threat to the autonomy of the members themselves) from those institutional forms whose objectives interfere with personal purposes and generate conflict in society. If we are to overcome our present preoccupation with conflict and learn to discover a personal and organized order that is natural to us as human beings, one that does not put us into a state of war with ourselves and one another, we must begin with an unclouded view of our present condition. I *am* suggesting that the explanations for our dilemma of social disorder are to be found in the institutional arrangements by which we have chosen, or consented, to live our lives, and that we can rediscover social peace and harmony by abandoning our dependence upon and subservience to institutions and moving toward unstructured forms of association. It is the *very existence* of *all* institutions, not the abuses of *some*, that underlies social conflict and disorder. To suggest the reform of institutional methods is to legitimize the anti-social and inhumane premises upon which they are founded. One cannot make slavery more humane, nor war more peaceable, nor tyranny more benevolent. To paraphrase the late Frank Chodorov, such reforms amount to little more than "wanting to clean up the whorehouse, but keeping the business intact."[4]

In a world increasingly characterized by organized conflict, the case for institutions can no longer simply be assumed. The consequences to human beings of an institutionalized, hierarchically-structured world have been disastrous. If we are truly interested in the quality of life upon this earth, we must be thoughtful and mature enough to face the discomforting truths that will foster a better understanding of our condition. To do so requires a clear and unprejudiced mind, a mind that is free from conditioning, a mind that does not require assurances that its herd of sacred cows will be sheltered during the inquiry.

This book is not intended only as a polemic against institutions. Neither is it designed as a blueprint suggesting how you ought to live your own life. The emphasis throughout will be upon our personal involvement with and contributions to human conflict. Though it may be less disturbing to our egos to look to others as the causes of our problems, the crisis of conflict faced by mankind demands a more mature response from each of us. There is simply too much at stake to permit us to continue ignoring our responsibilities for what we have become. My criticisms of institutional behavior, therefore, are made *not* for the purpose of pointing fingers at others, but to try to understand ourselves. Institutions maintain power over our lives only because we have allowed ourselves to become dependent upon their authority. It is not *institutions* we must confront if we are to end the conflict and disorder in our lives, but our own *dependencies.* We can put an end to our dependent state of mind only by taking responsibility for our own thoughts, decisions, and actions. The conflict, violence, and chaos of this world has *not* been caused by "them," but by *us,* by *you* and *me.* Trying to understand the nature of and reasons for our attachments to institutions, and the disruptive consequences thereof, is the purpose of this literary journey. It is undertaken with a sense of humility by one who, like Dorothy and her friends, has spent a good deal of time trudging the roads that lead only to hallowed temples, when all that any of us really wanted was to find our way home.

2

ON GETTING
ORGANIZED

"The fault, dear Brutus, is not in our stars,
But in ourselves, that we are underlings."
    —From *Julius Caesar*
    by William Shakespeare[1]

Popular sayings often have a way of mirroring our implicit understanding of reality. In folk wisdom and other vernacular expressions, our subconscious minds may be providing us with answers to questions our conscious minds are afraid to ask. I have noticed, in the bumper sticker and office poster philosophy that has permeated our society in recent years, what appears to be a gnawing disenchantment with organized behavior. Without too much risk of being accused of projecting my own impressions onto others, I have sensed a growing popular alienation from political processes; a dissatisfaction associated with one's work environment; an increased awareness of the insensitivity and unapproachable nature of established organizations; and an antagonism toward commercial advertising, bureaucratization, and computerized communication. The words "in structured chaos," spray painted on the side of a California Highway Patrol building by an anonymous social critic, revealed to me an increased public understanding of the adverse consequences of overindulging in institutional practices.

One of the deadliest habits we have gotten ourselves into is that of permitting our lives and our relationships with other people to become structured and controlled by various institutions. Just as the inhabitants of an ancient city-state were unable to conceive of life without the ministrations of their resident king and his cabinet-level temple priests, so too, most of us have developed an unshakeable belief in the necessity for political, religious, economic, educational, ideological, and other social institutions to direct and coordinate our behavior. There is scarcely a facet of our daily lives that has not been consumed by established authorities. We are born in hospitals, educated in schools, married in churches, employed in business establishments or government agencies, supervised by political authorities, retired with institutional pension plans and government security benefits, and we return to the hospitals to die.

As soon as we have drawn our first breath of life, we begin to get pulled into the institutional scheme of things. We receive a birth certificate, a document of no useful purpose to *us*, but necessary to inform institutions of the arrival of a new conscript. The birth certificate, which literally "certifies" our existence in an institutionalized world, locks us into the system of compulsory education, and is a requirement for our registering to vote, getting a marriage or driver's license or a passport, or for receiving other institutional "services." The birth certificate is also a prerequisite for getting registered with the social security system which, as anyone who has ever worked for someone else has discovered, is a requirement for getting a job.

Our birth certificate, social security number, and school records also lock us into the military draft system. The military and state motor vehicle departments fingerprint us, and this information, along with our driver's license and other data, ties us into the police system.

Our prospective employer will insist on seeing our military discharge papers as well as our school records, both of which reflect the degree of our institutional conditioning. The record we develop with our employer (including our social security number) pulls us into the taxing system. In order to gratify the taxing authorities, banks, investment houses, insurance companies, and other firms demand the identity of our social security number.

Registering to vote brings us into the system of compulsory jury duty, and as we get older we find that we must have a social security number in order to get medical treatment, and must agree to be covered by Medicare in order to purchase our own health insurance. We also discover that we cannot cash a check without a driver's license, that we must display our draft registration card upon demand by State authorities, and that something called a "credit rating" is distilled out of our financial records with various institutions.

We also learn that the political State is making efforts to "simplify" all of this by combining our institutional histories into computers and dossiers under the control of some secretive group known as "the intelligence community." Greater "efficiency" was no doubt the motive, as well, of the federal government official who, in the early 1960's, offered the chilling proposal that the federal government require each newborn infant to have its social security number tattooed on the sole of one of its feet. The Orwellian implications of this proposal become all the more disturbing when one considers that the same practice is now in vogue as a way for people to mark and identify *their own* property. Meanwhile, in a display of bipartisan support for a greater degree of police control over people, a number of Republican and Democratic politicians have advocated the creation of a national identification card, or "domestic passport," to be carried at all times by every American.

We can see, if we look closely, intricate patterns of institutionalization in our daily lives. We arise in the morning and prepare ourselves for a day of work within our employer's place of business. We conduct ourselves—including when we come and go, our style of dress, the content and manner of our speaking—in ways that conform to organizational expectations. Institutionalized news services, broadcasters, and publishers advise us of the information that business and governmental authorities believe we should have for the day. We drive to work along government-maintained and policed streets and highways, being careful to abide by State-established rules.

Meanwhile, our children are preparing themselves for their day in an educational establishment. We pressure them, as we do ourselves, to arrive on time and avoid any official stigma of tardiness. How early we learn to meet institutional expectations! We help teach our children to be obedient and "responsible," by which we mean for them to so internalize such expectations as to be able to compliantly respond without having to wait to be told to do so.

For the better part of each day, we (including our children) work within our respective organizational confines, meeting the deadlines and complying with the directives of our constituted authorities, and working to advance institutional purposes. At the end of our work day, we reverse the process, return home to again be informed of news important to institutional interests, then rest in order to renew our energies for yet another day of routinized work.

We purchase a house, car, food, clothing, electricity, entertainment, and most of the other goods and services we are expected to consume, from institutional sources. Like domesticated pets, we have made ourselves so dependent upon our masters for our basic provisions in life, that we would probably be unable to survive on our own. We conduct our business through banking establishments and communicate with friends, relatives, and business associates through telephone companies and the government postal system. We spend a portion of our spare time (i.e., time that our employer or the State has not otherwise preempted) working on behalf of religious or charitable organizations, political candidates or issues, or in some highly-structured form of recreation. Insurance companies and the political State endeavor to secure us against life's continuing hardships, even unto the grave, while religious institutions promise that, if we do as we are told, our *next* life will contain the happiness and serenity we are unable to find in *this* one!

The illustrations could continue. The point to be made, however, is that most of us are almost totally institutionalized people, living out our lives in furtherance of organizational objectives, and in accordance with the demands, expectations, ideas, values, opinions, tastes, and standards of conduct ordained by established officials. We are locked into an elaborate institutional network of interconnected registrations, certifications, licensings, reports, surveys, and other documented and computerized information. Government and corporate computers track our behavior, recording our correspondence and telephone calls; credit card purchases; reading and driving habits; bank transactions; psychological test results; school, work, family, and medical histories; and our religious, charitable, ideological, and political preferences. We work, shop, travel, play, bank, and become hospitalized under the ever-present electronic eyes and ears of institutional Big Brothers. Space satellites containing powerful telescopes, cameras, and heat sensors, are capable of detailed monitoring of virtually any location on the earth's surface. We are, far more than most of us are aware, little more than empty reflections of the institutions that have combined to shape and direct our lives. Most of us have become numbered parts in giant machines over which we have virtually no influence, but which integrate our energies and use us in furtherance of their ambitions.

We have made ourselves, in the literal sense of the word, *institutional* people: well-programmed servomechanisms whose points of reference are almost totally organizational in nature. Political and business institutions, schools and churches, and ideologies have impressed themselves upon our personalities. We have sworn ourselves a Boy Scout oath of allegiance to organizational purposes, and have sought to develop those character traits that reflect the internalization of their values. We have made ourselves "obedient and loyal" to governments, "trustworthy and diligent" to businesses, "punctual and scholarly" to schools, "faithful and self-denying" to churches, and "moral and rational" to ideological systems. The greater part of our lives is spent in service to external authorities. Our principal purpose for being has been to participate in the achievement of organizational objectives; our glory lies in dedicating ourselves to the glory of the State, the Church, our employer, or a cause. We take our subservience to institutions as a matter of unexamined faith, having accepted, without much inquiry, the agreed-upon lies and shibboleths that provide the foundation for their authority. We not only acknowledge the propriety of having institutions place fences around us, we believe that it is right and proper that we confine ourselves to our designated compounds.

To say that we have accepted for ourselves little more than the status of institutionally-serving machines would hardly be an exaggeration. Even our language reflects this reductionist mentality. We speak of getting "warmed up" for a job, and of "running out of gas" or being "worn-out" or "run-down" after prolonged exertion. We get "keyed up" for a particular task. Our emotions are passively "turned on" or "turned off" by others, and if we should get "overheated" we are likely to "blow a fuse" or a "gasket" or experience "burnout" unless, of course, we have been able to "let off steam" to relieve our "pressure." If things do not go right for us, we speak of having our "wires crossed," or a "screw loose," and of the need to get ourselves "in gear." We "blow our tops," "go to pieces," "fall apart at the seams," or become "unhinged." We may, in order to prevent a "breakdown," go out to a nightclub to "get oiled" or take drugs to "get fixed." We are more likely to observe that our minds are like computers than we are to state that computers are like our minds. We even consent to have ourselves regarded as national "resources" or "assets" to the community; to be a "big wheel" or "kingpin" in our place of employment.

We regard our body's physical or emotional cries for help as a weakness on our part, a failure to adjust. Not unlike the man who broke his car's temperature gauge in order to avoid the knowledge that the engine was overheating, we try to pacify or deaden our bodily warning signs with tranquilizers, painkillers, drugs, or alcohol. Failing in this, we turn to what we hope are more permanent forms of psychic adjustment: biofeedback, psychiatric therapy, or the counselors brought in by our employer to provide workshops to help us learn not to *eliminate* stress (an approach that would call into question our institutional commitments) but to *live* with it so that we can, like an older model car, get more institutionally-serving mileage out of our own bodies. We are also accustomed, in this age of advanced medical technology, to look upon our various bodily organs as expendable, replaceable "parts," not unlike the air filters, spark plugs, and fuel lines we so routinely replace in our automobiles. Now we are told that innovations in genetics may even permit us to produce not only custom-made children, but duplicates of our own selves. Imagine! An endless supply of Xeroxed people, ready to take the places of those who, at increasing rates, are being consumed by the ever-more-demanding appetites of organizational machinery. As Marshall McLuhan has stated, by embracing institutional systems "we relate to them as servomechanisms."[2] But we are paying a very dear price for our subservience.

Why have we become as we are? We may be tempted to conclude that we were *forced* into organizational servitude, that we had no choice in the matter. Such, however, is not the case. It is the innocence of our minds, not coercive power, that constrains us. We have allowed ourselves to believe that it is inappropriate to question the fundamental purposes or the legitimacy of institutions. We don't really want to know how, in fact, the Constitution came to be imposed upon the American people: we prefer the comfort of the delusion that it was accomplished, somehow or another, by the common will of everybody. We prefer mouthing our well-recited bromides about how "we, the people" run the government, than confronting the hard truth that institutions are beyond the control of individual persons. In spite of the rhetoric of popular sovereignty associated with democratic government, *we* do not control the machinery of the *State: it* seeks to control *us*. Those who doubt this are invited to stop in at the local Post Office and arrange to have the windows kept open until six o'clock, or pay a visit to a state or federal tax collecting agency to inform them of their decision to pay a reduced amount of taxes. Those who believe the high school civics class rhetoric that political authority rests with "the people," are encouraged to walk into a government office, or police station, or courthouse, or legislative chamber, or military installation, and begin issuing directives to their alleged servants. They will very quickly discover just who "the people" are who *do* exercise political authority! Believing in popular sovereignty is not unlike a pen of steers believing that the slaughterhouse was erected for their benefit, and that the butchers are there to serve them.

This lack of personal control applies to other institutions as well. What student has any control over *what* will be taught in the classroom, or *how* and *when*? What parishoner can direct the church hierarchy or change its policies? Neither individual customers, employees, nor investors have much influence in corporate decision-making. The individual investor who is bold enough to take his or her five shares to a stockholders meeting and actually propose a resolution is often treated as something akin to a village idiot by the corporate management. Even if such a resolution gets voted upon, this stockholder will discover that the effective voting power of most major corporate institutions is held by *other* institutions: banks, insurance companies, universities, foundations, mutual funds, union pension plans, and churches. Institutions tend to be owned and controlled either by *themselves* or by *one another, not* by individual persons. Our formally organized world consists of a mutually-supportive, symbiotic network of institutions arrayed, like the computer Hal in the movie *2001: A Space Odyssey*, in opposition to and controlling the very persons they were theoretically designed to serve. In a world *of* machines, *by* machines, and *for* machines, it is not so amazing that the interests of human beings would occupy a secondary position.

Even the titular heads of most institutions lack decision-making autonomy. Institutional leadership is bestowed upon those who, over the years, have reflected an institutional point of view. Persons who are not organization people are weeded out in the process but, of equal significance, even those who reach the top of the organizational pyramid are subject to removal should they cease to reflect the institutional *weltanschauung*. There is a life-force within every institution that transcends the lives of those within it. As Richard Nixon will confirm, even the commander in chief of the most powerful political institution on earth is subject to this impersonal force. My oldest daughter discovered this truth when she and two of her classmates tried to get an incompetent teacher replaced by one who was more intellectually stimulating. They began with their own school administrators and worked their way up to a meeting with the superintendent of schools and a school board member. While all of these school officials professed—quite sincerely, I believe—both an awareness of the problem and a desire to correct it, they admitted to an inability to do anything about it. My daughter, unable to understand how the top official of the school system was powerless to replace an incompetent teacher, kept asking: "what *can* be done?" "Nothing," she was told.

As we shall discover in subsequent chapters, patterns of institutional domination of people are to be found in virtually every area of human activity. However much we may delude ourselves with beliefs that institutions are essential to our well-being and responsive to our wishes, there is no denying the fact that such systems exert power and authority over all of us in order to get us to conform our behavior to their expectations. What begins as a simple *division of labor,* a system of specialization designed to allow the work of the group to get done more efficiently, becomes a *division of purpose,* with group members segregated into a chain of command. When this takes place, the organization is no longer a tool serving its members: the members have become conscripts in service to the organization. Conscripts though we have become, however, there is no denying the fact that our involvement in institutional activity has been that of willing participants, not innocent victims. An informal organization can become a formal institution only if we are willing to allow the organization to become an entity, and to interject its purposes into the group.

At this point, of course, one might respond: "so what?" After all, do institutions not provide us with all kinds of benefits? Have we not achieved the highest standard of living in the world? Do we not enjoy our air-conditioned-home-with-swimming-pool, Mercedes-Benz-with-leather-up-holstering, beach-house-at-Newport-with-the-sailboat lifestyle, and would any of this be possible without institutions? Have we not been well-paid for our vassalage?

We are, to be sure, the most materially-productive, "secure," and comfortable people ever to have lived on this planet. We have developed intellectual processes that allow us to stockpile knowledge at exponential rates of increase. We have produced a technology that spans the earth and gropes its way into the universe, a technology that has provided us with a minimally-acceptable standard of living far beyond the powers of the most despotic of medieval monarchs to command. We have highly-sophisticated health and drug industries to cater to our most trifling of symptoms. We have discovered many of the best-kept secrets of life itself, and now fashion ourselves the engineers of our own future evolutionary development. We enjoy so much leisure time that we have spawned entertainment industries whose earnings surpass the gross national products of entire nations. We enjoy split second communication with nearly any location on earth as well as various parts of our own solar system, and are privileged to witness, electronically, the live march of history through our living rooms. We have even taken to advertising ourselves to the rest of the universe, and contemplate the technology for exporting the wonders of our world to other parts of our solar system and beyond. We are, or so we like to believe, the healthiest and wealthiest; the most educated; the best informed; the best clothed and fed; the most analyzed, tested, and counseled; the most mobile; the most sophisticated and progressive; the most entertained; the most comfortable; the most self-pampered people in history, . . . and we assert the maintenance of these conditions as among our most "basic human rights." We are aglow with narcissistic pride at the capacity of our civilization to master nature itself and to subject it to our collective will. We reflect upon the conditions of our ancestors, as well as those we choose to call the "less-civilized" peoples of the world, and consider ourselves clever for having had the foresight to be born at this place and this time into such an intelligently-planned and well-ordered society.

Having a materialistic outlook, it is not at all surprising that we have been disposed to look upon the *benefits* we derive

from our institutionalization. But what about the *costs*? Not
just those narrow, quantifiable material costs that so engage
the attentions of institutional leaders, but those *personal* and
social costs that erode human dignity and autonomy; costs that
can only be felt by *people*, not by organizational systems; costs
that nevertheless affect what we refer to as "the quality of
human life." What about the costs, whether measured in
terms of lives or the physical and psychological suffering,
occasioned by wars; environmental pollution; group confrontation; incarceration in prisons, concentration camps,
and mental hospitals; the destruction of neighborhoods and
communities; and the increasing formalization of mandatory
and injunctive human relationships? It should be evident that
we humans continue to absorb a tremendous amount of
contrived misery; that we are, indeed, inhabitants of a world
of calculated chaos.

The personal and social conflict that permeates our lives is
made all the more unbearable for us because it contravenes
our expectations. We intuit that such disorder is not natural
to us. We are, as has been said, social beings with needs for
cooperation and closeness to others, and yet there is little
denying the fact that our social life has lost the sense of
community, of belonging, it once enjoyed. We are, as David
Riesman has so aptly put it, members of a "lonely crowd."[3]
Our neighbors are strangers who only happen to live near us,
and from whom we are quick to isolate ourselves. Though
we live in proximity to millions, we are close to very few.
We have cast ourselves adrift from others, and become little
more than a confederation of separate islands, fearful and
distrusting of one another's purposes and intentions. We deal
with one another at arm's length, maintaining the anonymity
of our true selves. We communicate little of substance to one
another, preferring the safety and security of meaningless
bromides to the expression of thoughts and feelings that
might reveal ourselves and upset the social detente that is

based upon our mutual agreement to appear to be other than who we are. Our social cement, in other words, is very tacky, the consequences of which are revealed to us in the social decay that has accompanied our increased institution-alization. We have become increasingly lonely, frightened, and unhappy human beings able to identify, to one degree or another, with the lament of Housman: "a stranger and afraid, in a world I never made."[4]

Most of us have grown up with the ethic that education, good motives, reason, and hard work would combine to assure our future well-being. Yet, we now experience uncertainty as one of the few constants in the world about us. We were taught to make sacrifices—of our lives if need be—in order to ensure our children a world at peace, but in our world of increasing prosperity, peace has become a scarce commodity, and *our* children are now told to make sacrifices. We find ourselves living in a society that dotes on the pursuit of pleasure, but few people appear to be truly happy. We demand an ever-growing cushion of security, but our lives are filled with much tension and fear. We have increased opportunities for learning, but we seem to understand less and less.

If we are to understand the nature of our present condition, we must resist any temptation to polarize institutions as the villains and individuals as the innocent victims of some social melodrama. While institutions provide the machinery and the impetus for organizing and directing conflict, we—you and I—are the ones who *cause* conflict as a result of the attitudes we have developed about ourselves and other people. Because of our attitudes, we have learned to live contrary to our natures, and to create within ourselves a sense of conflict, contradiction, and confusion which we have projected onto our social world with disastrous consequences. Institutions do not generate conflict wholly on their own. Rather, they have socialized—or nationalized—the private, internal conflicts we have within ourselves. Nation-States may declare the wars, but we are the ones who show up to fight them in order to relieve ourselves of the anger we have developed against some other group of people. Of course, institutions work to *encourage* this sense of conflict within us in order to promote their divisive interests. But this internal conflict can develop only with our active participation. If we feel a sense of conflict—whether we have generated it on our own, or adopted the quarrels suggested to us by others—we must regard ourselves as the fomentors. It is true, of course, that institutions flourish only because we believe in them, and that we do believe in their necessity because they have taught us to do so. Still, if we manage to get ourselves embroiled in institutional disputes, it is because *we* have chosen to embrace institutions and to make *their* quarrels and controversies our own.

3

RALLYING OUR EGOS 'ROUND THE FLAG

Once there was a man who said,
"Range me all men of the world in rows."
And instantly
There was terrific clamour among the people
Against being ranged in rows.
There was a loud quarrel, world-wide.
It endured for ages;
And blood was shed
By those who would not stand in rows,
And by those who pined to stand in rows.
Eventually, the man went to death, weeping.
And those who stayed in bloody scuffle
Knew not the great simplicity.
                    —Stephen Crane[1]

How did we manage to get ourselves involved in these lethal practices? Long before we became conscious of the fact, the adults in our lives began teaching us how to make all the proper distinctions among people, to make us aware of *differences* between ourselves and others. Our parents, teachers, church leaders, and government officials helped us learn to think of ourselves as unlike, and superior to, other people. Few of these adults would have endorsed such an elitist proposition when so bluntly stated; nevertheless, we were taught to regard *our* nation, *our* race, *our* religion, *our* ancestry, as better than any others. We were told how civilized, enlightened, and free *our* culture was, and how brutal, superstitious, and enslaved other cultures were.

While growing up in a predominantly white, middle-class city in Nebraska during World War II, I was told how fortunate I was not to have been born in another nation, or as a member of another race. I was reminded that my background provided me with advantages others would not share. To quiet my concerns over the war, I was informed that America was bound to win because God disliked tyrannies (i.e., the enemy nations) and favored those who fought for freedom (i.e., the United States and its allies).

Wasn't the truth of all this confirmed to me wherever I turned? No adult ever suggested to me anything to the contrary. My friends certainly expressed no doubts in the matter. My parents told me it was all so. My schoolbooks and teachers were in agreement. The Bible seemed to confirm what ministers and Sunday school teachers had been saying, especially concerning God's disposition for smiting wicked and evil people. And what about all the other evidence? Weren't the newspapers filled with pictures of starving, orphaned children in Europe? Weren't the fundamental differences between "our" side and the "enemy" well-documented in wartime news reports and Hollywood motion pictures that portrayed American soldiers as brave, noble, and humane, and German and Japanese soldiers as sneering, heartless butchers who machine-gunned helpless children as they prayed for salvation? And didn't America eventually prevail in the war, just as I had been promised would happen? And was it not also true that I enjoyed many economic, social, and educational advantages others did not; that I lived in a nation blessed by a standard of living that was the envy of men and women around the world? Was I not better off than the black children I saw living in run-down houses in the poorer sections of town? In the face of all that I had been told and experienced, why *wouldn't* I be expected to grow up believing in the superiority of *my* nation, *my* race, *my* religion, *my* way of life?

What I had been learning was to develop for myself what Frederick Perls calls "ego boundaries,"[2] or what Ludwig von Bertalanffy refers to as the "ego barrier."[3] I was taught, as were you, to become an *identity-seeker,* hoping to find personal perfection, security, or a vicarious sense of fulfillment in some institutional entity, ideology, or other grouping with whose purposes I could merge my own. The external authorities with which I might have identified myself included nation-States ("I am an American," "I am a Palestinian," "I am a Russian"); religions ("I am a Catholic," "I am a Buddhist," "I am a Presbyterian"); ideologies ("I am a Marxist," "I am a capitalist"); ethnic groups ("I am Jewish," "I am a Chicano"); racial groupings ("black power," "white supremacy"); social or political causes ("pro-" or "anti-abortion," "environmentalism," "pro-" or "anti-nuclear"); corporate enterprises (one businessman, when asked for whom he worked, replied "I am Xerox"); or sexual groupings ("I am woman," "I am gay"). My ego boundaries may also encompass my family, property, or ancestry; the school I attended; a labor union or profession of which I was a member; or an athletic team. More than likely, my ego boundaries would embrace multiple identities, as I aligned myself with, perhaps, a religion, nationality, trade or profession, social class, race, and ideology, at one and the same time (e.g., "white-Anglo-Saxon-Protestant-union leader," "third-world-lesbian-novelist"). To test the impact ego boundaries have upon our lives, try describing yourself without making reference to any subdivisions among people.

In the process of acquiring ego boundaries, we have learned to move *outside* ourselves, to define meaning, purpose, and success in life in terms of our *becoming,* in the literal sense of the word, the entity with which we have identified ourselves. We learn to see the world through the lenses of our ego boundaries, and to conform our thoughts and behavior to the demands of those who claim to represent this abstraction. Like dependent children, we have learned to invest these external agencies with the authority to direct our lives, as we pledged unto them our continuing subordination. We began to channel not just our energies, but much of our very being into these authorities. We learned to not only take direction from these entities, but to align *our* life purposes with *theirs*. We have come to believe that our personal weakness and subservience will be more than compensated for by our sharing in the power and glory of our collective identity.

If we look closely at what we are doing, we will discover that this process of identification consists of nothing more than chopping ourselves up into *words,* words that have absolutely no reality to them at all. We associate ourselves with fictions of no significance outside the minds in which they have been fabricated. If we had never learned to divide people into groups, would we have any reason to make distinctions among people on the basis of where they live, or what they think, or the color of their skin? Our minds, not nature, create the divisions that set Christians against atheists, Germans against French, communists against capitalists, and whites against blacks. Our minds, alone, are capable of attaching importance to what they have dreamed up. We fool ourselves with our own fantasies. We define and describe who we are by reference to these mental concoctions and, as a consequence, we become further fragmented and non-integrated beings. We learn to focus our attentions on those with whom we identify, seeking to know more about them than about ourselves, and being careful to accurately read their expressions in order to gain clues for our own behavior. We learn to conform to the expectations of others, and to repress any conflicting wants of our own through an elaborate network of self-imposed restraints. We learn to extoll the virtues of duty, sacrifice, altruism, and faith, and to renounce selfishness, doubt, and the pursuit of pleasure.

Isn't this pattern evident in our daily lives? Because we want to be thought of as faithful followers of a religion or ideology, we memorize catechisms or philosophic conclusions, and behave and speak in ways that will demonstrate to our intellectual leaders the consistency of our dedication. We want to be recognized as honor students, and endeavor to find out what our teachers want us to know, and what their biases are, so that we may conform our class participation and examination answers accordingly. In order that we not be looked upon as cowardly or irresponsible, we repress our own desire for living and allow political and military leaders to employ our lives as they see fit for the alleged greater interests of the nation-State.

Why do we choose to become so intensely involved with identifying ourselves through external agencies? The answer to that question lies, I believe, in the fact that we have far greater conscious mental capacities than we employ. Rarely, if ever, do we focus our total attention upon the present moment. The mind tends to wander, to play games, to recall both good and bad experiences from the past, and to anticipate the future. The mind becomes dissatisfied with things as they are, and begins to feel incomplete. But it *is* incomplete, for it is not totally energized, not intensely aware of the present. The mind can be analogized to an electric power plant operating at less than peak load: if we are being totally attentive to the moment, the mind has no excess capacity to employ either in remembering the pains and pleasures from the past or fantasizing about the future. But if we are not bringing our complete attention to bear upon the present, the mind begins to generate fears and desires: we wish to avoid future suffering and enjoy future pleasures.

It is at this point that the conscious mind begins to develop *images*. Perhaps the first image it fashions is of *itself* as an entity. The mind's awareness of its own existence provides a focal point for our anxieties and aspirations. Having conceived of its own primacy and the necessity of its own immortality, the mind begins identifying conditions that threaten or gratify its sense of well-being. We remember a friend who died under mysterious circumstances, and we imagine a human or superhuman agency that might have been responsible. Concerned that we too might die, the mind comes up with the threatening image of an "enemy," or all-powerful "god," and begins to think about possible methods of protection or appeasement. Or, we remember a time when food was scarce. Fearing that we might again be threatened by starvation, or anticipating the pleasure of future consumption, we imagine ourselves with a constant supply of food, and think of ways to assure that desire. Or, we meet someone who has acquired great wealth, and who lives in a luxurious home. We envision ourselves enjoying such affluence, and begin to resent the acquaintance who has what we would like to have. To comfort our wounded pride, we condemn him for his greed, and take pride in ourselves for not being the kind of ruthless and unprincipled person we convince ourselves one would have to be to amass such wealth.

Because our fears and desires are so closely associated with other people, this process of image-creation is also closely related to the development of ego boundaries and institutions. We begin to look for *security* or *fulfillment* in persons or things beyond ourselves. Being egocentric, the mind regards its own purposes and well-being as the *raison d'etre* of its commitments. We begin associating with those whose purposes are compatible with our own, and separate ourselves from those we perceive as threats, or who remind us of our feelings of guilt, inadequacy, or other fears. Having created an image of ourselves, we try to get others to conform to and reflect that self-image. We organize to promote and perfect our sense of self, investing our egos in a collective identity onto which we project our own image and, at the same time, reflecting that collective image back onto ourselves. The birthplace of institutions, then, is to be found within our psyches. Institutions have a profound psychological significance for us: we create them in order to gratify our mind's sense of its own importance, to make the rest of the world as predictable and consistent with our self-image as we can. We attach life-and-death meaning to these agencies of our creation; we value our relationship with these organizations, being careful to cultivate ties with those who share our institutional outlooks and avoid those who do not.

This is how institutions *develop,* but it does not fully explain the *continuation* of institutions from one generation to the next. Neither you nor I were the architects of the organizationally-structured world into which we were born. Nevertheless, the success of institutions can only be explained in terms of our identifying our individual self-images with their collective images. Having already been created, and having their own reasons for being, institutions become the dominant force in integrating *our* images with *theirs.* For the same self-image-gratifying reasons that men created institutions in the first place, institutions seek to promote *their* self-images through *us.* As soon as we are able to think, organizational authorities get their hands on us—initially through churches and government-mandated schools—and begin teaching us to develop institutional images of ourselves. After years of being consistently propagandized with their world view; of having their identities impressed upon us, we emerge with a collective, organizational definition of our very beings. So firmly is this institutional view engrained within us, that many of us are able to recite—with nary a twitch of doubt as to its verity—the well-rehearsed doctrine that *institutions* reflect *our* interests.

Our willingness to relate ourselves as institutionally-defined beings has provided us with an effortless substitute for understanding who we really are. These agencies have encouraged and pandered to the fears and cravings that have caused us to embrace them. We have become attached to so many external values in our lives, including the institutional systems that promise to protect and promote those values. Because of our attachments to things outside ourselves, our fears and desires become accelerated, initiating more intensely felt needs to adhere to these agencies. The consequence of all this is a vicious circle: the further removed we are from an understanding of our personal selves, the more attached we become to external authorities; and the more tightly we embrace these institutional entities, the less we know and understand of ourselves.

The harm that is caused by these practices goes beyond such personal disorientation. As we shall discover in greater depth in the following chapter, conflict is a necessary consequence of our willingness to allow institutional purposes to preempt our own. Whenever two or more persons seek to control the same exclusive thing at the same time, conflict will result. Anyone who has made the mistake of giving two children joint ownership in one toy has experienced the truth of this proposition. When the authorities in our lives try to compel us to act contrary to our wants, only one of us can prevail, with frustration, resentment, anger, and other expressions of conflict necessarily resulting. I remember, as a grade-school student, various incidents in which schoolmates vandalized the school building, such as by breaking windows or destroying the interior of the cafeteria. To my knowledge, there was little of such violence directed at homes or local businesses. It seems more likely that these children were reacting against the school system that compelled them to be where they did not choose to be.

On the other hand, if our individual interests and those of the institutions with which we are associated exactly coincide, we will experience no such internal division of purpose and, hence, no sense of conflict. This is why institutions are so anxious to have us identify with them. Because they have purposes of their own that transcend any conflicting personal interests, and because they can accomplish their purposes only through us, institutions have an incentive to promote those attitudes and conditions that will get us to subordinate our wants to theirs and submit to their authority. The expansion of our ego boundaries serves this end quite well. To the degree we identify our very beings with an institution, we are unlikely to experience any conflict between our interests and those of the organization. In effect, the institution *is us,* not just collectively, but quite personally. We lose our personality in the group with which we have identified, only to discover our new group-oriented self. We develop enemies who, like ourselves, are the personifications, the operating agencies of our respective images. As James Powell has stated, "[w]hen armies clash, it is not tank against tank, bomb against bomb, and man against man, but flag against flag, God against God, and symbol against symbol."[4] The men who go marching off to war are, for the most part, thoroughly convinced that, in defending the interests of the *State,* they are defending *themselves.* Their ego boundaries are so perfectly aligned with the State that they can regard the loss of their *individual* lives as insignificant when compared to the perceived threat to their *collective* life.

In an effort to strengthen our attachments to them, institutions endeavor to persuade us that their interests and ours are entirely compatible. Haven't political institutions, for example, helped convince us that "we are the government," and that the various authorities we are compelled by legal force to obey are our "agents" and "servants"? Don't police departments advertise "your safety is our concern" on the sides of the patrol cars that are used to help keep us all in line? Don't business firms try to convince us that "we do it all for you," and "the customer is number one"?

It should be clear that whenever we identify with anything, whenever we choose to live as externalized, other-directed persons, we are abandoning reality and embracing a gigantic lie. It should be obvious to us that, no matter how much we may choose to do so, we can never surrender the direction and control of our lives to other persons. Others may *influence* us, but they cannot make *choices* for us. There is no way that any human being, or ten million human beings, or a parent, or a President, or a teacher, or a Pope, or a bully, or an employer, or a guru, or a friend, can get inside us and energize our systems. It is our biological nature for each of us to be in control of our individual energies. No one else is physically capable of causing us to do anything. We have to choose whether we will conform to the demands and expectations of others. We may, as children so often do, seek to discount our responsibility for our actions by pleading "I couldn't help myself; they made me do it." But we are adults now, and ought to be able to understand that in employing such an excuse we are only trying to take comfort in a lie. That frail argument did not avail the Nuremburg defendants following World War II. It is deserving of no greater respect today.

The most severe consequences of our institutional attachments are those that comprise the social conflict in which our world is immersed. Ego boundary identification is premised upon our distinguishing ourselves from others, a process characterized by a sense of both *integration* and *alienation*. We learn, through subtle means, the importance of associating ourselves with all the right people, groups, and ideas, and avoiding or withdrawing from those who do not share our world view. Whatever the particular abstraction with which we have come to identify ourselves, we learn to have favorable responses to all that is within and, as a corollary, unfavorable responses to all that is outside our ego boundaries. We regard those who share our ego boundaries as comrades, or brothers, or sisters, or colleagues, or countrymen. Those outside our ego boundaries are enemies, or foreigners, or competitors, or infidels, or simply misguided. During the war years of my youth, there were otherwise intelligent adults who insisted they could, by looking at faces or asking value-laden questions, tell the difference between persons of Japanese and Chinese ancestry. At the same time, I recall the unsettling problem many of us in the neighborhood had of figuring out whether the German immigrants who lived on our block were "Americans" or part of that enemy group of "Germans" we were being taught to hate.

The tendencies for conflict should be evident in any practice that employs the double-edged sword of cooperation and a sense of belonging, on the one hand, and distrust and unfamiliarity on the other. Wars; racial, religious and ideological disputes; terrorism; genocide, . . . these and all other forms of social conflict arise from our willingness to identify ourselves with words that represent our ego boundaries. Whenever we embrace one group of people or ideas, no matter how well-intentioned our purposes, we separate ourselves from all others who do not share our identity. Through ego boundaries, we enlarge and extend ourselves outward, increasing the territorial size of our egos as we learn to distinguish ourselves from more and more people. Through this process, we develop and refine our sense of who we are.

Because our ego boundaries are designed to separate us from others, there is an enhanced likelihood of social conflict occurring along the boundary lines that distinguish us from other ego collectives. This is not simply to make a theoretical or abstract statement regarding collective responsibility. Our lives are, in fact, subjected to conflict as a result of our identifying with groups. Once we identify ourselves with anything, we develop a need for enemies, for the same boundary lines whose configurations help us define our friends, also separate out our adversaries. One cannot be devoutly religious, or patriotic, or moral, without differentiating oneself from the ungodly, the disloyal, or the immoral. To be *for* one's own group, or nation, or race, requires that one be *against* strangers. Just as we can only identify where we are, spatially, by reference to the positions of other persons or objects, our ego boundaries have meaning only insofar as they distinguish us from others. The moderate and the extremist, the socialist and the capitalist, the conservative and the liberal, are in paired dependencies upon one another for their places on the political spectrum. In the words of a philosopher friend of mine: "we cannot define *moral* behavior: only that which is *immoral.*" Institutional success, then, is conditioned upon the careful cultivation of enemies, for *outsiders* are the necessary benchmarks for identifying the *insiders;* we need men and women who are *different* to tell us how the rest of us are the *same.*

The strengths of our attachments to institutions or beliefs are directly related to our need to distinguish ourselves from those outside our ego boundaries. For this reason, the conflicts between friend and foe, good and evil, countryman and foreigner, are most pronounced along the contact points that divide one group from another. Frederick Perls has noted the tendency for wars to start along boundary lines as boundary disputes. India and China, he tells us, are more likely to go to war than are India and Finland.[5] As our ego boundaries expand to encompass a wider range of identifiable interests, we multiply the conflict. Such nation-States as the Soviet Union and the United States, for example, both of whom have expressed world-wide definitions of their respective national interests, experience conflict and the threat of war far more frequently than do Switzerland, Sweden, or Liechtenstein.

Human society comprises interconnected networks of people in a myriad of social settings. As men and women are pressured into mutually-exclusive, artificial subdivisions, their existing ties with others may be disrupted or cut off

altogether, resulting in both personal and social fragmentation and conflict. During World War II, for example,
Japanese-Americans were expected to renounce their cultural and ancestral bonds—including family connections—
within Japan. Even as our social networks are being torn
apart, institutional interests are busy forcing people into
fictitious groupings that do not represent genuine social
relationships among humans. In this way, to quote David
Bohm, we end up fragmenting our world, as we seek "to
divide what is really indivisible" and "to unite what is not
really unitable."[6]

The trespasses that ignite conflict need not always involve
physical boundaries. The violation of our ideological boundaries often evokes the most violent reactions. The truth of
this can be found in the cold war struggles between private
capitalism and communism; or the present Iranian government's struggle to defend the Islamic culture against what it
regards as the decadence of western values; or the religious
differences that have blazed a trail of blood through the
pages of human history, continuing in recent times in the
natural jungles of Guyana and the man-made jungles of
Belfast, Jerusalem, and Beirut. Ideological boundary clashes
also fuel the hostilities between pro- and anti-abortion advocates, as each group seeks to have its particular philosophic
conclusions certified by the political State.

The interrelated nature of institutions, ego boundaries,
and conflict should be evident. Peace consists in our leaving
one another alone, not committing trespasses upon one
another. Order in society is dependent upon our confining
the scope of our actions to our own selves, our own territory,
so to speak. If, instead of being externalized through
mutually-divisive groups with rigidly defended ego boundaries, we are *inwardly*-directed and content to restrict our
decision making to our own selves, we reduce the potential
for conflict.

But our institutionally-structured society has been any-thing but peaceful. Institutions have been the principal sub-divisions into which we have organized and identified our-selves. They are made more powerful by an increased willingness on our part to play their vicious games, a willing-ness that has been fostered by institutions desirous of having us embrace the abstractions upon which their existence depends. The history of institutionalized society has been principally one of the *organization and management of conflict.* Do institutions not encourage the duality in our thinking that promotes the practice of projecting good and bad character-istics onto others? Do they not encourage and exploit both scapegoating and authority worship, continually reminding us of the presence of some object of fear or hatred, or some other source of conflict, and consoling us that they, alone, can make our lives secure? Do they not teach us to distrust our minds and to rely on the omniscience of institutional authorities? What political institution does not tell us that it offers us protection and order and freedom and abundance, while other political systems threaten us with harm and chaos and slavery and pillage? What religion does not pro-mise its followers the "one, true, all-knowing, all-powerful" god, and caution that the followers of other religions will suffer eternal hell and damnation—or, at the very least, nonpreferred treatment in the hereafter? What philosophy or ideology does not claim to be following "right reason," and to be consistent with the "moral imperative," while discounting competing belief systems as irrational or immoral? What business does not accept, at least implicitly, the asser-tion of former GM president Charles Wilson that "what's good for General Motors is good for the country"?

In our carefully nourished innocence, we believe that institutions exist for the purposes they have taught us, namely, to provide us with goods and services, protection, security, and order. But in fact, institutions exist for no other purpose than their self-perpetuation, an objective requiring a continuing demand for their services. In the words of Herbert Spencer, "within every society, each species of structure tends to propogate itself."[7] If institutions are to sustain themselves and grow, they require an escalation of the problems that will cause us to turn to them for solutions. The police system *needs* crime; the national defense establishment *needs* wars; the health-care industry *needs* sick people; dentists *need* overbites and tooth decay; schools *need* ignorance; the legal system *needs* disputes; the welfare system *needs* the poor and unemployed; religions *need* sin. Unless one is aware of the symbiotic relationships between mutual enemies, between problem solvers and their problems, one's understanding of institutional behavior is bound to be superficial. Labor union officials and management consultants need one another as constant adversarial threats around which to organize their respective constituencies. If racial discrimination ended overnight, civil rights organizations would have to find other social injustices to overcome, just as the sudden departure of all racial minorities from American soil would send the Ku Klux Klan into a frenzied search for new hateworthy groups. Marx and Lenin needed the capitalists' exploitation of labor to the same extent that anti-pornography groups require the continuing exploitation of sex.

Because their continued and prospering existences are their very reasons for being, institutions have vested interests in keeping the conflict game going while, at the same time, carefully avoiding any disclosures that would reveal it all *as being* just a game. After all, if the show is given away, people will stop buying tickets! Institutions, then, have an incentive *not* to *solve* problems, but to carefully *manage* them, doing just enough to create in the minds of the rest of us the appearance of at least minimal efficiency. To actually *overcome* major social problems would bring these games to an end, for there would be eliminated the conditions that caused us to embrace institutions in the first place. And so we continue playing our vicious games at one another's expense. With the problems continuing unresolved, and with our unquestioning faith in organizational authorities to take care of our interests, we dutifully respond to their failures with a willingness to grant them even *more* power and resources over our lives!

Because we have derived so much benefit from our associating with one another, most of us have no doubt expected that bringing people together into institutional collectives will foster greater social unity. But this has not been the case. Our expectations have failed to materialize because we have failed to distinguish between those spontaneous, unstructured organizations in which people *come* together for their mutual interests, and the structured institutional systems that *mobilize* people, inducing them—through intimidative or coercive means—to sacrifice their individual interests in favor of the alleged collective good. But on close examination, what is purported to be the *collective* good ends up being only the narrow good of the *institution* itself. One of the consequences of our being *pushed together* by institutional pressures has been an increased social isolation, a *pulling away from one another.* Perhaps Newton's third law of motion offers some explanation for the paradox of a society *disintegrating* as a result of its *organization.*

Having learned to be externalized, it may be tempting to blame others for the causes of social conflict. It is easy to blame governments for wars, churches for religious discord, the business system for economic dislocations, or ideologies for terrorist practices. But to disassociate ourselves from such conflict while criticizing the agencies we have helped to energize is but to continue avoiding the responsibility for our own behavior. While institutions are the principal instruments for organizing and conducting social conflict, and while such organizations could not long survive without disharmony, *we* are the indispensable fuel for keeping their fires ablaze. Consider the insanity of what we are doing: we introduce division into our lives and begin to experience conflict. In order to resolve the conflict, we become externalized, other-directed persons. We learn to look upon other people as both the causes of and the answers to the very problems *we* have created.

But rather than seeing the absurdity of what we are doing and putting an end to it, we continue the practice. We thus reinforce not only the divisions that precipitated the conflict in the first place, but the neurotic delusions that assure our continued participation. We have made ourselves like helpless children dependent upon a dominating parent, looking to others for purpose and direction as well as the unity and wholeness we cannot find within us, and taking comfort in the certainty and regularity of our own abuse. Without our willingness to live beyond ourselves, identifying our ego boundaries with institutions, social conflict would come to an end. Though institutions encourage us to play the game, we are the ones who actually create the divisions among people that cause the conflict. We do so whenever we identify with *anything* for *any* purpose whatsoever. When we identify with any group or organization, incorporating into ourselves the official friends and enemies and all the other assorted preferences and prejudices of such groups, we are doing more than merely *participating* in social conflict: *we are* social conflict!

It is fashionable to lament the growing popular disenchantment with institutions, and the withdrawal of men and women from socially-motivated behavior in order to indulge in those self-centered pursuits that preoccupy what some have disparingly called the "me generation." We are so unaccustomed to being self-assertive that our initial efforts, like a baby's first steps, can indeed prove awkward or even downright silly, like viewing those old movies of mankind's initial experiments with flight. But rather than joining in the

Dutch uncle ridicule of those who dare to get off their knees and stand on their own feet, or moralizing about the alleged failure of human character, we might offer encouragement to those who are willing to ask serious questions about their own behavior and psychological commitments. Instead of sneering at those who have made the choice to withdraw from traditionally unquestioned conduct in favor of experiments with alternative practices, we might be better advised to question our *own* actions. If we are to be responsible human beings, we might begin addressing the underlying causes of our social discontent. The question we should be asking ourselves is whether it is possible for us to continue identifying ourselves with institutions and their self-serving abstractions, without contributing to social conflict. If we do so, we may come to understand how the institutional interests that force us together are tearing us apart, and destroying human society.

4

IDENTIFYING
PERSONAL CONFLICTS

The centipede was happy quite
Until a toad in fun
Said, "Pray, which leg goes after which?"
That worked her mind to such a pitch,
She lay distracted in a ditch,
Considering how to run.
—Mrs. Edward Craster[1]

Identifying ourselves with anything inevitably causes personal conflict. Whenever we engage in this practice, we discover that we *are* not only our individual selves, but the embodiment of that with which we have identified. This creates a sense of inner conflict as we struggle to accommodate both our individual and group purposes. We become fractionalized by contrary ideas, by one set of expectations that are incompatible with other wants we have, or judgments we have learned to make about ourselves. Because of such divisions, we develop feelings of uncertainty, inconstancy, or guilt as we seek to reconcile our contradictions, quiet our apprehensions, and overcome our felt inadequacies.

If we had to regularly experience erratic alternations between gravity and weightlessness, or deadly heat and freezing temperatures, the parallelism with our institutionally-fostered psychological uncertainty would be complete. We vacillate in a sea of moral and philosophical confusion as our minds struggle to accommodate conflicting institutional norms. Religions issue commandments against killing, but the State orders us into bloody wars. Business and political institutions stress materialistic values in life, while educational and religious institutions counter with emphases upon intellectual and spiritual values. Churches preach against the sins of greed, while business firms reward us for its pursuit. Social organizations stress the need for cooperation, but businesses and governments thrive on competition. If we ask institutions for direction in resolving these contradictory expectations, the State tells us we must be *responsible* and yet *obedient*; churches tell us to adhere to God's will and have faith, but to "render unto Caesar"; schools teach us to use our own minds, but to respect authority; business firms emphasize individual self-interest, but demand the loyalties and sacrifices of their employees; while ideologists and philosophers confirm to us that reality is unknowable and moral relativism is the only certain norm. As young people, we might have been attracted to drugs, sex, or other pleasure seeking activities, only to be met by religious leaders and government officials who warned us of the immorality and illegality of such pursuits. We might have resisted the military conscription that would send us into life-destroying combat, but for the fear of our being labeled a coward, a traitor, or a criminal. Is it any wonder that we are so confused and divided?

In an effort to find some order amongst these competing demands upon us, and to provide us with guidelines for our actions, we begin to make *judgments* about ourselves and other people. This is a habit most of us learned in our youth. Because our parents, teachers, and other adult authorities wanted us to conform to their expectations, they began tagging our compliant behavior as good, and any deviance from their standards as bad. In reality, of course, there is no such thing as a "good" or "bad" anything. It is evident that, without wanting to satisfy the demands of the adults around us, few of us would have been attracted to the proposition that there could be a bad side to our characters. In time, however, we learned to internalize these expectations and to pass judgments upon ourselves and each other, a practice most of us dutifully continue to engage in even as adults.

It should be apparent that making judgments about ourselves implies a duality within our personalities; a division between the judge and the judged, with the judge applying standards that have been fabricated out of nothing more than subjective preferences. Whether we have created the standards ourselves, or have adopted those that others have created, the result is the same: we end up structuring our behavior around words and ideas. We manufacture such manipulative and intimidative devices—as we do so many other fantasies—in an effort to control ourselves or others. Because we believe that the agencies that represent our ego boundaries are more important than our own selves, we learn to repress our personal sense of being. We strive to become personifications of the intellectual inventions of other people, a habit that helps to both reinforce the divisions already within us and to deepen the rifts that separate us from one another. If, for example, we judge our self-seeking conduct as bad or immoral, we create a division within us based upon a perceived dichotomy in our character. We conclude that we have a good side and a bad side to our personality, but that by rigorous effort, self-control, and stronger attachment to our external authorities, our good nature can be made to prevail over the bad. We learn to doubt and fear ourselves and come to believe, as a result, that we are not in control of our own lives and that, even if we were, we could not trust our own judgments. We become *fragmented* human beings, without a sense of integrity or direction. We become *neutralized*, believing that we are unable to act without contradiction, or to discover peace and order within ourselves. Convinced that we are incapable of harmonizing and integrating our lives, we begin to *reject* ourselves, to move away from who we are. So busy have we been being other than who we are, living in the fantasy of an abstraction, seeking to satisfy the expectations of others, and taking our direction from anyone and everyone but our own selves, that we discover we know the external being better than we do our own persons. In an effort to find relief from internal conflicts, we intensify our search for answers outside ourselves. Unfortunately, rather than *reducing* conflict, such an approach only reinforces the divisions within us and increases our resolve to exert more control over what appears to us to be the sources of our problems.

Once we start this dangerous practice, we begin embracing external definitions of purpose and success in life. We learn to live *outside* ourselves—as though in a state of suspended animation—thinking, being, feeling, and acting in conformity with mandates of external origin that we have accepted and imposed upon ourselves, and which we faithfully enforce through a process of critical self-evaluation. All that is truly meaningful or can provide us with happiness is *out there* someplace. We want wealth, or power, or fame, or love, or status. We want to be popular, or thought of as successful, or intelligent, or creative, or heroic, or a benefactor to mankind. We seek, in other words, happiness or purpose in life by *comparing* ourselves to other people or their expectations. We learn, through a lifetime of "what will other people think?" admonitions, that what we *are* and what we *want* is always measured by reference to other people. We become little more than empty shells, made up of fragile, polished mirrors that do no more than reflect the world outside ourselves.

If you or I had wanted to make our lives confused and strife-ridden, could we have dreamed up a better formula than that under which we grew up? We have allowed institutions to manipulate us into experiencing internalized, self-directed conflict, but only because we have used our conscious minds to splinter us with divisive thoughts. We have learned to believe that it is possible for us to act contrary to our self-interest. We have been taught that what we want is not necessarily consistent with our *true* interests, and have been exhorted to resist temptations to deviate from the pursuit of what is in our own good. We have learned to be responsible by surrendering our spontaneity and autonomy, conditioning ourselves, in the words of Harold Laski, to "check our impulses at their birth lest they involve us in departures from the norm."[2] Our belief in such notions internally polarizes us, thus immobilizing us and making us more susceptible to external direction. We regard any lessening of our commitment to institutional objectives as a signal to increase the mechanisms of self-control with which the Dr. Jekyll side of our schizoid being endeavors to subdue the Mr. Hyde. We content ourselves with authoritative explanations of our "antisocial" or "irresponsible" nature, and learn to reject the voices that cry out from our subconscious mind. We begin casting overboard that precious cargo of our very beings, which we have come to regard as unwanted, burdensome freight. If, along the way, we should exhibit any tendencies to break out of our mental prison, we treat this as a symptom of our failure to adjust, and busy ourselves with tearing down any other barriers to the swift dispatching of our cargo. We have, as a result, turned ourselves into firmly-anchored sinking ships. We have damned our own rudders, compasses, and sails as we hasten to scuttle our very souls in order that we prove ourselves to be no hindrance to the onrushing and consuming sea.

Why do we go about concocting standards of behavior to control our lives, making life miserable for ourselves and others as we strain to make our personalities fit the mold? Why do we busy ourselves with conducting seances in our minds, calling forth ghosts and other dead spirits to speak to us and frighten us into compliant behavior? Isn't the answer to be found in the fact that we have become dissatisfied with ourselves, and that such dissatisfaction is purely a fabrication of our conscious minds? We have become so externalized by our willingness to accept institutions that we respond to our self-induced internal conflict by turning against our own selves. In desperation, we turn to psychiatrists and other gurus to help us resolve the frustration and guilt we feel at being unable to "adjust," or turn to new religions or ideologies that will reprogram us for less demanding sacrifices of our selves.

In trying to resolve our *internal* conflicts by *externalizing* ourselves, we engage in "projection," a practice defined as "an alienated aspect of the self which is attributed to someone else."[3] Stated another way, projection involves our imputing our own attitudes and personality traits to other persons. We can project either good or bad, positive or negative, desirable or undesirable qualities onto others. From the habit of projection, we learn to *be* something *other than* ourselves. We come to externalize all that is good within us; to project our own capacities for responsible, self-directed, self-controlling, efficacious, happiness-seeking behavior onto others whom we perceive as more perfect beings possessing the virtue and competence we feel we lack. Though we are fully capable of discovering order and harmony for our lives, we idealize these qualities in gods and gurus, political leaders and other authorities.

Whenever our well-being is dependent upon what *other* people do, a sense of *powerlessness* emerges within us. Although, as we have seen, it is impossible for others to actually govern what we do, still, if we *believe* that our happiness and well-being *are* controlled by others, we will feel increasingly inefficacious and less and less capable of making the decisions that will promote our interests. *Others* —whether we regard them as the problems or the answers in our lives—become the source of our welfare. *Their* behavior, not our own, becomes increasingly important to us. Our feeling of powerlessness is compounded by the realization that those whom we believe control or influence *our* lives are, themselves, beyond *our* personal ability to control. We end up fighting the life processes within us, as we discover that we are ever more dependent upon established authorities who, alone, can provide us security from the dread terrors of our own responsibilities. Perhaps it is no more than the continuation of our childhood dependencies that we fear the loss of our attachments to these external agencies, and continue to worship them as the sources of the qualities we find lacking within ourselves.

We have also learned to project onto other people those attitudes or qualities (whether real or imagined) that have created so much frustration and self-alienation within us. We see in others the personification of those discomforting aspects of our own lives that we have learned to reject. We conclude that other people are greedy because they put *their* selfish interests ahead of our own, and we advance the belief in the malevolent nature of mankind. The doubts and criticisms we have of ourselves often produce one of the more unpleasant consequences of projection: the feeling of *persecution*. Being unable to deal with our feelings of self-condemnation, we may project these attitudes onto others and assume that *they* are out to punish *us* for our felt inadequacies. If we feel incompetent in our work, for example, we may ascribe this self-criticism to our employer and conclude that he is planning to fire us. We then go about reading our self-induced fears into everything our employer does or says, interpreting facial expressions or voice tones or silence or changes in work assignments as confirmations of these fears.

We may also seek to alleviate our pent-up anger and frustrations by projecting our felt undesirable traits onto a "scapegoat" (i.e., another person or agency upon whom we bestow the evil quality we fear is within us). Political and religious institutions, in particular, have prospered at the

expense of scapegoats. The popularity of this practice is
enhanced by its adaptability to so many situations. The
scapegoat is a marvelously versatile creature, capable of
becoming whatever anyone wants it to become: businessmen, hippies, communists, blacks, whites, extremists, Jews,
Arabs, rock music, nuclear-power stations, atheists, Iranians, Alaskan pipelines, drugs, labor unions, OPEC nations,
television, Wall Street, feminists, Ivy League professors,
robber barons, the ACLU, homosexuals, scientists, doctors,
illegal aliens, lawyers, male chauvinists, bureaucrats, dirty
books, oil companies, environmentalists, social workers,
your next door neighbor, teenagers, . . . and institutions.

Scapegoating, then, is but a trick we design for our self-
deception. By unloading our internal conflicts onto others,
we seek to make them the embodiment of the fears and
contradictions we feel within ourselves. We do so in the hope
of thus finding our own inner peace. But it never works out
that way. In the first place, scapegoating—like any other
form of projection—is almost never a conscious undertaking:
few of us are aware that we are engaging in the practice. In
fact, if one *was* fully aware that he was projecting, he would
likely experience the absurdity of the practice and put a stop
to it. Instead, projection takes place at a subconscious level.
To one who has learned to project with regularity, the
activity becomes almost automatic. But even if it becomes
habitual, it is nevertheless founded on a delusion, the underlying fallacy of which remains within ourselves. We can no
more rid ourselves of our conflicts by a process of transfer
than we can unlearn what we know by teaching it to others.
If, for example, we harbor a fear that we might be capable of
engaging in violent conduct, we may project this fear onto
others and conclude that *they* are violence-prone and not to
be trusted. But does this really alleviate our own fears about
ourselves? Do we no longer experience a sense of inner
turmoil and contradiction? Or, is it more correct to suggest

that the practice of projection only compounds our own felt sense of conflict by further removing us from an understanding of ourselves?

Because internal conflict is discomforting, but acknowledging ourselves to be the source of that conflict is even more unbearable, we tend to hold others accountable for the distress from which we seek relief. Having convinced ourselves that others are responsible for our sense of uneasiness and are ill-motivated towards us, and distrusting our own capacities for self-direction, we are inclined to the proposition of subjecting these other people to some form of control. Whether we characterize ourselves as missionaries, or activists, or organizers, or vindicators of injustice, or progressives, or other varieties of true believers, we become driven by our cause, having not a spark of doubt about the propriety of what we are doing. Of course, our actions often persuade these other persons to take a similar course of action against us, a response that only confirms to us the legitimacy of our fears. The all-too-frequent result of such thinking is that we seek formal, institutional means of exercising such control over one another. As we intensify this practice, we give institutions more and more power to act in what we like to imagine are our interests. This further dilutes our sense of personal efficacy, of being capable of making decisions in our own behalf. Our feelings of individual powerlessness are further reinforced, leading us to the realization, as noted by Rollo May,

> that we cannot influence many people; that we count for little; that the values to which our parents devoted their lives are to us insubstantial and worthless; that we feel ourselves to be "faceless others," as W.H. Auden puts it, insignificant to other people and, therefore, not worth much to ourselves. . . .[4]

In looking outside ourselves for the wisdom and competency

to resolve our self-generated turmoil, we end up institution-alizing our servile dependencies upon one another. In order to change or control other people, and to shore up our own beliefs, we intensify our attachments to institutions, thus renewing the same vicious circle of organized conflict. Through such practices *we create our own conflict.*

That our lives are interwoven with group conflict can be demonstrated with the hypothetical example of two men, one of whom lives in Salt Lake City, Utah, and the other in Tripoli, Libya. The former identifies himself as an American, and the latter as a Libyan. In the event the American and Libyan governments get into a dispute that escalates into a full-blown war, these two men will each likely regard the disagreement as their personal quarrel. Each may now be prepared to march off to the other's country to lie in foxholes and shoot at one another, *not* because either has personally injured or threatened the other, but because each regards the other as a trespasser upon his ego boundaries.

Or imagine two men, one of whom is Jewish and the other an Arab, who live next door to one another in an American city. These men may be the best of friends until hostilities erupt between Israel and an Arab nation. Depending upon the degree of their identification with the principals in this dispute, these two may become enemies, refuse to speak to one another, and may even take to fighting with each other. This is not because of any actual transgression either has committed upon the other, but because the nation-States with which each identifies have an argument. If the political leaders of Israel and the Arab nation should later embrace one another and announce the reestablishment of friendly relations, these two men will likely do the same thing.

Or let us suppose that a white man, living in Los Angeles, reads in a newspaper that a group of black demonstrators in an African nation burned an American flag. He reacts with anger toward these demonstrators and, perhaps, to other citizens of that same country. He regards this action, in a very real sense, as a trespass to himself—even though he was half a world away—because he identifies with, he *is,* the object of the demonstration.

This man may also choose to react against blacks in general, viewing the flag-burning as an attack by members of another race upon what he considers the symbol of both his nation and race. He may be inclined to view all blacks as personal threats, and may go so far as to take retributive action against, let us say, a black woman living in Los Angeles. If he does so, the reports of his attack may result in a black man—living in New York City, and identifying himself with the racial abstraction "black"—reacting with righteous indignation. The New Yorker, upon learning that the man in Los Angeles is a member of a particular religious sect, may choose to direct his anger against members of that same group living in New York City. Meanwhile, a feminist in Boston may react to the attack by the Los Angeles man as an attack upon the abstraction "woman" and, as a consequence, consider *her* ego boundaries to have been violated. If she makes a public criticism of this man, a self-proclaimed male chauvinist living in Houston may react against the feminist's stance and come to the defense of the Los Angeles man believing, by some twisted logic, that the feminist's attack on *his* identity provided ex post facto justification for the original attack upon the black woman!

If you are inclined to regard this as a straw man hypothetical that is too unrealistic to be meaningful, try doing a careful reading of your daily newspaper. Isn't this sort of intergroup squabbling a major portion of what we call news? Try to recall the responses of members of various groups within America to the takeover of the American embassy in Iran. Iranian students at American universities defended the holding of one group of Americans for the alleged wrongs of others; Jewish Defense League members attacked Iranian students on the streets of Los Angeles; many blacks sided with the Iranians because of their shared Muslim beliefs; men and women of Armenian, Egyptian, or Turkish background clearly distinguished their national origins; Marxists seized upon the opportunity to renew the rhetoric of capitalist imperialism, while conservatives reminded us of the menace of communist subversion; bumper stickers afforded four-lettered opinions of Iranians or advised nuclear solutions to the hostage problem. We might also recall the 1982 assassination, in Los Angeles, of the Turkish consul. This official had been murdered, apparently by members of an Armenian-American group, as a reprisal for the Turkish government's 1915 massacre of Armenians. One man of Armenian descent sought to rationalize the assassination by declaring: "one of his ancestors may have been responsible for the murder of my grandfather."[5] Such events demonstrate not only the interrelated nature of the conflict that exists throughout the world, but the impossibility of pointing to any one person or group as the cause of that conflict.

To better understand the personally disruptive consequences of dividing ourselves from others, let us take the example of a woman who, after having been introduced to feminism, comes to the realization that she has lived most of her life accepting a socially-defined role as housewife and mother. Until now, she has never questioned the ranch-style-home-in-the-suburbs-with-the-station-wagon, taking-the-boys-to-Little-League-on-Monday, the-girls-to-Camp-Fire-on-Wednesday, bridge-club-on-Thursday life-style she has been trained to live. Now, however, she becomes aware of alternate life-styles that offer greater fulfillment, and she seeks to change her life to get away from the *Stepford Wives* style of living that she perceives others have established for her.

This woman may come to her conclusions through a process of introspection, of observing and being aware of every aspect of her life and the world about her. In seeking to understand herself—openly, and without reacting to or passing judgment upon what she observes—this woman is likely to realize that she is in control of her own life, a discovery that confirms to her her own responsibility for her behavior, including the roles she has been living all these years. Through this process of awareness, of nonjudgmental observation, this woman may develop the understanding that will cause her to effect fundamental changes in her life-style without, at the same time, experiencing any internal conflict. Such understanding produces a state of mind that is free of debilitating psychological dependencies. Nonjudgmental awareness puts an *end* to conflict, and provides the only basis for a truly liberated life.

On the other hand, this woman may be less interested in understanding herself than in fixing the blame for what she has become. She may react against her life-style and all that she associates with it, and vow to liberate herself from it. As a result, she will engender division and conflict within herself, as her traditional and liberated selves confront one another and as her previous attitudes do battle with her enlightened views for the supremacy of her mind. This conflict will accelerate into self-directed anger, as her new self passes judgment upon the old. She may try to rid herself of her anger by projecting the source of it onto others (e.g., male-dominated institutions), whom she has been told are responsible for her plight. How much more comforting it is for her to believe that women have been wronged by male chauvinist inclinations to oppress and subjugate them. It is much easier to accept the idea that men have forced women into particular life-roles than to confront the reality that, even if men *had* manipulated women into accepting such roles, their purposes could only have been carried out with the cooperation of women. It is less distressing for this person to believe that men disrespect women, than to acknowledge and deal with the disrespect she may have for herself, a disrespect occasioned by the internal conflicts she has been unable to resolve. This is not to minimize the dehumanizing nature of institutional behavior, or to suggest that women— or any of the rest of us—have "deserved" what has happened to them. It is, however, to stress that most of us have been willing participants in our own victimization; that we have consented to be manipulated and pushed around by institutions because we have chosen to identify ourselves with them.

One of the most vulgar and crudely vicious examples of how ego boundary identification creates division and conflict within society is found in *racism*. We are close enough in history to the wholesale brutality of Nazi Germany that there is a tendency for many people to react indignantly to the savage butchery or man's inhumanity to man implicit in the practice of incarcerating and murdering people on the basis of their ancestry. Few can deny that racism exemplifies the most barbaric form of collectivizing people, or that the effects of the practice are usually quite severe. But do we truly *understand* the nature, the reality of racism, or are we content to call it names, to deal with it only as an *abstraction*?

We watch a movie depicting the Nazi holocaust and we react against the evils (one abstraction) done by Nazi Germany (another abstraction) to Jews (yet another abstraction). We speak of the horrors of six million dead Jews (one more abstraction), as though a higher number correlates, consistent with our materialistic outlook, with an increased intensity of feeling. We cry out for justice (still another abstraction) and come away thoroughly convinced that our intellectual catharsis has provided us with an understanding of the vicious nature of racism.

But do we really understand *anything* when we deal with it only in abstract terms as ideas? Can we really experience the personal nature of the suffering involved? Can we understand that murdering six million people is not a greater crime than murdering just one person; that increasing the numbers of victims does not *increase* the suffering but only *repeats* it? Can we truly understand these things, or are we content to stand at a comfortable distance and play our intellectual games, treating human suffering only as a problem to be talked about, lamented, debated, and calculated? As long as human misery serves only to shock our sensibilities or arouse our moral indignation, we will derive from it little more than intellectual stimulation and entertainment. As long as we treat the matter as a philosophical or moral issue, and refuse to experience its harsh, personal reality, it will never have enough of an impact on our lives to help us understand its causes.

If we want to know what causes racism, and if we are willing to observe, with clarity, the nature of such practices, it should be apparent that the same processes of group identification that produce other forms of conflict are at work here as well. Dividing people into groups separated by ego boundaries *always* generates conflict, whatever the basis for the division might be. Unfortunately, we have been taught to believe that bad motives or malicious dispositions have been the causes of racist conduct. We look to the evil or psychotic or vicious nature of the Hitlers, Eichmanns, Goebbels, or percaled Ku Klux Klan fanatics, hoping to find explanations for their behavior in aberrated mentalities. But were the motives or mental states of such persons the root cause of racist sentiments? Could an Adolph Hitler have mobilized public prejudices unless those prejudices were already present in well established and defined ego boundaries? Motives may well tell us how severe an impact a particular practice may have, but they do not alter the inherent nature of the conflict that arises whenever—and for whatever reason— we choose to divide ourselves into mutually-exclusive groups.

It is always more comforting to regard trespasses upon us as the consequences of other people's malice. We do not like to call into question our psychological commitments, or acknowledge even the possibility of our own complicity in our suffering. But if seeking our identities in divisive collectives creates an environment of separation, fear, and distrust among people which results in conflict, then it should be obvious that many of the *victims* of racism and other forms of violence have contributed to the creation of this climate. It should be clear to us that, regardless of motives, the man who embraces the ego boundary of "Jewish" and the man who identifies himself with the abstraction "Aryan" are both playing the same deadly game; that the implications of "black pride" and "white supremacy" are identical. No matter how peaceful the intentions of the man who identifies himself with a group, the very process creates the we-they, good-bad divisions that produce human conflict. The pairings that match the P.L.O. and the J.D.L., the loyalists and the rebels, the Ku Klux Klan and the Black Panthers, and the "left" wing that necessarily implies a "right" are all mutual contributors to the discord and violence that are tearing the human race apart. We fail to see the consequences of what we do and say. We are willing to stand and shout for patriotism because we perceive no cost to us in doing so. It does not appear to harm anyone, and brings us so much in the way of social returns. We do not see the real and direct connection between our flag-waving and the machine-gunning of children. We believe that we can enjoy the benefits of the former without bearing any responsibility for the latter.

Racism—like any other form of conflict—will come to an end *not* through moral preachments or appeals to such vague abstractions as brotherhood. It is not bad intentions that keep us apart, but our willingness to live outside ourselves, and to identify with groups. We are willing to inflict death and suffering upon others *not* because we are filled with *hate*, but because we have such an intense *love* for our collective identity. We have subdivided our minds into "exclusive developments," complete with restrictive covenants to keep out the "undesirables." We have created rigid, spiritual ghettoes, designed to keep ourselves and everyone else in his or her place.

Why do we do these things to ourselves and one another? That institutions have an interest in having us identify our ego boundaries with them, and to the exclusion of competing institutions, should be evident by now. We have learned to divide ourselves into antagonistic groupings and, like other territorial animals, to discern the subtleties of the boundary lines that separate us. We have learned to accept aggression as part of our biological nature, conflict as the norm in human society, and to attribute to institutionally-defined "outsiders" the source of that conflict. The success of institutions has been at the price of peace, harmony, and human autonomy. The organizations we have regarded as being virtually synonymous with *order* have been the principal agencies of *disorder*. In trying to impose order on society, we have fostered the very problems we sought to prevent.

As long as our focus is upon what *others* are doing (or should be doing), we shall fail to see that *we* are the cause of our own conflicts. We—you and I—are the source of our problems, a truth we can comprehend if only we will look inward instead of outward. We have made ourselves both the gods and the devils in our self-authored Miltonic psychodrama, and we stage our tragic performance with a cast of millions. Whatever the social condition of which we disapprove, it originates *within us* , not from without. If it is your desire to end wars, then discover the conflict within yourself, and, by so doing, put an end to it. Peace comes only from within yourself, not from rearranging other people. If you wish to end discrimination, then discover the racial, religious, sexual, or nationalistic divisions you have created within yourself. In so doing, you will put an end to your contribution to racism, sexism, nationalism, bigotry, and other forms of discrimination.

Why we permit ourselves to play these lethal institutional games of divide and conquer is a question we must be willing to ask if we wish to understand the nature of conflict. It should be evident to us that, if any one of us were the last human being on earth, there would be no occasion for the group divisions into which we have pigeonholed one another. We would be neither an American nor a German, a black nor a white, a man nor a woman, a Jew nor a Christian, a patriot nor a traitor, a communist nor a capitalist, a manufacturer nor a consumer, a Catholic nor a Protestant. We would be but an individual who is, at the same time, all that remains of mankind. When we realize that that is who each one of us is *anyway*, we shall have ended our own involvement with the conflict that is destroying mankind.

5

THE CARE AND FEEDING OF THE COOKIE CUTTER PEOPLE

[They] try frantically to order and stabilize the world so that no unmanageable, unexpected or unfamiliar dangers will ever appear. They hedge themselves about with all sorts of ceremonials, rules and formulas so that no new contingencies may appear. They are much like the brain injured cases, . . . who manage to maintain their equilibrium by avoiding everything unfamiliar and strange and by ordering their restricted world in such a neat, disciplined, orderly fashion that everything in the world can be counted upon.

—Abraham Maslow[1]

In our adult years, we sometimes get allegorical glimpses of the institutionalizing processes to which we were subjected in our youth. For example, I recall how, as a child, I would stand by the kitchen table and help my mother make sugar cookies. I shared with sculptors and potters the anticipation of being able to cut from that flat, colorless mass of cookie dough the patterns I wanted; but before doing so I had to endure the seemingly endless preparation that always managed to precede fun activities. In due time, I was wielding an assortment of cookie cutters—stars, hearts, circles, trees, and a variety of animal shapes—with which I began imposing designs upon my pasty and prostrate victim. In hindsight, it was as if I were reenacting the creation myth from the book of Genesis: from the primordial mass in front of me, I was able to create a universe that suited my particular fancy.

Of all the cookie patterns available to me, however, I enjoyed most those human-shaped characters I have since come to refer to as "cookie cutter people." Like little gingerbread men—their arms raised either to invite an embrace or to offer surrender—these creatures were cloned with flawless accuracy by the master cutter I held in my own hands. What power I wielded! I could stamp out my own Adam and Eve, stain them with whatever original sin suited my tastes, and, if I noted any character flaws, could cast them out of my earthly paradise and back into that amorphous confectionary gene pool from which they had come.

Upon reaching maturity, i.e., that adult stage in which our behavior reflects our acceptance of institutional expectations, I was able to reflect back upon this earlier experience and draw an interesting analogy: the pleasure I derived from my cookie cutter people was not unlike that realized by the manipulators of *real* people. That kitchen table and pile of cookie dough represented a social engineer's dream. Armed with the super-race model of the master cutter, I could fashion a limitless supply of ideal people who met my most arbitrary of expectations. Like my real world counterparts, I was in control of my own "conscript clientele":[2] a faceless, mindless, uniform, obedient society; mass-produced samples of industrial man; those soulless and indistinguishable proletarians who passively awaited the exercise of my unquestioned authority.

I was my own trinity of God, philosopher king, and social planner, capable of continuing my progressive programs as long as the dough held out. I had achieved that most perfect state of equality for my people and, unlike Adolph Hitler, I had discovered that ovens could be used to *perfect* rather than *destroy* life. I had an unerring system of population control: I could choose to limit either the *birth* rate—by controlling the size of the dough pile—or the *death* rate—by a cannibalistic-genocidal program that satisfied both my social preferences and appetite at the same time.

I became a little uncomfortable, though, when in later years I began noting the similarities between the cookie cutter people and myself. Had I, in fashioning and decorating those doughy forms, only been playing out what had been happening to me? The parallel was certainly there, whether the innocence of my early years had permitted me to see it or not. It may be that in those confectionary characters for whom I had such affection, I had projected something of myself.

I have since become convinced that a happy, eager, inquisitive child cannot grow up to become a structured, tightly controlled, fearful, confused, and depressed adult without a lot of help from a lot of well-meaning and dedicated people. We begin, as inexperienced and uncertain children trusting in the love of our parents, to learn to live contrary to our natures, to reject our own beings, and to rationalize our internal confusions and institutionally-mandated contradictions. We learn how to submit ourselves to the authority of others and to accept the insanity of normal behavior: in short, to become confused, conflict-ridden adults, ready to take our assigned places—like submissive cookie cutter people—in an institutionally-directed society.

It has not been by happenstance, of course, that we have become such disciplined and inflexible people. Since institutions are the established order, it is in their interests to instill in people those values of restraint and inhibition that serve to reinforce the status quo. Whatever differences otherwise exist among such established agencies, they are fueled by a common purpose: to control and manipulate people. There is no passion so lustful as the ambition for power to rule over other people: it dominates murderers, rapists, and pimps, as well as monarchs, presidents, judges, priests, legislators and city council members, bureaucrats, welfare administrators, policemen, prison wardens, school teachers and administrators, and military people. An environment premised on individual freedom, self-control, and decentralized social organizations is incompatible with their interests in centralized authority. As a result, institutions have not only attracted those persons who find purpose and satisfaction in directing and disciplining others, but have carefully and painstakingly inculcated the human race in the value system of social control.

Growing up in an institutionalized society has always been a process of inculcation in the established belief systems and the psychological manipulation of children. It has been the purpose of schools, religions, and ideologies to dull the edge of human awareness, to anesthetize the mind, and put to sleep the human spirit, all for the purpose of molding human behavior to conform to institutional expectations. Beginning when we are young enough to know no better and incapable of resisting, we are subjected to a consistent and virtually unchallenged indoctrination in the need for institutionalized authority in our lives. The same adult authorities who helped us fashion our ego boundaries also taught us that institutions are an essential part of civilized and orderly society. We began learning, at a very young age, ritualized, catechismic definitions of reality, familiarizing ourselves—in the words of Albert Jay Nock—with "certain poetic litanies" which, "provided their cadence be kept entire," causes us to be "indifferent to their correspondence with truth and fact."[3] We were also taught that our lives and our interests and our purposes are always subordinate to some obscurely-defined greater good which, had we examined the concept closely, turns out to be but a reflection of institutional interests.

Through such practices we learned not only to become structured and controlled people ourselves, but to believe in the need for controlling other people as well. So strongly are these ideas impressed upon our minds that the matter is not even regarded as a question to us: the proposition is simply considered self-evident.

As a result of our indoctrination, we have developed a pyramidal concept of human society, with wealth, status, and power reserved for the few who manage to get to the top, while powerlessness and indistinction await the so-called masses at the bottom of the social structure. This pyramidal design is reflected in organization charts, constitutions, and bylaws. It is found in many of the nursery rhymes and fairy tales (e.g., powerful fairy godmothers, handsome princes being married to young maidens, noble kings being served by brave young men, etc.) and games (e.g., chess, king of the mountain, "Monopoly," computerized video games, etc.) that help reinforce upon the minds of children and adults alike the sentiment so aptly expressed by former Defense Secretary (and corporate executive) Robert McNamara: "[v]ital decision-making, particularly in policy matters, must remain at the top. This is partly, though not completely, what the top is for."[4]

Our belief in the necessity for a "top" derives from the commonly-held proposition that some external agency of control is necessary to every process in nature. We find it difficult to think of things just "happening" in an orderly manner, without someone or something "running" the show. We are unable to comprehend a self-generating, self-organizing universe, and so imagine a deity who creates and directs everything. (Of course, when pressed to explain the origins of the deity, we have no problem accepting the idea of *its* self-creating, self-regulating nature!)We cannot conceive of a society of people functioning in a well-coordinated and orderly fashion, and so insist upon a variety of rulers, judges, social planners, and other "law-givers," whose common purpose is to manage society.

It is our failure to understand the spontaneous and self-ordering processes at work everywhere in the universe—processes we do not *direct*, but which we can *interfere with* at our peril—that underlies most of our personal and social grief. We have, as a consequence, learned to distrust ourselves and others, to fear the absence of supervision and authority as harbingers of chaos and disorder, to submit our lives and our interests to the whims of ambitious exploiters of people, and to regard our exercise of power over others as a definition of our own success. Our reluctance to allow life—including our own—its natural, unplanned, and unrestrained expression is no doubt the product of our self-centered egos projecting their demands for dominance upon the rest of nature. While our minds are disposed to such a view, institutions have seen to it that we thoroughly learn these attitudes, because their survival is dependent upon it. We structure *ourselves* in order to solidify the foundations of a structured *society*.

The processes of structuring are encouraged by another attitude many of us have expressed at one time or another: the desire for *certainty*. We want our world to be as predictable as possible, we say, so that we can anticipate the consequences of our actions. On first impression, this attitude can be said to reflect the intentional, non-instinctual nature of human behavior, as well as our comprehension of the orderly nature of the universe. We observe patterns of apparent consistency about us and try to understand those patterns so that we can forecast results. We learn from our experiences, and we catalog that information in ways that will permit us to carry the accumulated benefits of our prior learning into future actions. Because we desire to accomplish a given result ("y"), and have observed, on previous occasions, that "x" has always resulted in "y", we feel justified in concluding that "x" will lead to "y" the next time as well. This process has generally proved adequate enough to provide us with a workable approximation of reality, and when we employ it in technical and mechanical settings, it permits us to approach problems with skill and competence. Because of this, we have developed a great deal of confidence in the sciences, technology, engineering, commerce, and industry from their own demonstrated proficiencies in being able to predict from past experiences.

The problem with this approach is that all of our knowledge is *past*-related, never *present*-related. No matter how clearly aware we are when we are experiencing anything, what we learn always becomes—within an instant of our experience—a part of our *past*. No matter how faithfully we try to repeat a prior experience—even one that may be but a few moments old—the present always differs from the past, not only as to time and place, but as to the people and the objects involved. Our universe does not stand still for a moment, not even to accommodate the scientist who used to believe that a portion of it could be frozen in time in a clinically pure laboratory setting. Nor can what is learned be separated from the subjective learning processes of the observer, meaning that the learning experiences of two persons in the same location will be different. We are, as many others have observed, an inseparable part of the universe we are studying.[5] In addition, our lack of complete information about anything, and the fact that all conclusions involve some degree of simplification, limit our ability to predict with certainty. As meteorologist Eric Kraus has stated: "uncertainty increases with the number of possible answers to a question. . . . One can get a good prediction only in answer to a relatively crude question. There is always a trade-off between information content and reliability."[6] David Ehrenfeld's characterization of the "uncertainty principle" provides this further limitation on the predictive value of prior learning: "we do not solve problems as we acquire new technologies because new technologies simultaneously make our problems worse."[7]

Kraus's statement reflects a movement by many contemporary scientists away from the more traditional view of a fixed and certain universe which could be studied objectively, and from which studies could be made providing accurate predictions of the future.[8] Before modern equipment made it possible to study the makeup and behavior of subatomic particles, scientists were fairly confident in extrapolating from what they had previously learned about matter to the characteristics of the atom. But with more sophisticated technology came the startling realization not only of the limitations of their prior learning, but of their limited abilities to predict how such particles would behave. The *certainty* of atomic behavior gave way to discussions of *probabilities,* and the *certainty* associated with the existence of matter itself was replaced by references to *"tendencies to exist."*[9] The epistemological implications in such discoveries are potentially shattering: *the more we know about the behavior of distinct particles, the less able we are to predict future behavior.* Stated another way, *we can take comfort in the certainty of what we know only if we do not know too much!* Albert Einstein was a bit more poetic in observing that "as a circle of light increases, so does the circumference of darkness around it."[10]

The lack of complete certainty that pervades our efforts within the so-called hard sciences becomes even more pronounced when we try to understand human behavior. Our desires for certainty and predictability, when applied to social and psychological behavior, provide the base for the institutional structuring that has generated so much conflict and disorder among us. The illusions of the behavior modification advocates to the contrary notwithstanding, we know very little about the causes of individual decision-making and conduct, even our own. Because each one of us is autonomous and self-controlling by nature, it is very difficult to predict—with any degree of certainty—how any particular person will respond in a given situation. The difficulties associated with trying to forecast how any given individual will behave is made all the more impossible when institutions try to anticipate the wants, the likes and dislikes, and the conduct of millions of people. The miscalculation, confusion, and disruption that invariably accompany any effort at national economic planning, for example, is less a result of the incompetence of the planners than it is of the fatuous belief that political institutions have the capacity to predict the future preferences and actions of millions of persons. Because we are biologically self-controlling, our behavior is very unpredictable.

But institutions cannot live with uncertainty and unpredictability. They demand a rigid, unchanging, stable environment in which people are tied down by long-term commitments. The self-serving nature of all institutions fosters a process of "ossification" in which, according to Snell Putney, "the decision-making centers of a system come to derive their decisions independently of the information inputs and feedback." Putney goes on to state that "[t]here seems to be no way of preventing ossification. It is a natural process in social systems."[11] The implications are apparent: institutional behavior leads, invariably, to a structuring process in which the activities of people are increasingly *restricted*, and the activities of institutions are increasingly *insulated* from the influence and control of people.

Institutions have their own special interests which can only be advanced by homogenizing the individuality and diversity of people. Humanity has been compressed into molds that shape people to serve institutional purposes. It has been the common experience of mankind that people have been taught, pressured, and threatened "to give up being their own persons and to become whatever the game requires them to be."[12] Organized society has always been too involved in collectivizing and harmonizing millions of wills into uniform social orders to have much patience with individual preferences. As a result, institutions have always found it advantageous to structure human behavior by engineering a consensus in favor of institution-serving attitudes. As R.D. Laing has observed:

> Once people can be induced to experience a situation in a similar way, they can be expected to behave in similar ways. Induce people all to want the same thing, hate the same thing, feel the same threat, then their behavior is already captive—you have acquired your consumers or your cannon-fodder.[13]

In furtherance of their purposes, institutions have helped train us to fear uncertainty and doubt, and to insist upon fixed and certain knowledge. Dogmas, moral and philosophic systems, taboos, credos, organizationally-centered life-styles, and other doctrines and beliefs have been designed to convert the unpredictability and diversity of millions of autonomous human beings into a unified, predictable, and controllable whole, a "behavioristic herd to be conditioned and indoctrinated into virtuous conduct."[14] Men and women, who now search for moral and intellectual certainty, reinforce the herding process by dividing themselves from those whose views of reality do not coincide with their own. Then, in an effort to reinforce their *own* commitments, the true believers demand that the mavericks remaining outside the herd—and who are usually designated as unprincipled, or irrational, or insane—be rounded up and branded with the appropriate institutional insignia. With little question as to the wisdom of their doing so, millions upon millions of loving and responsible men and women have helped one another to look upon prison walls *not* as confining barriers, but as a security against the unknown dangers beyond. Through such attachments to their own ignorance, institutional prisoners have assured their keepers the existence of future generations of inmates by inculcating youth in such dubious virtues as organizational loyalty and subservience, obedience to authority, and the ultimate sacrifice of one's very sense of being a person.

We preoccupy ourselves so much with changing the lives of others *not* out of proclaimed sentiments of selfless human charity, but out of our selfish desire to validate our own identities. There is, of course, enormous ego-gratification in the exercise of power over other people, but such satisfaction is rooted in our need to have others believe and behave as we do. Our contemporary efforts to westernize the so-called "underdeveloped nations"—like our ancestors' attempts to Christianize pagan societies—reflect our need to have the rest of the world live as we live. Though we proselytize with computers instead of Bibles, our purpose remains the same: to confirm our sense of who we are. This need for self-verification through others, firmly incorporated into our organizational attachments, makes us enthusiastic agents for institutional ambitions.

The static, conservative nature of institutions causes them to favor not only a uniformity of practices among their members, but the maintenance of a firm and settled body of ideas supportive of the established order. It is for this reason that institutionalized society has always depended upon the existence of priestly classes who claimed to possess knowledge unavailable to others in society. Whether such knowledge was revealed by the gods or, in this scientific age, was the product of specialized study, the result was the same: by virtue of this superior knowledge, the priesthood was able to comprehend the subtleties and complexities of life and advise institutional leaders of the appropriate policies for avoiding chaos and catastrophe. The shamans and witch doctors of primitive societies gave way to the formal priesthoods of organized religions which, in turn, have been replaced by the priestly classes of our scientific and technological age: the scientists, academicians, and professional "experts" (e.g., physicians and medical researchers, economists, engineers, psychiatrists and psychologists, investment and marriage counselors, lawyers, "sexologists," et. al.). Throughout history, the institutional priesthood has helped to organize mankind with a common doctrine: that life is too complex for men and women to make decisions for themselves; that modern society requires organized leadership. Though we chortle disdainfully at the superstitious innocence of our primitive ancestors, we continue their habits of genuflection before priestly authorities. Was the man who sought the restoration of his health through a witch doctor possessed of fright masks any different from a contemporary who seeks a return to emotional stability by calling in a practitioner bearing Rorschach cards? Were the men who thought alchemists could turn lead into gold any more gullible than those of us who believed that government economists could produce prosperity from paper currencies? We may have more sophisticated superstitions than our ancestors, but have we a rightful claim to a superior exercise of intelligence?

Since it is, ultimately, our belief systems that sustain institutional power, it is understandable that these social organizations would want to promote and safeguard the body of ideas upon which their existence depends, and to resist innovation. Institutional success has always necessitated being at war with nonconforming individuals. Institutions cannot tolerate dissenters and non-believers who challenge the established attitudes, beliefs, and knowledge that provide the theoretical base for institutional existence. Nonconformists are living denials of the myth of the collective identity; their presence raises doubts in the minds of others that threaten the institutional scheme of things. In Harold Laski's words, "unwonted opinion or behavior is dangerous. It shocks men out of their accustomed grooves. It leads to the examination of basic principles, and that, in its turn, to the sense that contemporary institutions are not inevitable or final institutions."[15]

For these reasons, the political State has always had its categories of traitors, extremists, and radicals; religious organizations have had their heretics, sinners, and formal processes of excommunication. Business organizations ostracize or dismiss the man who is not a team player, and hold out promotions to those who best represent the corporate point of view. The military severely punishes as cowards and deserters men who place the value of their own lives above obedience to constituted authorities; while educational institutions have used the dunce cap, the "myth of the hyperactive child,"[16] and the power to flunk or expel those students who have their own views as to what is relevant to learn. Variation, novelty, change, and innovation—factors that reflect human diversity—have always been looked upon with suspicion by institutions. While they have had to tolerate a certain amount of diversity in order to maintain the sanction and approval of their members, they have never been willing to condone the sort of individuality that would substantially threaten the established institutionalized social system. Many who dared express an understanding that threatened or troubled the established order, came to their deaths upon the cross, the rack, the burning stake, or with a cup of hemlock. Though we like to believe that modern society has risen above such blatant efforts to destroy the men and women who challenge the prevailing doctrines and settled lore, it is closer to the truth to observe that there has only been a refinement in repressive methodologies. The religious inquisitors who perused the writings of dissidents for evidence of heresies have been replaced by State psychiatrists seeking—through practices leading to no less preordained conclusions than those arrived at by medieval

clerics—evidence of the psychotic tendencies that will justify the incarceration of contemporary nonconformists. Psychiatrist Thomas Szasz has offered the astute observation
that the persecution of witches died out only when modern
psychiatry emerged as a more scientifically acceptable substitute for ridding society of those persons whose unorthodox
views or behavior threatened the institutional order.[17] The
beheadings that rid the power structure of such minds as Sir
Thomas More have been replaced by lobotomies and other
forms of psychosurgery that seem to satisfy our preferences
for clinical-State methods of torture and tyranny.

Does the despotism of this century come any closer to the
basic standards of human decency than that practiced by our
ancestors? How different were the experiences of Tom
Paine—forced to flee England because of his criticisms of
British institutions, only to be imprisoned by the French
government for his anti-Jacobin views—from those of the
renowned psychiatrist Wilhelm Reich—forced to flee Nazi
Germany, only to die in an American prison, and to have his
books and research journals burned for having disobeyed a
federal Food and Drug Administration-sought injunction
that prohibited not only the promotion or sale of his orgone
energy devices, but many of his theoretical and philosophical
writings?[18] How different was the hemlock-induced death of
Socrates from the apparent drug overdose death of comedian
Lenny Bruce, two men who had been hounded unto their
deaths by an established order that feared their influences
upon the minds of young people? The arbitrary authority of
feudal kings to summarily punish critics for "treason," has
given way to White House "enemies lists," politically-
inspired tax audits, and the employment of other "dirty
tricks." Despots no longer poison one another in the manner
of Lucretia Borgia or the fictional Macbeth: such work is,
today, secretly hired out to government assassins working
for what are referred to—surely with a grotesque sense of

humor—as "intelligence agencies"! Those who oppose wars are no longer imprisoned without trial as they were by Abraham Lincoln, but are indicted—as were Dr. Benjamin Spock and others—for alleged "conspiracies" to encourage others to violate draft laws. Men and women who communicate to others about alternative health and medical practices that are inconsistent with the interests of the medical establishment are no longer hauled before ecclesiastical courts on charges of "sorcery": they must now answer to industry-dominated administrative agencies—such as the Food and Drug Administration, or state medical boards—to charges of "unlicensed medical practices." We fail to understand the fundamental nature of all institutions if we fail to perceive their inherently conservative, change-resistant characters, or note the viciousness with which they will respond to a significant threat.

On the other hand, the progress of what we are fond of calling civilization has been based upon a continuing challenge of the prevailing beliefs, practices, and institutions. Socrates, Christ, Copernicus, Galileo, Luther, Paine, Darwin, Marx, Einstein, and Gandhi, are among the more visible personifications of this tendency. The emergence of new religions and philosophies, the Renaissance, the industrial and scientific revolutions, and classic liberalism, were all occasioned by a questioning of the existing order and, in time, became the prevailing orthodoxy. The history of organized society has reflected the pattern discerned by Thomas Huxley, for "new truths to begin as heresies and to end as superstitions."[19]

Though institutions require certainty and inflexibility, why are *we*, as individuals, attracted to systems of fixed and certain ideas? What would cause *us* to want a durable and stable body of knowledge and beliefs? Perhaps our attraction to structured thinking and behavior is only a carry-over from our biological past, in which our pre-Homo sapiens ancestors functioned on the basis of instincts instead of conscious thought. Fixed patterns of behavior serve well those species that have become specialized for survival in a given environment, but the predictability of their conduct also assures the absence of any significant variety or change. Because we humans are *not* specialized, we are able—in fact, compelled—to use our minds to overcome many of our physical limitations, and adapt our conduct to a variety of environments. But with the flexibility that permits us to greatly transform our lives comes a loss of the undisturbed certainty associated with programmed behavior. The distress of an unsettled mind is aggravated by the fact that we have been carefully trained to believe in the need for intellectual certainty. Such training has been facilitated by the need all of us have to understand the nature of the world about us. But we have made the mistake of assuming that our desire for *understanding* requires *answers*. We tell ourselves that we are searching for answers to various questions, expecting that the answers will provide us with the understanding we seek. But understanding is not based upon *answers* as much as upon *questions*. Our formal education has emphasized learning how to provide *answers* (e.g., the ability to answer test questions, to respond to a teacher's inquiry, to recite catechisms or formulas, to recall memorized data, or to engage in problem solving) rather than learning how to ask the right *questions*. If we do not know how to ask relevant questions, how can we expect to come up with relevant answers? One is reminded, in this connection, of Gertrude Stein's classic deathbed utterance. In response to the query, "what is the answer?" Stein asked: "what is the question?"[20] What is more significant, however, is something the eastern philosophers have helped us to comprehend: *the answer is to be found in the question itself.*

When we insist upon answers, we forget that reality is never constant. It does not come in fixed, unalterable segments. Everything within the universe is part of a continuous process, and what we observe today is, at best, only a partial and fleeting glimpse of an instant of reality. To begin with, our mind and senses are limited by time and space. We observe reality *selectively*, not only because our observations tend to be conditioned by our prior experiences, but because of the physical limitations of our sensory organs (e.g., many light and sound waves are imperceptible to us). Furthermore, what we see today is not the same reality that we saw yesterday, nor will it be the same tomorrow. Nor can we disassociate ourselves from the observation process. We are a part of the reality we are observing and, like the rest of nature, we too are a continuing process of change. How and what we observe do not remain constant. As soon as we glimpse the answer we have been seeking, that answer (which is always only a partial one) becomes a part of our *past* and interferes with the processes of observation that are always in the *present*. Even if we reexamine the same thing, *what* we see after we have already found our answer, and the *intensity* of our continuing observation, will be different from our initial inquiry.

What this suggests, then, is that we learn more when our minds are *uncertain* than when we trust in settled conclusions and that continuing doubt fosters understanding. Many of us have, at one time or another, faced some crisis in our life in which we no longer had confidence in our prior learning, attitudes, or commitments. The crisis might have been associated with one's choice of a career, dissatisfaction concerning one's role in a marriage, or the loss of one's innocence about the nature of various institutions. Such crises, however, have often proven to be periods of "creative chaos," during which major transformations occurred within us. Having lost our sense of certainty about what we knew, we had to rediscover much of our world. We could no longer afford the luxury of kidding ourselves that everything was "just so," for our psychological survival depended upon a forthright questioning of our past learning. All that we had known was thrown into doubt. When we do not know something, we energize our minds to learn. When we are *certain* in our knowledge, on the other hand, we no longer inquire. It is in spontaneity and exploration—not rigid adherence to fixed truths—that our minds are best able to understand reality.

Why do we believe that we need certainty in what we know? Why do we have this preoccupation with being right? It may be answered that our knowledge must reflect reality in order that we might survive. But is this true? We humans have managed to institutionalize so many alleged fundamental truths that have later been demonstrated to be terribly in error (e.g., the shape of the earth and its relationship to the rest of the universe; the origins of the universe and life; the divine character of political rulers; etc.). Our understanding of many other basic matters (e.g., the nature, origin, and treatment of diseases; the causes of weather and natural disasters; the psychological makeup of human beings; etc.) has also been proven clearly erroneous on more than one occasion. But in spite of being so wrong about so many important things, we human beings have managed to survive. Primitive men possessed only a fraction of our formal understanding of reality, and yet were fully capable of sustaining themselves. To paraphrase a line from Hal Holbrook's *Mark Twain Tonight*, think of all the pre-Christianized tribes who managed to live happy and healthy lives without ever knowing there was a hell![21] The truth is that we humans have been very resilient people, capable of absorbing a great deal of error, falsehood, and plain ignorance. In what sense, then, can it be said that we have ever had a need for certainty? Is this an actual *physical* need that we have, or is it only a *psychological* need that we have learned to express as part of our structured and controlled training?

It is not settled and immutable truths from our *past* that we require in order to live well, but understanding of the *present*. Our answers are only intellectual abstractions, after-the-fact explanations of reality. Since our experiences are necessarily tied to the past, it becomes evident that our understanding of the present depends upon our *questions*. But, since the form and content of our questions also tend to be influenced by the past, our questioning must take the form of nonjudgmental, nonevaluative *observation*. This is the method of learning employed by very young children: to observe reality with the totality of one's senses; to taste, to feel, to smell, to watch, to listen; to approach reality with the attitude expressed by my oldest daughter when she was but three years old—"my think is always 'why?'."

To understand reality, then, we must first learn how to observe without imposing our past experiences upon the present. In other words, we must learn to observe, to experience the substance of reality itself, without allowing our thoughts (which are always based upon the past) to get between ourselves and what we are observing. When our thoughts intervene, we end up *not* with an understanding of reality, but with an understanding of our *ideas* about reality. What we see becomes filtered, divided up, and categorized on the basis of our prior experiences and intellectual constructs. We accept or reject facts on the basis of their compatability with what we already know, including our ideological commitments. Our inquiry, then, becomes little more than an exploration of our own mind. We compare and contrast ideas, or play logic games, or amuse ourselves with twentieth century variations of medieval inquiries into the number of angels capable of dancing on heads of pins. We operate on the assumption that understanding is a product of *reasoning* rather than *observation*. What is crucial to our understanding of ourselves and the universe of which we are an indivisible part, on the other hand, is our continuing inquiry, our never ending process of observing, searching, and asking.

To do this requires a mind that is not only free of the prejudices of prior experiences, but is aware of the pitfalls associated with discovering answers.

How does all of this relate to institutions and conflict? As we have already seen, both of these phenomena are occasioned by the way you and I view ourselves, other people, and the world about us. In the most realistic sense of the word, institutions exist only in our heads. They are a product of the way we think about things. They are words surrounded by people. They represent our past rolled in gold leaf. We cannot understand institutions until we understand the intellectual processes within our own minds that sustain them. The human crisis, in other words, is within our consciousness.

If we can observe how our conscious minds deal with reality, we may be able to see a parallel between institutional structuring and our own intellectual structuring. When we try to live in the *present* on the basis of our structured knowledge from the *past;* when we try to enforce ideological consistency upon ourselves, struggle to conform our actions and beliefs to the ideas firmly-entrenched within us, and impose restraints upon the full and autonomous expression of our very souls, we are behaving just like institutions. It is the nature of intelligent life to function with energized awareness; to be free, searching, and naturally spontaneous. Not being burdened by a sense of allegiance to prior learning, an unfettered mind is capable of a greater range of possible responses to new experiences. Institutionally-dominated minds, on the other hand, tend to be characterized by passivity and discipline; by a rigidly-structured conditioning designed to conform present behavior to the demands of previously learned institutional values. Because they no longer possess the natural resiliency of presently-focused, unstructured minds, such people tend to reflect the pathetic patterns of behavior identified in Abraham Maslow's words at the beginning of this chapter.

It ought to be clear to us, then, where institutions origi-
nate: they are mirror images of our conscious minds. We like
to imagine that there are men and women—or other superhuman beings—who, unlike ourselves, are possessed of both
factual and moral certainty, and in whom we can invest the
responsibility to make the right decisions for our lives. In
spite of evidence that the universe began in a spontaneous
"big bang," and will likely end in a "big crunch," we still
refuse to acknowledge the inherent uncertainty of reality.
We would rather play tricks upon ourselves by pretending
that someone or something is—or ought to be—in charge of
everything, and that this authority can provide what nature
neglected: absolute certainty. Our consciousness, in other
words, provides the breeding ground for institutional authorities. Those who are inclined to blame others for their trou-
bles would be better advised to look inside themselves. Until
we can learn to not be afraid of being apprehensive, and to
experience the euphoric sense of liberation that comes with
being able to live with psychological uncertainty, we shall
continue being the designers of our own personal and institutional confinements.

I recall an incident from my youth that is relevant here. I
was taking swimming lessons, during which I first had to
learn, within the more certain surroundings of the shallow
end of the pool, how to float on my back. After accomplishing this task, my instructor pulled me (via a long pole he held
from the side of the pool) into the deep end and told me to
relax and do what I had already learned to do: float on my
back. I did so without any difficulty until my conscious mind
reminded me that (1) I was at the deep end of the pool, and,
(2) I did not know how to swim. My fears took over and I
began to struggle, hoping to find a fixed landmark onto
which I could hold. As long as my past-oriented mind was in
control, I struggled and kept going under, looking for land-
marks or my teacher for security. When I learned to shut off

my conscious mind and just float in my sea of uncertainty, I was able to deal with reality and learn to swim. Paradoxically, it was not my *lack* of knowledge, but the knowledge I carried with me from my past, that most threatened to take me under.

As long as our inquiries into the nature of reality are based upon nonjudgmental, nonevaluative observation, rather than proceeding from our ideas and other prior experiences, our minds would have no need for certainty. We would actively consume reality, as a sponge absorbs the water around it, until we and what we are observing become indistinguishable. We would take it all in, as does a camera, without concern for whether the consequences will be compatible with what we have seen previously. A need for certainty arises only when we allow our mind to make judgments—based upon our past learning—about what we discover. Certainty becomes important only if we are seeking to confirm our prior experiences or other prejudices. But even if our prior experiences continue to approximate present reality, what benefit is there in reconfirming our past? And if they do not, who would benefit from our doing so?

6

PRAGMATISM DOESN'T WORK

*Some of the owner men were kind because they
hated what they had to do, and some of them
were angry because they hated to be cruel, and
some of them were cold because they had long
ago found that one could not be an owner unless
one were cold. And all of them were caught in
something larger than themselves. Some of
them hated the mathematics that drove them,
and some were afraid, and some worshipped the
mathematics because it provided a refuge from
thought and from feeling.*
—From *The Grapes of Wrath*
by John Steinbeck[1]

There is a dichotomy about institutions. On the one hand,
they exist only by virtue of the production of individual men
and women. Institutions succeed only by using people, by
extracting, through various means, the energies or the material resources of human beings. Without our participation,
organizational activity would cease. At the same time, however, because they have the machinery for mobilizing
our skills through the division of labor principle, many
institutions—particularly economic ones—are able to combine our efforts to greatly multiply the amount of production
over what individuals could do on their own. This dichotomy
provides one of the major hurdles to our efforts to come to
grips with the disruptive nature of institutional behavior.

The organizational structuring of our lives has, of course,

provided us with many material benefits. But in recent years, many people have become increasingly aware of the physical and psychological costs mankind—and the rest of the planet—has had to incur to obtain such benefits. In the name of efficiency, business firms have been permitted to dump their unprofitable by-products into rivers, oceans, the atmosphere, or the lands of others, imposing upon us all hidden taxes that threaten not only the *quality* but the very *existence* of life on earth. The interests of the political-industrial system have also precipitated murderous wars, with hundreds of millions of men, women, and children being sacrificed for the aggrandizement of organizational power. Institutions of every type have, to one degree or another, abused and degraded human beings with their coercive, intimidative, and manipulative practices designed to get people to surrender their wills to organizational authorities. But none of these problems would likely have developed had we not imposed upon ourselves an even deadlier influence: institution serving beliefs and attitudes. We have polluted our minds with ideas about the propriety of our subservience to organizational purposes, and have cooperated to twist and contort ourselves from self-directed, autonomous beings into self-denying institutional robots.

One of the ideas we have accepted in our institutionally-oriented upbringing is the central role of *pragmatism* as the basis for decision-making. The emotional and other human costs involved in directing, compelling, and manipulating people in furtherance of organizational objectives, are not generally considered by the pragmatist who, according to one dictionary definition, "test[s] the validity of all concepts by their practical results."[2] What politician, businessman, or other institutional official, has not tried to rationalize the repression and victimization of people in terms of practical necessity? Philosophic premises, moral arguments, sentiment, intuitive or emotional appeals about the dignity of man or the quality of human life, and value judgments, do not figure in the calculations of the "real-world" pragmatist who is only concerned with "getting things done."

The limitations of the pragmatic approach to decision-making were pointed out in an example brought to my attention by a friend. The illustration he used was from ancient Syria, and involved a prescription for steelmaking discovered on a parchment at an archeological site at Tyre:

> Let the high dignitary furnish an Ethiop of fair frame and let him be bound down, shoulders upward, upon the block of the God Bal-Hal, his arms fastened underneath with thongs, a strap of goatskin over his back, and wound twice around the block, his feet close together lashed to a dowel of wood, and his head and neck projecting over and beyond the end of the block. . . . Then let the master workman, having cold-hammered the blade to a smooth and thin edge, thrust it into the fire of the cedarwood coals, in and out, the while reciting the prayer to the God Bal-Hal, until the steel be the color of the red of the rising sun when he comes up over the desert toward the East, and then with a quick motion pass the same from the heel thereof to the point, six times through the most fleshy portion of the slave's back and thighs, when it shall have become the color of the purple of the king. Then, if with one swing, and one stroke of the right arm of the master workman it severs the head of the slave from his body, and display not nick or crack along the edge, and the blade may be bent round about the body of the man and break not, it shall be accepted as a perfect weapon, sacred to the service of the God Bal-Hal, and the owner thereof may thrust it into a scabbard of asses' skin, brazen with brass, and hung to a girdle of camel's wool

dyed in the royal purple.[3]
My friend—an engineer with many years experience in
industry, but intensely sensitive to human values—noted that
the procedure satisfied the technical requirements for steelmaking, including heat-treatment, quality control, and
packaging, and invited his readers to draw the rather obvious
conclusion about the limitations of pragmatism as a standard
for human decision-making.

The example was a poignant one, and its message was not
lost. Some may respond that the illustration only set up a
straw man; that the vicious and inhumane nature of this
practice is so apparent that not even the most insensitive
industrialist could countenance its use. This is undoubtedly
so. But that is precisely what makes this example so valuable
in trying to understand the costs of contemporary practices.
If ancient steelmakers could employ such a method without
any hesitation, how much conflict, dissatisfaction, anger,
pain, and unhappiness do *we* help to engender because we are
not sensitive to the human costs associated with our actions?
What lesser offenses than those writ on Syrian parchment do
we regularly sanction against one another simply because we
are not aware of the consequences?

If we are to understand the nature of our personal and
social problems, we must learn that what is important to us as
human beings, and what is important to institutions, are not
always compatible. Institutional decision-making is pre-
occupied with attention to those objectively-described,
quantifiable costs that directly affect organizational success.
As organizational decision-making becomes more specialized
and divided, officials tend to more narrowly define the
parameters of factors to be considered in making decisions.
They learn to consider only the *material* consequences of their
actions, and become increasingly inattentive to anything that
is not directly related to solving the problems before them.

Such decision-making tends to minimize the significance

of psychic and other human costs, as well as the emotional and aesthetic effects of organizational activity. Most institutional authorities are not inclined to weigh heavily such nonmaterial factors as individual resentment of their own manipulation, intimidation, and loss of dignity, autonomy, and respect. Institutions, after all, do not have feelings, philosophic principles, or souls. They do not bleed, hurt, cry, laugh, or feel pain, joy, exhiliration, sadness, or indignation. As a result, the men and women who have become organizational leaders because they best reflect the institutional viewpoint have had to repress such nonmaterial considerations within themselves. Such repression produces fragmentation and a sense of being incomplete. Having learned to efface their own humanity and personality in favor of the standardized group consciousness, such persons are unlikely to be sensitive to the feelings, dreams, and psychological pains of others. It is little wonder that such officials are often seen as being inconsiderate or even malevolent, or that the organizational decisions they make are often fragmentary, conflict-ridden, and lacking in coherence.

Institutional behavior, in other words, is lacking in *integrity*. By "integrity" I refer not to that more popular usage that speaks of one's adherence to legal or moral codes of conduct, but to the broader sense of being complete and undivided, of being integrated, of being whole. Institutional decision-making lacks this sense of integration because of the division, separateness of purpose, and conflict that is inherent within it. Organizational insensitivity to human costs is but one manifestation of this lack of integrity.

Many businessmen would, I believe, be quite willing to return to a legalized system of slavery—provided it was dressed up in a less provocative name, such as "alternate service" under the draft laws—if such a system were to appear more profitable to their firms. Those who regard this as too harsh an accusation are invited to review the history of the I.G. Farben Company, and its willingness to use State-supplied slave labor in its factories in Nazi Germany.[4] Those contemporary business leaders who are prepared to sanction the involuntary servitude of a system of military or "public service" conscription would no doubt be equal to the task of rationalizing a legalized scheme for industrial conscription. The public school system already has its "conscript clientele," over which it rules with the unassailable authority of the most autocratic plantation overlord. Governments and business firms routinely gather the most personal information about people, and many retail establishments have begun emulating the brutal methods initiated by police departments in efforts to confront suspected shoplifters. Governments around the world have exhibited little restraint in the use of concentration camps, torture, hired assassins, or the wholesale slaughter of men, women, and children in advancing whatever they choose to characterize as their "national interests."

Perhaps pragmatism *is* the appropriate standard by which to measure institutional conduct, for if we consider *all* the consequences, our well-organized madness hardly serves as a practical model for social living. If peace, cooperation, order, love, and mutual respect are important to us, our established practices are terribly ineffective. If those who profess to be realistic pragmatists would become aware of all the costs of institutionalism—the long-term, the human, and the intangibles, as well as the short-term, the organizational, and the quantifiable—they would soon understand just who are the hard-headed realists and who the fuzzy-minded visionaries! It is because our awareness is so limited that we so often fail to comprehend the contradictory nature of our practical undertakings.

Because we have developed an institutional view of the world, we are not disposed to think about matters that have no relationship to the pursuit of organizational purposes. We insulate our emotions with a hidebound cocoon spun from platitudes about real-world practicality. Because they are concerned only with so-called "bottom line" considerations of profits, losses, and power, institutions have taught us to be motivated only by externally-derived systems of rewards and punishments. We have accepted the view that "life is an all-consuming race for money, status, acclaim, perhaps for bare survival," and that our very worth is measured "by acquisition and conquest, by *having*, never by *being*."[5] It is no wonder, then, that when our protective shield is occasionally penetrated by grim and painful evidence that we can no longer ignore, we tend to respond with rationalizations about the failure of *leadership*, not of our *institutional premises*. As a consequence of all this, we have accepted the inherently contradictory notions that competitive discord is nature's way of providing order, and that the human race has survived and evolved through a process of the strong destroying the weak. But it is *ideas*, not our biological *nature*, that are destroying us. We are eating ourselves alive, from the inside out, in the name of advancing successful and responsible careers within institutional hierarchies.

The manner in which institutional officials deal with persons within their respective organizations is, for the most part, a reflection of the assumptions they hold regarding the basic nature of human beings. While institutions tend to attract, as leaders, those who enjoy the exercise of power over other people, the willingness of such agencies to engage in human structuring reflects not so much a *maliciousness* as an *insensitivity* to the personal consequences of such practices. In the words of two observers, *"the intentions of managers are decent and . . . they want the best, not only for themselves and their organizations, but for all people as well."*[6] It is not in simplistic devil theories that one will find an explanation for dehumanizing institutional practices. Like the ancient Syrian steelmakers, many officials are simply unaware, unconscious of the human consequences of coercing and manipulating other people. This lack of consideration can be seen as the product of the operational premises of institutionalism which, as Steinbeck reminds us, involve processes as dehumanizing to the authority as to the subordinate.

It is probably impossible to begin calculating the pain and suffering, or the sense of indignity and humiliation brought on by our being dominated by institutional interests. The greater the degree of *power* being exerted over us, the greater the degree of our own contrary *free will* that is being subdued, and the stronger our resentment. The feelings of anger and personal worthlessness we experience as a result of the suppression of our own sense of self, have been observed by psychiatrist Viktor Frankl in connection with his own imprisonment in Nazi concentration camps. "Under the influence of a world which no longer recognized the value of human life and human dignity," said Frankl, people "lost the feeling of being an individual, a being with a mind, with inner freedom and personal value."[7] While Frankl was discussing a world of torture, gas chambers, and other calculated cruelties, his words have significance for every situation in which any person is exploited or sacrificed for the benefit of others. It is such feelings of resentment, however, that institutional officials have learned to disregard.

No one has done a better job polarizing the underlying premises of organization managers than Douglas McGregor. He has identified the more traditional, externally-directed view of management as "theory x," and the alternative, self-directed approach as "theory y." The "theory x" managers assume, in McGregor's words, that:

> 1. *The average human being has an inherent dislike of work and will avoid it if he can.* . . .
> 2. *Because of this human characteristic of dislike of work, most people must be coerced, controlled, directed, threatened with punishment to get them to put forth adequate effort*

toward the achievement of organizational objectives. . . .
3. The average human being prefers to be directed, wishes to
avoid responsibility, has relatively little ambition, wants
security above all. . . .[8]

By contrast, the "theory y" manager assumes that:

[t]he expenditure of physical and mental effort in work is as
natural as play or rest. . . . Man will exercise self-direction
and self-control in the service of objectives to which he is
committed. . . . The average human being learns, under
proper conditions, not only to accept but to seek responsibil-
ity. . . .[9]

The basic tenets of "theory x" are most evident in highly-
structured forms of social organization. They are, in fact, the
implicit assumptions held by every form of political institution
regarding the nature of human behavior. Those who operate
on such premises assume that the accomplishment of organizational goals requires the supervision, direction, and control
of human beings through the exercise of coercion, fear, and
punishment. The public school teacher or principal, judge or
police officer, priest or pastor, foreman or personnel director
who does not see mankind through "theory x" lenses is,
indeed, the exception within most institutions.

All of this should reveal to us something about the institutional perception of man. Those who are willing to *use* other
people—whether through manipulation, coercion, or other
exploitative means—to accomplish their purposes, must
surely have a dismal view of human life. From such a perspective, the ideal human personality must be something resem-
bling the "Pringle." Pringles are those uniformly-processed,
uniformly-textured, uniformly-shaped potato chips that
come uniformly-stacked in round containers. Pringles are
constant, undifferentiated chips with a commitment to the
unvarying conformity we expect from institutions. Pringles
belong to the same family as the cookie cutter people: cut
right out of somebody else's mold. Not a bearded, long-

haired radical in the group; not a black sheep among them to embarrass the rest of the family; not a deviate or extremist in the crowd to threaten the social order; not a one among them stepping to the beat of a different drummer: they are straight out of *Brave New World.* When you open a can of them you hear a sound not unlike that of a whispered "shhhhh," as though to deter the utterance of a heresy, or even a discouraging word.

Perhaps this is the fate of us all: to become institutionally Pringleized; to be turned into uniform, unchanging beings who dutifully take our rigidly-defined places in tightly-packed, stifling, airtight organizational containers. There were overtones of such prospects in some research done a number of years ago with retarded patients at a state mental institution. The retarded persons were provided with paying jobs in industry doing routine, light assembly work. These people proved to be very serious, punctual workers. They arrived at work on time and went straight to their work stations. They took work breaks only when scheduled and promptly returned to their work when the breaks were over. Unlike their less-handicapped counterparts, they diligently tended to their work without interruptions of horseplay, goofing off, or clock-watching. Their work was of good quality. What is more, these retarded workers clearly enjoyed what they were doing: they smiled almost constantly. When their work day was over, they promptly left the plant and returned to the mental institution from whence they had come. The experiment was generally regarded as a success, leaving us to contemplate the disquieting fact that the attentive behavior of such retarded persons exemplified what most businessmen would doubtless consider that of the ideal employee!

If what has been said thus far is true, the question remains: since both work and social organization are natural to us, why have institutions so consistently developed personally-restrictive and highly-structured organizational practices? Why have institutional authorities tended to reflect "theory x" managerial styles? It may be that such methods reflect a natural evolutionary process within any organization. Size may prove to be a catalyst for helping to convert a cooperative, informal organization into a rigidly-disciplined, hierarchically-structured institution. As any organization grows in size, the contribution and influence of each member of the group becomes diluted. People perceive a less direct correlation between their contribution to the group and the benefits they receive. It becomes possible, in other words, for the members of the organization to share in group benefits without contributing their full share to the effort.

The implications of this have been explored by economist Mancur Olson, whose inquiry raises serious doubts about the validity of the folk wisdom that suggests that the interests of the group are but a composite of the interests of the individual members comprising that group. Olson's analysis demonstrates that, even where individual members of the group have a common interest in realizing the group's objectives, it is in the interests of each member to allow the *others* to incur the costs associated with such activity. This is the so-called "free rider" problem familiar to labor unions, trade associations, and voluntary cartels: the self-interest incentives of each member to not have to pay any of the costs (whether in the form of dues or higher product prices) will undermine the group's purposes *even though each member would be better off if everyone did contribute his or her share of the costs.* As Olson states it: "unless the number of individuals in a group is quite small, or unless there is coercion or some other special device to make individuals act in their common interest, *rational, self-interested individuals will not act to achieve their common or group interests.*"[10] He adds:

> The larger a group is, the farther it will fall short
> of obtaining an optimal supply of any collective

good, and the less likely that it will act to obtain
even a minimal amount of such a good. In short,
the larger the group, the less it will further its
common interests.[11]

Olson's analysis may help us to understand how and why
even *voluntary* organizations have a tendency to become
structured and institutionalized. It may be that true, unstructured cooperation is possible only when the size of the group
is small enough that each of the members will be motivated
to contribute to the joint effort in order to accomplish what
each wants individually. But as the group increases in size—
as it must with any institution with which more and more
people are willing to associate themselves—the incentives
for true cooperation are diminished. Relationships become
less personal; face-to-face dealings with one another dissolve
into formal rules and chain of command directives; there is
less and less correlation between individual effort and group
output.

The less people perceive that their personal objectives can
be satisfied by helping the group to achieve its goals, the
greater the likelihood that "coercion or some other special
device" will be employed to compel or manipulate group
members. By that point, a division clearly exists within the
group, with the members and the organization, the employees
and the management, looked upon in antagonistic roles.
Accentuating this conflict is the introduction into the organization of a managerial class, whose function is not to *augment*
the work of the other members, but to organize and coordinate and supervise it. What this amounts to is placing the
group under the control of an elite trained in the art of
managing, i.e., manipulating and controlling other people in
order to get them to work on behalf of the organization.
Whether the motivational tools consist of such carrots as
rewards, incentives, promotions, or other prizes, or punishments, penalties, demotions, or other applications of the

stick, the manager's function is to induce persons under him to pursue those organizational objectives they might not otherwise be inclined to pursue. Institutional supervision and control may be necessary, in other words, only in those situations in which some people want to get others to do things that the latter really do not want to do.

Once this occurs, the spirit of cooperation quickly gives way to threats, punishments, persuasion, and other forms of manipulation; individual self-interest is replaced by notions of duty and sacrifice; the pleasure of teamwork melts in the fear of sanctions; the enjoyment of *work* becomes the misery of *servitude*. When the group no longer functions as a cooperative venture, but is under the control and direction of an elite of managers; when the organization is looked upon as something more than a tool or a convenience for its members, and is regarded as having rights or interests separate from and superior to those of its members; when, in other words, the organization takes on the character of a depersonalized entity with an identity and purpose of its own, it has become an institution. The human consequences of such practices have been noted by the late E.F. Schumacher:

> That soul-destroying, meaningless, mechanical, monotonous, moronic work is an insult to human nature which must necessarily and inevitably produce either escapism or aggression, and that no amount of "bread and circuses" can compensate for the damage done—these are facts which are neither denied nor acknowledged but are met with an unbreakable conspiracy of silence—because to deny them would be too obviously absurd and to acknowledge them would condemn the central preoccupation of modern society as a crime against humanity.[12]

One may suppose, at this point, that the appropriate response to such systems of structuring is to join with those

other critics of industrialism who have attacked the techno-
logically-dominant, growth-oriented premises of western
society. But it is to misconceive the nature of the problem to
lay the blame upon technology itself. The prognosis for
humanity has been made increasingly grim by the fact that
our enhanced technological capacities have not been tempered by any significant improvement in our psychological
maturity. Technology and institutions are both products of
the human mind, consequences of the ways in which we think
about things. A repressive and dehumanizing technology is
but a reflection of the premises we have brought to the
designing boards. As long as our minds are divided, confused,
and angry, we will continue to produce tools of violence and
control. Technology, in other words, has not fashioned *itself*.
Machines have not forced us into their service; they have not
reached out and grabbed us like marauding, mechanical
slavers. We have chosen our indentured servitude, having
been enticed by the many trinkets and treasures that were
dangled before our dazzled eyes. It is not *technology* that has
subordinated us to institutions, but our self-induced *dependencies* upon technology, and our willingness to believe that
technology must be housed within institutional walls. We
have been unwilling to question present methods of production on the assumption that institutions *themselves* will provide us with any needed innovation.

But institutions are designed to *resist* any substantial innovation deemed threatening to their established interests. As
we shall discover in chapter 9, most business institutions
have regarded open and unconstrained economic environments as impediments to their growth and power. They have
helped indoctrinate us in the view that any obstacles to their
expansive ambitions were problems for all of us. Without
inquiring into the consequences, we have sanctioned all
manner of politically imposed restraints designed to eliminate such barriers. We have accepted the economies of scale,

natural monopolies, and free rider rationales for institutionally-centralized production, without considering that such factors—rather than justifying the *extension* of organizational power—may represent natural forces that help keep organizational size to within limits compatible with the interests of people. In our innocence and dependency, we have failed to see how institutions develop a vested interest in the maintenance of their existing systems and technologies, and how they resist efforts to adopt methods inconsistent with such established practices.

None of this is to suggest a neo-Luddite, emotionally reactive approach to technology: quite the contrary. Computers, lasers, space engineering, and other emerging forms of technology can, like our present machinery, become either tools of assistance and understanding, or weapons of control and violence. It is not *technology* that needs changing, but our *attitudes* that cause us to be dependent upon technology, or upon the institutional ownership and control of technology. This is the real lesson of Schumacher's *Small Is Beautiful.* Neither blind faith in the "bigger is better" doctrine of industrialism, nor a modern-day equivalent of the machine-breaking riots will suffice. Rather, we must learn to become more sensitive to all the personal, social, and environmental consequences of our efforts to sustain ourselves on this planet. We must learn to question the assumption that the subordination of our thoughts, our emotions, our actions, and our very beings to organizational purposes offers the most practical and least cost method of living. For when we examine *all* the costs—particularly those that affect the quality of human life—we will likely discover that our most efficient methods are far too costly, and that pragmatism really doesn't work.

7

THE PEOPLE PUSHERS

*Government is actually the worst failure of
civilized man. There has never been a really
good one, and even those that are most tolerable
are arbitrary, cruel, grasping and unintelligent.
Indeed, it would not be far wrong to describe the
best as the common enemy of all decent citizens.
But there will be small hope of gaining adherents to this idea so long as government is
thought of as an independent and somehow
super-human organism, with powers, rights
and privileges transcending those of any other
human aggregation.*

—H.L. Mencken[1]

As I best recall, my introduction to the realities of politics
occurred during the 1944 presidential campaign. I was a
nine-year-old with the courage of my parents' convictions
that the reelection of Franklin D. Roosevelt would be disastrous to the nation. At that young an age, however, politics
was only some vaguely understood game, with our selection
of sides being somewhat akin to making a choice between
cheering for the Yankees or the Cardinals in the World
Series. Or so I thought, at any rate, until one fall day when I
went over to the school playground and discovered two
eleven-year-old boys—the revered "big kids"—engaged in
a no-fooling-around fistfight. This was the first serious fight
I had witnessed other than on a motion picture screen, and
the ferocity with which these boys were willing to attack one
another was quite frightening. Curious as to the purpose of it
all, I inquired of one of the onlookers, who informed me that
the fight was between the leader of the pro-Roosevelt group

and the leader of the pro-Dewey contingent. The Roosevelt crowd was on one side of the fray, glowering at the Dewey-ites, and the Dewey faction was on the other side, staring back contemptuously. And there, in the middle of every-thing, were the leaders of these two gangs, pounding away at one another, each seeking to pummel the other into submis-sion. I was beginning to understand what politics was all about.

Almost all of us have been raised in the belief that political institutions are necessary to provide order and harmony in society. In fact, we have been taught that the political State is synonymous with society itself; that the political State energizes and organizes society, creates and protects human rights, and makes economic and social life possible. We have even learned that civilization is something equated with (or at least the product of) sophisticated systems of political organization. We have, in other words, been taught that political institutions are a benefit to us, and that political leaders exist to serve us by harmonizing our differences and coordinating our energies in order to maximize our interests and promote the general welfare of all of us.

But is any of this true? Do political institutions exist to promote *our* interests? In order to answer this question, let us consider how officials of the political State deal with us. If the State *is* our agent, and State officials are indeed con-cerned with furthering *our* welfare, we should expect the actions of these officials to reflect *our* wishes. We would suppose that they would be highly solicitous of us, and regard their opinions and desires in matters affecting our interests as subservient to ours. But this is not the way in which State officials function. They behave as anything but dutiful sub-ordinates, or agents desirous only of obeying our wills.

When we scrape away the high school civics class veneer and examine how, in fact, officials of the State behave, we discover that, instead of them helping us to realize our objectives, they coerce, threaten, and intimidate us to get *us* to do what *they* want in order to further the purposes of the State. Their time is spent directing, warning, taxing, ordering, enjoining, confiscating, penalizing, arresting, preventing, punishing, incarcerating, mobilizing, compelling, conscripting, killing, surveilling, trespassing, denying, deceiving, rationing, and mandating. This is not what the *words* we have learned to associate with the political State *say* they do: the words tell us that State officials only *serve* and *protect* us. These people are, we are told, public servants. But if we look to the reality of how political institutions function, it becomes clear that their essence is to be found in the exercise of coercive power against *us*. *We*, the theoretical beneficiaries of political systems, are the ones who must obey, who must subordinate our wishes and desires to the dictates of our alleged agents.

While we are fond of reciting litanies about our free and voluntary political institutions (even the Internal Revenue Service points with pride to the taxpayers' "voluntary" compliance with income tax laws!), it should be quite evident that the political State tries to regulate our lives by violating our free wills, by imposing legal standards of conduct upon us, and by threatening us with punishment if we do not obey. It is the person who does not voluntarily choose to be subservient to State authority who is of greatest concern to government officials.

How have political institutions managed, throughout history, to maintain such a nearly universal power to threaten, compel, tax, and punish its own citizens? Why have we been so willing to cooperate in our own subjugation? Is the power and authority of the State sustained by our fear of its capacities to punish us or confiscate our property? I think not. A gang of brigands or mobsters could, for example, loot and coerce a given group of people for a limited period of time, but the fear of such attacks would not be enough to convert such gangs into permanent political institutions. As long as the victims viewed their attackers as criminals, they would likely oppose or seek to evade their assaults. The hostility of their victims would likely cause whatever power the gang enjoyed to disintegrate. If these marauders wanted to maintain a permanent position of power, if, in other words, they wanted to institutionalize their rule, they would have to reduce or eliminate such hostility. To accomplish this, they would seek to develop a consensus among their victims that their authority is *legitimate*, their exercise of power *justified*. It is the acquiescence, the *approval*, of the victims of State action in the purposes and processes of political control that sustains the political State and gives it permanence.

The emergence of political power can, perhaps, be traced to the power of the spoken word. Many of the more intelligent members of early cultures may have foreseen that power could be acquired over their fellow tribesmen by *institutionalizing* the tribe, by cloaking it with metaphysical significance.[2] Through their efforts, such men helped to transform primitive man's perceptions and attitudes about the nature of human society. They understood that the process of controlling others through the exercise of political power could not be made permanent until those who are to be subject to such control grant their *sanction* to the institution. This sanction requires not simply lip service to the entity, but the internalized belief by the individual that this entity has a *right* to rule him. In a very real sense, the political State is born of our belief that it *should* exist. This is ordinarily accomplished through the individual believing that his identity is wrapped up in the State; that the *State* is an extension of *himself*. The State amasses its power *not* through the appropriation of wealth or other property, or through the mobilization of bodies, but through collectivizing the identities, the ego boundaries of those to be governed. How manageable and obedient people become; how willing they are to surrender their lives or their property or their judgment to the State, when they truly believe that, in doing so, the *State* is serving *them*; the *State* is fulfilling *their* purposes in life.

The political State can engage in coercive and manipulative practices against its own citizens, then, only because these same citizens are willing to cooperate with it. But why do people sanction this exercise of political authority over their lives? It is understandable that one might *obey* an armed brute who was threatening him with harm, but what would cause him to *approve* of the practice, to be willing to accord it *legitimacy*? What would cause people to march off to war and participate in the mass annihilation of millions upon millions of other persons—total strangers—and at great risk of their own death or dismemberment? What do people expect from political institutions that can lead them to regard their submission to the coercive, violent, life-destroying authority of the State, as their highest act of honor and virtue?

Many people sanction the political State for purely pragmatic, economic self-interest motivations. These people seek a structured form of social order because, in one way or another, they stand to benefit (or at least believe that they will benefit) from having the State restrict the actions of others. To the businessman, this order means a system of laws to restrict the practices of one's competitors; to the educationalist, it means the adoption of State-enforced standards of instruction applicable to all; to the moral reformer, it means the banning of drugs, alcohol, and pornographic books; to the labor union, it means the elimination of lower-priced labor through minimum wage laws, as well as a monopolistic status as bargaining representative for all employees of a particular employer; to the manufacturer, it means the restriction of competitive foreign imports through tariff and import quotas; to the environmentalist, it means restriction of the development of natural resources; to the railroad or telephone company executive, it means the assurance of restricted entry of would-be competitors and the comfort of knowing that existing competitors may not engage in effective price competition through reduced rates; to the farmer, it means governmental maintenance of artificially high prices for farm products; to the consumer advocate, it means the imposition of his preferences on all other consumers; to the doctor, lawyer, barber, dentist, funeral director, electrician, and car dealer, it means control over the trade practices of one's competitors (as well as the entry of other would-be competitors) through systems of licensing; and to the real estate developer, it means the regulation, through zoning laws, of the use that others may make of their property. To such people, the State functions as a mechanism for ordering, restricting, and regulating human conduct in order to protect advantages they might lose if other people were free to pursue their interests. These people can hardly be considered victims of State action: they are profiting from it, and their belief in the necessity for political institutions has rather apparent self-interest motives.

Most people, however, have come to sanction the political State for reasons unrelated to the advancement of their economic or ideological interests. The endorsements of this second group are the products of personal attitudes and beliefs, although many may also share the pragmatic motivation for supporting the State. Such persons subject themselves to the exercise of State authority because they have learned to become externalized, other-directed persons whose life-focus is outside themselves. Consistent with our previous discussion of the establishment of ego boundaries, these people have come to identify their very beings with the State. For them, the State reflects the projection of the personal images they have of themselves. In obeying the edicts of political authorities, they believe, they are fulfilling themselves.

Most of us have grown up believing in the need for political institutions because the State has helped teach us to think this way. Even though other supposedly less intelligent animals have managed to live quite well without violent, conflict-ridden, and oppressive political organizations, we humans do not question their absolute necessity. The State has fostered this belief by encouraging us to live outside ourselves, to look to other people as the sources of our problems and our salvation. The State, in other words, has had a vested interest in promoting attitudes that would tend to make us skeptical of our own abilities, fearful of the motives of others, and emotionally dependent upon external authorities for purpose and direction in our lives.

In order to encourage us to become externally oriented, political institutions have always had to manufacture vague abstractions, and seek to persuade us to identify ourselves with such abstractions. This practice has gone on throughout recorded history. In the name of "America," or "the father-land," or "democracy," or "the majority," or "the proletar-iat," or "the true religion," or "the Inca," or "Pharaoh," or "the free world," or "black nationalism," or "white suprem-acy," or "manifest destiny," or any of untold other national-istic, ideological, or religious generalizations, most of the people who have ever occupied this earth have been willing participants in their own victimization by political institu-tions.

Political authorities have, in the pursuit of their interests, found it profitable to mass-market fear and distrust of others. In doing so, they have generated the division and collectivi-zation of people that is the essence of social conflict. Whether the fear objects have consisted of the "Nine Bows" or the "robber barons"; the "international communist con-spiracy" or "Zionist bankers"; "capitalist imperialism" or the "warlike Germans"; the "drug-crazed yippies" or the "over-thirty crowd"; the "establishment" or the "anar-chists"; or simply their own neighbors or those persons who are trying to become their neighbors, the political State has always sought to create in the minds of people a fear of other persons, groups, ideologies, or nations and, at the same time, the assurance that *their* political authorities—if only given enough power—are capable of protecting them from such threatening forces.

We have already seen that conflict arises whenever people divide themselves into groups. Whether the division is along nationality, religious, racial, sexual, ideological, or geographical lines; or whether it is based on employer/employee, manufacturer/consumer, or management/stockholder sub-divisions (or any of a seemingly endless assortment of other factions), the result is always to foster the we-they, if-you're-not-with-us-you're-against-us attitudes that do more than *promote* conflict: they *are* conflict.

We have learned to think of conflict as the normal state of human affairs, and to look upon the State as a necessary catalyst for whatever peace and harmony people may be able to find with one another. As we increase our demand for government to resolve differences, we increase the flow of both resources and power to the State. Since this gives the State a vested interest in having us increase our demand for its services, it ought to be apparent that the State also has a vested interest in fostering social conflict. If it is true that we huddle together more when we are fearful, we should expect the State to find it in its interests to provide us with an endless supply of bogeymen and other fear objects. For these reasons, the State both encourages and exploits the practice of people looking outside themselves for direction and seeking their identities within groups.

It is our innocence in comprehending the reality of State-generated conflict that interferes with our understanding of social conflict. We are familiar with the role of the *agent provocateur* —the undercover agent employed by the State to infiltrate a group in order to incite illegal activity that would justify retaliation by the State. The American government apparently made substantial use of such functionaries during the anti-war and anti-draft demonstrations during the 1960's and 1970's. We tend, however, to be unaware of the more general conflict-provoking character of all political institutions. Once we start playing the institutional game of divide and collect, we set ourselves up to be manipulated by a State apparatus having the capacity to set one group against another in order that the State may enhance its position by intervening to resolve the very disputes it has helped to create! We are familiar with the international examples of the United States and the Soviet Union each arming *both* sides in various wars between third world nations, but these practices have their domestic counterparts as well. Governments have established programs to promote the interests of one group (e.g., labor unions, tenants' organizations, bankers, natural gas consumers), then turned right around to legislate on behalf of groups adversely affected by the first intervention (e.g., employers, landlords, borrowers, natural gas producers). Such practices have helped people develop a political consciousness. Society itself has become increasingly politicized, as groups have come to regard legislative halls, courtrooms, and administrative agencies as appropriate forums for gaining advantages over their adversaries. Since the power and influence of the State is advanced by such attitudes, politicians and other government officials have had an incentive to help foster the continual group conflicts that encourage endless political solutions. If the medical profession were able to introduce viruses into the water supply in order to then treat the resulting illnesses, the role of the political State would be no better analogized.

The political State receives its sustenance from *conflicts*—real or contrived—conflicts born out of State-induced fears designed to solidify herd-impulses into a consensus for social rule by political institutions. Throughout history, governments have organized their citizens with promises to protect them from their enemies, both foreign and domestic. The *appearance* of social disputes—assuming they are plausible enough to be believed—provides the stimulus for combining individual wills into a unified, State-directed social structure; for converting millions into One; for transforming people of diverse backgrounds into nations. Those who seek to exercise political authority over others must, if they are to gain and keep popular sanction for their rule, create the impression that they can bring harmony out of conflict; that they can introduce predictability and certainty; that life without their intervention and oversight would be "nasty, brutish, and short";[3] that political institutions, alone, can socialize mankind and make for noble living; and that *order* is synonymous with obedience to *political authority*, while discord, confusion, and violence must necessarily accompany any weakening of such authority.

Discord, then, is the lifeblood of all political organizations. Rather than eliminate conflict, the State must encourage and promote threats against which it can mobilize and control its own populations. Though its public relations image is to the contrary, the history of the State has been *not* one of conflict *resolution*, but of conflict *management*. Governments have always employed what James Madison termed "the old trick of turning every contingency into a resource for accumulating force in the government."[4] California governments, for example, have learned to treat every variant in weather as a potential problem calling for the intercession of planners. If there is too *much* rain, there will be mud slides and floods to contend with, along with the destruction of agricultural crops and the enhanced growth of plants that produce the creosote that fuels brushfires. If there is too *little* rain, there will be water shortages and crop-destroying drought to deal with, as well as an insufficient growth of hillside underbrush that will encourage mud slides.

If there is too *much* snow in the mountains, the costs of street and road clearance go up, along with the threat of spring flooding. If there is too *little* snow, the reservoirs will not fill up, leading to water shortages in the cities, and the ski resorts will suffer financial hardship.

To the State, then, every condition becomes a conceivable problem; every group or type of behavior becomes a potential threat to the general welfare. Furthermore, each attempted political solution to a problem generates a multitude of *new* problems, once again escalating social conflicts which our well-conditioned minds call upon the State to resolve! For example, minimum wage laws have created increased unemployment,[5] leading to the enactment of unemployment compensation legislation, job training programs, and other welfare programs, as well as repressive "law-and-order" proposals to deal with the street crime engaged in by people unable to secure employment at artificially high wage rates.

For such reasons, political institutions have a vested interest in seeing that disputes exist. If there were none, the State would have to fabricate them. Through this process, competing groups—each seeking to promote their respective interests or to defend themselves in the face of a perceived threat —vie for the support of the State, each seeking to outbid the others with tribute that aggrandizes State power.

We do not like to admit these things to ourselves, of course. Like the victims of a bunco scheme, we resist acknowledging our own gullibility. We soothe our bruised egos with all kinds of lies, one of the principal being that "the system works," (i.e., it operates in harmony with the established folklore). When Vietnam, or Watergate, or Abscam reveal the devious, corrupt, and unprincipled nature of political power, we focus our attentions on the personalities involved, and ignore the system that produced them. We cling to our faith in the falsehood that *we* control the government, and seek a change through the very political processes that provided us with the incumbent scoundrels! But what is the nature of the change that we effect when we replace one fungible politician with another? Was Richard Nixon an improvement over Lyndon Johnson? We amuse ourselves with jokes about the Tweedledum and Tweedledee quality of candidates, not recognizing that the real joke is on *us*: the *State* controls and directs *our* activities, and not the other way around. We maintain the illusion of controlling government because we are permitted to vote for either of the institutionally-cloned candidates who will serve as our wardens and keepers. By voting, you and I do not control the State, but we do help to maintain the *appearance* that we do, and thus help to legitimize State authority over our lives. Believing that the political process can bring about a significant change in the problems it has caused, is not unlike an alcoholic trying to effect a cure for his cirrhosis by switching to another brand of bourbon.

If we wish to understand the nature of political institutions, we must be able to observe them with minds that are willing to abandon many of their most cherished illusions. In so doing, we will discover that we have been sanctioning the greatest of irrationalities: placing our lives and well-being at the disposal of men and women with appetites for power over other people, and who amuse themselves and gratify their egos while others suffer and die. We may learn that the police system does not protect you and me: it protects the established order *from* you and me; that the courts are not organized to guarantee our freedom, but to enforce our obedience to State authority. The political State represents nothing more than the institutionalization of unprincipled power and naked force. Though we delude ourselves with trying to measure differences between fascism and communism, democracies and dictatorships, conservatism and liberalism, moderates and extremists, authoritarian and totalitarian regimes, the fact remains that *every* form of government is a police-State, *every* political system is tyrannical. *Every* political institution—regardless of its particular form and constitution—suffers from the same defect: the presumption of *the right to rule other people.* It is the asserted *right to make forcibly-imposed decisions for others* that unites all governments in a common conspiracy against mankind. It is our concession of such a right that breathes life into these Frankensteins of unbounded power.

By institutionalizing violence, theft, corruption, murder, deceit, and manipulation, the State has helped to erode the more decent traits of human character and, as a consequence, to debase the general quality of social relationships. Few of us would be prepared to personally do to one another the sorts of things political institutions routinely do to each of us. We have sanctioned acts against ourselves that we would not have tolerated for a moment from our best friend, and acts against others that we would not have had the stomach to inflict upon our worst enemy. We are properly revulsed by the savagery and inhumane nature of a few mass murderers who occasionally terrorize cities. On the other hand, we exalt those who terrorize entire *nations*: the political leaders who have been responsible for the systematic and calculated butchery of hundreds of millions of men, women, and children during times of war. We honor those who have been most successful at both manipulating minor disputes into full-blown conflicts, and directing the warmaking machinery of the State, by designating them statesmen and national heroes. We decorate, as courageous patriots, those soldiers who have displayed great perseverance at killing the soldiers for whom other nations and families mourn. We do all of this even though political institutions have been responsible for the intentional infliction of more death and suffering than all other deliberate and accidental causes combined. We seem to regard highly the planned suffering inflicted by political leaders because they are institutionalized, and hence sanctified, actions. The utter confusion in our understanding is no more clearly expressed than in awards of the Nobel Peace Prize to such political leaders as Gen. George C. Marshall, Henry Kissinger, Le Duc Tho, Menachem Begin, and Anwar Sadat (all of whom had been actively involved with their governments' making of war), on the one hand, and to such genuine humanitarians as Albert Schweitzer and Mother Teresa, on the other.

The result of our political structuring has been to depersonalize and dehumanize society; to substitute, in human affairs, compulsion for cooperation, plunder for trade, suspicion for trust, confrontation for consideration, force for persuasion, hatred for love, deception for honesty, fear for hope, war for peace, slavery for freedom, inquisition for inquiry, restraint for liberty, and destruction for creation. The State has activated the fears, hostilities, weaknesses, and ignorance of the least psychologically mature people, and reinforced gloomier assessments of the depraved nature of mankind. It has glorified the use of force, intimidation, and manipulation in promoting one's interests, and has elevated obedience, suffering, and sacrifice to the highest planes of social virtue. It has fostered the basic totalitarian premise of the propriety of some people exercising authority over others.

Had all of this been accomplished by a vicious gang of fiends, one could dismiss it as an accident of history, or an isolated flaw of human character. The tragedy is that such anti-social and inhumane acts have been sanctioned and carried out by good people; by well-meaning people; by people who love their parents and their children and are good neighbors; by people who would not tolerate the suffering of animals or the impairment of the environment; by people who do volunteer work for charities, stop to help fellow motorists in distress, and pay their bills on time; by people who are hardworking, responsible, competent, decent, honest human beings; by you and me.

Such perversions have, unfortunately, been the product of our willingness to believe the importunities of those who seek power over us. Even if we assume the very worst of motives on the parts of those who manage the State apparatus, it is nonetheless certain that they have been able to accomplish their purposes only because we have willingly made ourselves dependent upon, and acknowledged the legitimacy of, their rule. We have not been *coerced* into subservience: we have been *seduced.* We have been willing to become externalized, other-directed persons; willing to separate ourselves from others by organizing into groups; willing to suspend personal judgments and abandon the responsibility for our own lives. We have learned to project onto politicians our capacities for favorably directing our lives, and have come to identify political action as our most effective attribute. If governments are *strong,* it is because *we are weak.*

The State has encouraged us to develop expectations of other people, and promised to compel the fulfillment of those expectations. It has persuaded us that *others* are the cause of our failures, and that *others* should be responsible for our happiness and well-being. It has offered to save us the effort of developing self-discipline, convincing us of the superiority of institutionally-imposed discipline in providing for social order. It has pandered to our worst fears about ourselves and others, concocting bogeymen and perilous threats from which it has promised protection. As a result, we have learned to live on the edge of disaster, in an ever dangerous and threatening environment in which crisis is the norm, fear is the medium of exchange, and the only certainty is of an increasingly hostile, malevolent universe.

The State has, in other words, sold us snake oil cures and fountain-of-youth escapes from the harsh realities of nature. We have, like bib-overalled bumpkins in the big city with the egg money, been bamboozled by sharpies trying to sell us the Brooklyn Bridge. We have succumbed to their advances not just because of our innocence, but because, in our desire to get rich quick, in our appetite for being flattered and sweet-talked, and in our willingness to believe in sideshow illusions and fast-shuffles, we set ourselves up to be fleeced.

8

FUELING

THE

ENGINES OF WAR

A prince should therefore have no other aim or thought, nor take up any other thing for his study, but war and its organisation and discipline, for that is the only art that is necessary to one who commands.
—Nicolo Machiavelli[1]

War is the health of the State. It automatically sets in motion throughout society those irresistible forces for uniformity, for passionate cooperation with the Government in coercing into obedience the minority groups and individuals which lack the larger herd sense. . . . [I]n general, the nation in war-time attains a uniformity of feeling, a hierarchy of values culminating at the undisputed apex of the State ideal, which could not possibly be produced through any other agency than war.
—Randolph Bourne[2]

There is a life force present within all matter and energy in the universe, and our failure to live in harmony with that force puts us into a state of war with nature itself. This statement is not intended as simply poetic expression, but accurately reflects how we have lived. For millennia, we humans have distinguished ourselves from the rest of nature, believing that we were apart from and superior to all else. We convinced ourselves that this entire planet was put here for our special benefit, and that all other matter is ours to master and subdue for the gratification of our narrow purposes. We have maintained our egocentric wars against other life forms, inorganic matter, and the forces of nature, telling ourselves that life is a struggle against the elements, that rivers had to be subdued and the land conquered, all to the end that nature surrender to our sovereign authority.

We are beginning to understand the fallacy of living in hostility to nature. We are becoming more sensitive to the interests of other life forms, recognizing that our interests are more mutually beneficial and interdependent than they are competitive. We have even begun to question the validity of our categorizing matter into "living" and "nonliving" groupings. Physicists studying subatomic particles have discovered not only very energetic and animated behavior-patterns within the atom, but an unpredictability and seeming independence that can almost be likened to free will. Geologists familiar with plate tectonics—the mechanics of change undergone by the earth's crust—have observed renewal processes that can be analogized to the birth, growth, and death cycles of living systems. When the so-called "inanimate" substances about us are seen characterized by such intense activity, we begin to wonder whether what goes on inside us is significantly different from what goes on inside an atom of hydrogen.

Many of us resist such an unpretentious view of mankind. To suggest that we have no more exalted place in the universe than does an earthworm or even a block of granite is, to say the least, a blunt denial of our species' manifest destiny, as well as an affront to our collective ego. We are too accustomed to separating ourselves from the rest of nature to take comfort in the proposition that we have only a plebeian role in the scheme of things. As one of my favorite professors used to say: "man is the noblest creature in all of nature. But, of course, the rats have not been consulted."[3]

Just how common our interests are with the rest of nature became very apparent to me one late fall day a number of years ago. I was living in the midwest at the time and, consistent with common practice in that part of the country, I was in the process of sealing up our home for the oncoming winter months. I raised one of our bedroom windows to clean out the sill area when I noticed a large number of box elder bugs huddled together next to the storm window. My first inclination was to take the whisk broom and simply sweep these intruders out onto the ground. After all, *they* were in *my* house; they didn't belong there: let them go get their *own* place to stay. But just as I was about to evict these sleepy creatures, I became aware that they were only doing what I was in the process of doing: preparing to ride out a cold and bitter Nebraska winter. By happenstance, the box elder bugs and I had chosen to occupy the same space. I shut the window and let them be, but as I did I felt a strange sense of elation. I had been familiar with *words* that described our common interests with the rest of nature, but I had just experienced the *reality* of the proposition.

Because we have chosen to divide ourselves from other people and the rest of nature, we have created a state of war with one another. So accustomed have we become to our personal and institutionalized sources of conflict that we have simply accepted the inevitability of leaving behind us a trail of corpses and crippled victims. Whether we are considering box elder bugs, or the animals we routinely slaughter as we speed along the highways in our rush to go nowhere, or the aborted fetuses whose only offenses were to be impediments to our self-indulgent life-styles, or the victims of more formalized systems of conflict, we seem increasingly indifferent to the consequences of our conflict-ridden lives. Because we have separated ourselves from these faceless "others," we find it easy to rationalize the suffering we so thoughtlessly inflict. After all, we convince ourselves, *they* did get in *our* way, did they not?

Nowhere, though, do we indulge ourselves in such a vicious and unquestioning piling up of victims as in the system of political warfare. Perhaps it is the enormity of the harm caused by war that anesthetizes our minds and permits us to overlook its obscene and monstrous nature. Even those who are rightfully horrified by the psychopathic butchery involved, often fail to understand how war is both the ultimate expression of institutional superiority over the lives of human beings and, at the same time, the natural consequence of classifying ourselves into mutually-exclusive groupings.

War is an activity with implications for the institutional control of people that have rarely been understood by even its most ardent critics. Far too many opponents of war nevertheless believe that society could not function without political supervision and coordination. What they fail to understand is the necessity of the war system for solidifying political authority over a population. We have seen how people identify their ego boundaries with the political State, coalescing their individualities into a unified whole. Similarly, the world becomes divided into "we-they" relationships that generate conflict and a fear of others. In order to resolve these perceived conflicts in their favor, people sanction the exercise of power by the political State.

It is not sufficient for the maintenance of their power that political institutions have only a *theoretical* capacity or *formal* authority to deal with conflicts. The State must be able to constantly exercise its control over conflict situations, and to demonstrate its capacity for violence, in order to reinforce both the herd-identity of its citizens and the force of its own authority. The State is as dependent upon conflict for its survival as the medical profession is upon illness. If conflicts do not arise in any other way, the State must concoct its own.

War is, indeed, the health of the State, the means by which the State maintains its existence. Politics feeds on conflict like a parasite, drawing its life-sustaining blood from the wounds it has inflicted.

This same conclusion was reached in what were reportedly the results of a secret, government-funded study—conducted over a period of some three years by prominent scholars from various disciplines, as well as people from non-academic fields—of the likely consequences of a general condition of peace. Even though the group's report was published without authorization and without identifying any of the purported participants—thus raising questions of its authenticity—it nevertheless contains (like Orwell's *1984* and *Animal Farm*) a perceptive understanding of the essential relationships between political institutions and the war system. Bearing the title *Report From Iron Mountain*,[4] this professed study reflected a rather dim view by the group members of a condition of universal peace. Such a situation would, they feared, serve to dilute the power of political institutions.

Acknowledging war to be the principal means for the organization of nations, the Iron Mountain group declared that the war system has been indispensable for governments securing a popular sanction for their rule. Wars and other threats to the national interest provided the sense of necessity making possible the state of mind that would gain the allegiances of men and women to a politically organized society. War, in other words, "is the basic social system," and "the end of war means the end of national sovereignty." Because "[a]llegiance requires a cause," and "a cause requires an enemy," the report goes on, the "war-making societies require—and thus bring about—[international] conflicts."[5]

Since the health of the State is dependent upon its war-making capacities, and a "healthy" military system "requires regular 'exercise,'" what would be the likely political consequences of an abandonment of war? The answer to that question was, of course, the primary charge to the Iron Mountain group. If the State was no longer able to rely on military "threats" from foreign governments as fear-òbjects for maintaining control over its own population then, the group suggested, "alternate enemies" would have to be found.[6] Demonstrating its capacity for practical as well as theoretical solutions, the group provided a list of such possible enemies that included threats from interplanetary creatures, environmental pollution (which, it was suggested, the State itself might have to secretly engage in in order to make such a threat plausible), ethnic minorities within the population, and the use of blood games. Should the State be unable to identify any existing group as a substitute enemy, the report continues, *"such a threat will have to be invented."* Other methods of social control mentioned by the group included the use of "selective population control" and the "reintroduction of slavery," to be accomplished through a form of "'universal' military service."[7]

What more damning indictment of institutions could be offered than this? What fiendish monsters concocted in the dreariest recesses of a psychopathic imagination could begin to match the evil inherent in the systematic and calculated slaughter of millions of human beings? More importantly, what evasion of reality do *we* practice when we choose to acknowledge the propriety and even the glory of such institutionalized savagery? When the State can engage in its murderous exploits with no other purpose in mind than the aggrandizement of its own power, how can we continue to embrace such agencies as being essential to the maintenance of social order? Do we really believe, as we have been taught, that the absence of such agencies of mass-extermination would lead to *dis*order?

Is it possible for us to look at the war system through clear, focused eyes, rather than the red, white and blue lens filters that have been implanted in our minds, and see this vicious game for what it is? It should become evident to us that the governments of the United States and the Soviet Union, for example, are organized *not* so much against one another, as against their own respective citizens, and that each government carefully guards against the disclosure of those State secrets that would reveal to their own people the nature of the game being played. It should also become apparent that, in spite of the heated rhetoric of the cold war, the American political and corporate systems require a healthy and vigorous communist bloc of nations, a fact that helps to explain the Reagan Administration's assistance to the Polish government during the "Solidarity" strikes. Political oratory about the "Red menace" may have frightened many Americans into surrendering more of their liberty to the State, but it has certainly not dissuaded western bankers from lending billions of dollars to communist regimes, loans that might become worthless should these governments succumb to the emerging spirit of human liberation. Nor would the disappearance of this purported monolithic threat bode well for the beneficiaries of the national defense racket: the defense contractors who have amassed great wealth in supplying the equipment for this game; the educational institutions that have been well paid to train the players (even the federal government's student loan program bears the name "National Defense Education Act"); and the politicians, warlords, and bureaucracies, into whose hands are centralized even greater power and authority.

It can hardly be denied that we have willingly been bamboozled into State-directed war frenzies conducted against whomever our political leaders have selected as our current enemies. During my lifetime, I have been told that Germany and Japan were my "enemies," and that Russia and China were my "friends." No sooner was that war concluded, though, and the roles were reversed: it was Russia and China that were now my "enemies," while Germany and Japan were my "friends." During the Korean and Viet Nam wars, I was told that if these nations fell under the rule of the Chinese government, the rest of the free world would be threatened. But even now, as southeast Asian nations are brought under communist control, I learn that the American government is concluding agreements for arms sales to China, which is really my "friend" after all. A Richard Nixon who, as President, was ordering the sacrifice of American lives in order to arrest the fall of dominoes, now preaches the doctrine that a militarily strong China is in the best interests of the United States. As this is done, we are asked to look elsewhere for our latest "enemies list," perhaps toward Iran, Libya, or some Central American nation. To those who are willing to subject millions of human beings to pain, misery, and death, for no other purpose than to maintain their own power, it really matters little *who* the war is against, or *what* the issues are.

The vicious nature of what the political State is up to should be obvious. If the ABC grocery chain went on television with a series of commercials to convince us that they were our friends, while the XYZ grocery chain was our enemy, few of us would be inclined to believe them. And if they tried to persuade us to go to a neighborhood shopping center with our fellow ABC customers and shoot at the XYZ customers as they came in to shop, even fewer of us would likely do so. The self-serving nature of their proposal, as well as the absurdity of our own participation in their scheme, would be so apparent as to evoke no interest on our part. Why, then, do we not question the State when it seeks to send us or our children off to a foreign land to die for the glory of the State and its leaders? Those of us who carefully lock burglars out of our homes, allow predators with more voracious appetites into our very souls. Those of us who would not think of permitting our daughters to go out with known rapists, willingly turn our sons over to those who wish to place their lives in mortal danger in order to gratify their self-serving ambitions for power.

If we were aware of the contrived nature of the State's bloody conflicts, we would lose our enthusiasm for participating in war games. When two people understand the logic of a game, it is usually pointless for the two of them to thereafter play that game with one another. One sees this in tic-tac-toe and computerized chess matches: when all the consequences of every move are known in advance by each player, it becomes impossible for either to win. The game remains meaningful to only two groups of people: those who do not understand the game, and those who *do* understand it and seek to take advantage of those who do *not*. Continuation of war games, then, is dependent upon widespread ignorance of the fundamental nature of politics.

It is certainly *not* in the interests of the State to encourage—or even tolerate—any substantial questioning by its citizens. From the State's point of view, the ideal citizen is the kamikaze pilot; the unthinking, obedient lemming capable of being programmed for its own self-destructive marches to wherever the State directs. The State cannot abide a thinker, an independent individual, a person who refuses to lose himself in the herd. In order to inculcate the attitudes upon which such mindless subservience to political authority rests, schools, churches, youth organizations, the entertainment industry, and business groups have carefully taught us to march in straight lines, to come to attention on command, to respect authority, and to do as we are told. As a consequence, we have become the kind of people who value the security that comes from the certainty of our own institutionalized suffering, who prefer "the devil we know" to the uncertainty of being deprived of our emotional crutches. What we have turned ourselves into was noted so dramatically and pathetically in the movie *Holocaust*, when one of the concentration camp victims declared, while being ordered to march to the gas chambers, "why do we still obey them? We're finished anyway."[8]

The extent of our moral paralysis in the face of established authority was alarmingly identified in the now-classic study conducted by Stanley Milgram. Following a series of experiments in which subjects were directed to inflict pain upon others participating in the project, Milgram concluded that many people do as they are told, regardless of the nature of the act, as long as they regard the source of their orders to be a "legitimate authority." It was neither anger, hatred, nor vindictiveness that caused people to be willing to inflict such pain, Milgram said. Rather, man tends "to abandon his humanity . . . *as he merges his unique personality into larger institutional structures.*"[9]

To the political State, human beings have never amounted to anything more than resources available for exploitation on behalf of institutional purposes, a sad truth made no more evident than in plans to develop the neutron bomb. In case there are any doubts as to the arrogance and human insensitivity of the State, or of the proposition that institutions have interests of their own which take priority over the interests of people, consider the implications of this ultimate weapon: a bomb that only kills *people*, while leaving buildings and equipment intact! A bomb capable of making distinctions between what is institutionally essential and what is dispensable. "Responsible" men and women will be able to be disintegrated for the glory of the State, comfortable in knowing that their homes will remain intact and thus not disturb the mortgage interests that secure their obligations to banks and loan companies, or provide a postmortem threat to their personal credit ratings. The agonizing screams of dying children will not be aggravated by their disquieting fears that the White House, or the Washington Monument, or their school building will suffer damage. At last, war shall have been made more "peaceful" for institutional interests. Wars are, it must be conceded, bad enough without insurance companies having to pay out billions of dollars for damaged property, or manufacturing firms having to suffer production line shutdowns. Neither should banks and insurance companies be left without tangible assets with which to guarantee repayment of corporate bonds, nor should governments be deprived of property on which to foreclose for unpaid taxes. Neither should we countenance the blasphemy inherent in toppling the Mormon Tabernacle or St. Peter's Basilica: religious "values" must be maintained. Wars do have a way of causing problems, and we must be prepared to exhibit that sense of "responsibility" with which institutions have carefully imbued us. Far better that the government develop a nice, "clean" bomb, one that is not so "messy" and "destructive," one that kills people off by "peaceful" means! Someday, perhaps, the State may even be able to design a bomb that does not leave bodies around to litter public parks![10]

The neutron bomb is not so much the product of some State-subsidized cadre of mad scientists as it is the logical extension of the basic premises by which we have chosen to live our lives. Once we accepted the idea that our lives ought to be subordinated to the purposes and control of institutions, once we subscribed to the proposition that "meaning" in life is only to be found in subservience to those "greater" purposes outside us, we also accepted for ourselves the status of fungible human "resources," means to the ends of others. It was *our* individual decision to place our lives at the disposal of institutional interests, as coequals with such other resources as buildings and machines and mineral deposits and other forms of wealth. I wonder if we really fell in love with the *Star Wars* robots because of *their* human qualities, or because we saw something of *ourselves* in their roles of institutionally-created and programmed servomechanisms.[11]

When the political State introduces its neutron bomb, it is telling us the same thing it tells us in every war, if only we will listen, namely, that the institutional hierarchy has taken inventory of all its assets, and that the bottom has fallen out of the market for human beings.

The political history of mankind has consisted of little more than a recycling of the war system. We continue to mistake for "progress" our escalating technological sophistication for clawing, clubbing, and slashing one another. If Attila the Hun or Genghis Khan were to return today, they would no doubt be amazed by the design and power of modern weaponry. They would have no lack of familiarity, however, with the logic or the organizational structure of the war system itself.

Though we do not love war, many of us are uncomfortable considering the factors that can lead to peace, for to do so would require us to confront all of our institutional commitments. And so we do nothing to change ourselves. We keep honoring dead soldiers as a way of reinvesting our own lives in the purposes of the State, never asking whether the Chinese are better off today than they would have been under Japanese domination, or whether eastern European nations suffered less under the tyranny of Stalin than of Hitler. We are more comfortable with the illusion that our relatives and friends died in wars fought to advance important principles, than we are with the harsh truth that they were exploited and consumed for no other purpose than to feed the insatiable appetites of the machines of war. And so we remain in our State-induced sleep, dreaming of "national honor" and "glory" bought with the broken bodies of our children. We dream, as well, that peace will come to the world . . . *somehow*; that it will occur as a result of fundamental changes in thinking . . . by *someone*, . . . *sometime*.

Theodore Roszak has commented upon the suicidal implications of our preoccupations with power and politics, suggesting that we are behaving as though we did not choose to survive. "Power," he suggests, "is the enemy of life," because power would "make life what it would not be."[12] We profess our ignorance of the lethal nature of political systems, as though our innocence exculpates us from the responsibility for our unthinking involvement with the destruction of mankind. But if we are to be responsible people we must *overcome* our lack of awareness, not take refuge in it. The threats to human life posed by the war system are too great for any of us to continue indulging ourselves in our innocence of what we are doing.

Some may argue that conflict is natural to us as territorial animals, and that we ought to accept our periodic mass-suicide ventures as simply one of the costs of being human. Again, such attitudes only help us to evade the responsibilities for our actions, and neutralize our efforts to change ourselves. We need to understand that aggression is the product of our *conscious minds*, of our ego boundary image-making. Our diabolical madness is the product *not* of natural selection, but of our preferences for the security of our collective images over the existence of life itself.

But even if our tastes for blood have come to us through the processes of evolution, to embrace our biological phylogeny affords us no assurance of our continued survival. Most of the life forms that have ever lived on earth are now extinct—in spite of their fidelities to their natures—and mankind has been provided no greater guarantees of special immortality. If conflict and violence are indeed a part of our genetic chemistry—which I doubt—then we had best learn *not* to control or suppress our nature, but to rise above it. For along with whatever other attributes we have been provided, we humans also possess minds capable of transcending the present limitations of our conscious thought processes. Evolution, after all, is a continuing process in which we are active participants, not simply end products. If we are to avoid the fate of being the only species to deliberately engineer its own extinction, we must begin to think more in terms of making fundamental changes in our understanding than in incremental modifications of existing policies or strategies. It is not new programs or systems that we so desperately require, but a radical transformation within our consciousness. We need to become aware of what we have been doing to ourselves and to one another as a result of the fragmentary and enervated habits of our minds. Though we have taught ourselves to feel menaced by enemies, the threat to our survival as a species comes from *within*: it is not us against *them*, but us against *ourselves*.

I have no doubt that the war system will come to an end someday, and that the earth will experience total and unconditional peace. The only question is whether mankind will be around to enjoy it. If the human race is to survive, we must be prepared to abandon the political, religious, and ideological divisions that have nourished the war system. Those who persist in their efforts to reconcile peace with the interests of the State in organizing and controlling people should learn that there is no such thing as a peaceful form of conflict. In the past, the political State has asked "who will defend our nation," or "who will defend freedom," or "who will defend democracy?" But if life on this earth is to continue, we must now ask "who will defend mankind?" Those who were prepared to march *into* war in order to save the interests of their respective nation-States must now be willing to *walk away* from war in order to save humanity itself. In the name of *life*, we must find the courage to move beyond all those sanctified divisions that are tearing the human race apart. We must be willing to transcend political authority itself, to challenge the legitimacy of the machinery that has universalized human suffering, and to deny all institutional claims of sovereign power and control over people.

Over the untold centuries of our existence, we humans

have committed almost every conceivable form of violence upon not only our planet, but one another. We have tried *conquering* and *dominating* anything and anyone that served our apparent interests. While our ancestors were *exploiting* nature as well as their neighbors, we have felt more comfortable *managing* them. No matter how well-intended we have been in using other people or our environment for our purposes, all of such methods have been for *controlling*—and keeping us in a state of continuing warfare with—our universe. We live in what the Hopi call a state of "koyaanisqatsi," of "life out of balance." Because of the enormous technological and organizational power we have invested in the agencies that conduct these wars, we must now choose between *destroying* one another—if not our planet—or learning to *live with* one another. At no other time in human history have the consequences of our thinking been so immediate and pervasive.

If mankind *is* to survive, you and I will have to take the responsibility for ending our participation in violence. The character of any society can never rise higher than the character of the individuals within it. If our world is disorderly and violent, it is because you and I have learned to be conflict-ridden and aggressive. Institutions are blessed with no mysterious powers that would enable a society to transcend the division, discord, and confusion of its members. Only by transforming ourselves can our world become peaceful and orderly. The task is ours, yours and mine. We have no one else to whom we can turn for salvation. No international organization of nation-States can be expected to curb the appetites of its own members. *We* must save mankind, for *we are* mankind. Our leaders, our gods, our ideologies, our laws, our thinkers, our experts, our institutions have all failed us—or, to be more precise, because of our dependencies upon these agencies we have failed ourselves. But if we are to end war, we must be prepared to do more than talk and moralize about the subject. We will not accomplish our purpose with humanely-inspired resolutions, nor by creating institutional scarecrows to ward off conflict. We cannot oppose war on a piecemeal basis, opposing "unjust" wars while sanctioning "just" ones, opposing nuclear weapons but favoring conventional methods of killing. We cannot oppose war while worshiping the engines that produce the agony. We must understand the nature of conflict and the conditions that make for peace. This means that we must be able to discover and deal with the conflicts we feel within *ourselves*, for those who cannot find peace for themselves will never help to secure it for the rest of mankind. But in the process of our inquiry, we must not be afraid to ask the questions we are not supposed to ask. We can no longer make a pretense of opposing war and, at the same time, fail to see that war is inherent to all political institutions. We must learn to be aware of how others embroil us in their disputes. We must learn to be more skeptical of those who teach children to march.

9

MANIPULATING
MARKETS AND PEOPLE

The bigger the unit you deal with, the more
brutal, the more mendacious is the life dis-
played. So I am against all big organizations as
such, national ones first and foremost; against
all big successes and big results; and in favour of
the eternal forces of truth which always work in
the individual and immediately unsuccessful
way, underdogs always, till history comes, after
they are long dead, and puts them on the top.
— William James[1]

One cannot fully comprehend the scope of institutionalism
without understanding how government regulation of economic activity helps to structure our lives. Government
control of production and exchange does not simply restrict
such depersonalized abstractions as the business community.
It restrains us from pursuing our personal interests, suppress-
ing individual behavior in ways we would not tolerate if
political dissent or religious beliefs were the subjects of
regulation. Though we have become more familiar with
many of the material consequences of these practices—e.g.,
the inhibition of growth, innovation, and the efficient use of
resources, not to mention the thousands of dollars spent by
the average American family each year in the form of higher
prices directly attributable to such regulatory schemes[2]—
most of us do not understand how such controls have helped
to fashion our social environment, and have ever more
tightly locked us into corporate-State patterns of living.

As with our indoctrination in the necessities of the war system, our minds have been carefully conditioned to accept government regulation for our protection. Most of us grew up steeped in the high school civics class folk wisdom that the regulatory system emerged as a countervailing influence to the growth of corporate power. Political controls were imposed on business institutions, we were told, in order to preserve competition, restrain unfair trade practices, conserve natural resources, and protect the economy from the sinister forces of monopoly power. The business community was powerful and ruthless, and certainly not to be trusted, it was said, but the government was on *our* side, the side of the weak, the powerless, the common man. *Our* government would step in and protect us from the greedy and corrupt ambitions of businessmen.

Having already accepted a condition of helplessness and dependency, most of us found comfort in such a proposition. We were content to kid ourselves that, when one institution imposed controls upon another, it was all done for *our* benefit. Like children, we snuggled up to the security blankets given us by paternal authorities. Most of us grew up believing ourselves to be the beneficiaries of a political protectionism, the basic tenets of which are well represented in a leading textbook in the field of government and business:

> It is not always safe to leave business to its own devices; experience has shown that its freedom will sometimes be abused. . . . Competitors have been harassed by malicious and predatory tactics, handicapped by discrimination, excluded from markets and sources of supply, and subjected to intimidation, coercion, and physical violence. Consumers have been victimized by short weights and measures, by adulteration, and by misrepresentation of quality and price; they have been forced to contribute to the profits of monopoly. . . . [T]he

nation's resources have been dissipated through extravagant methods of exploitation. These abuses have not characterized all business at all times, but they have occurred with sufficient frequency to justify the imposition of controls. Regulation is clearly required, not only to protect the investor, the worker, the consumer, and the community at large against the unscrupulous businessman, but also to protect the honest businessman against his dishonest competitor.[3]

Such interpretations of the regulatory process are about as valid as the notion that governments conduct wars in order to protect the lives of their citizens. Modern economic historians have helped to dismantle many of these traditional myths regarding business and political institutions. The rest of us now know what politicians and businessmen always knew privately, namely, that government regulation of business activity is only an expression of economic self-interest. It has been members of the business community—not a united front of fear-ridden shopkeepers, farmers, and proletarians—that have most often gone to the government for protection. The protection they have sought has not been from monopolies and high prices, but from competition and low prices. It was not the *failure* of competition, but its *effectiveness*, that prompted business leaders to endorse a closer working relationship with the political State. It was the inability of businessmen and trade associations to restrain and short-circuit the competitive influences that kept prices lower than industry leaders desired, that ultimately led to the enactment of antitrust and other regulatory legislation.[4]

Until government stepped in, competition among business firms was very intense. In the early 1900's, for example, major new industries were emerging—including the automobile, the airplane, electrical power, motion pictures, radio, the phonograph, and a variety of consumer appliances.

Petroleum, which had served mainly as a source of lighting in previous years, became the principal power source for the internal combustion engine, while electricity and natural gas developed as alternate power and lighting sources. New methods of distribution also came into being, including chain stores, vertically integrated retail operations, and new consumer credit practices. Innovations in manufacturing methods also occurred, while competition among industries became more intense (e.g., steel and concrete competing with lumber as sources of building materials).

As long as competitors were free to enter an industry, or to develop new products that made existing ones obsolete, or to aggressively pursue customers in such a way as to undercut the prices of other firms, the positions of the established firms would always be threatened. As a consequence, the older firms found themselves under continuing pressures to remain innovative, efficient, and capable of responding to any competitive challenge. Unrestricted competition, in other words, meant that firms had to remain ever vigilant and resilient in order to survive in an industry in which lower prices were the norm.

But, as we have already seen, institutions do not like to have to be responsive to change. They are conservative by nature, desirous of maintaining the status quo because they represent the status quo. Institutions favor an *established* environment over a *developing* one. They have a need for certainty and permanency that requires, from their perspective, the structuring and control of others in order to insulate themselves from the existence-threatening processes of change. An environment of innovative, competitive freedom was, consequently, viewed by leaders of commerce and industry as a threat to be brought under control. In the words of economist Walter Adams, business leaders "quickly and instinctively understood that storm shelters had to be built to protect themselves against this destructive force."[5]

In order to overcome such threats, many established firms turned to *voluntary* methods of restraining competition. Mergers, consolidations, pooling arrangements, trade association codes of ethics, and the more subtle understandings exhibited in the steel industry's "Gary dinners," were a few of the more significant efforts to bring competition within limits acceptable to business leaders. Such arrangements proved futile, however, for two basic reasons: (1) the inherent antagonisms between individual and group interests meant that, even if every firm desired the collective result being sought, each would nevertheless find it to its self-interest to violate the agreement; and, (2) the group was unable to enforce effectively its collective decision because of a lack of coercive power. Each firm was free to ignore the arrangement, knowing that the power to fine, enjoin, enforce, or punish was unavailable to the group.

It was this failure of the marketplace to succumb to business efforts to restrain competition that provided the major impetus for regulatory legislation. Business leaders discovered, in the political State, the coercive power that could overcome their competitors' reluctance to subordinate the pursuit of their own self-interest in favor of the collective good of the industry. Businessmen also discovered that the political and administrative realities were such that industry control of the regulatory agencies could be assured. They found, in the political State, not only a willing ally in their efforts to structure and control economic life, but the only effective means of corraling those industry mavericks who would not play the game. In short, the business community discovered that their cartellizing ambitions could be accomplished only through a permanent, incestuous marriage with the State.[6]

There is nothing new about the willingness of business institutions to employ the political State to promote their self-interest. The practice is a centuries-old custom whose presence has never been more poignantly noted than by a Kansas farmer who observed, in the 1920's: "Paternalistic schemes of government are agitated, not at farmers' meetings, but in businessmen's organizations. I have heard more socialism preached at meetings of commercial bodies than in socialistic gatherings."[7] Though businessmen may complain about a specific piece of legislation or the over-bureaucratization of a given agency, almost all of them are committed to the proposition that government should intervene to promote or protect their interests. Very few are willing to leave the marketplace open to the free play of their competitors and customers.

The intervention desired by businessmen has taken many forms. A partial listing would include the following:

1. Tariff or import quotas to restrict foreign competitors.

2. Licensing of business firms in order to limit the entry of would-be competitors and to control their behavior.

3. Regulation of competitive trade practices in order to stabilize prices.

4. Land use planning or zoning laws to restrict real estate development.

5. Establishment of wage, working condition, or product standards in order to universalize cost factors and thus restrict price competition.

6. Antitrust laws to control the more aggressive competitors in an industry.

7. Government contracts, subsidies, price supports, and research and development grants.

8. Conservation laws to control production in order to help stabilize prices.

Given the power of political institutions to confer artificial advantages that circumvent the disciplines of the market place and thus affect the profitability of firms, it should come as no surprise that businessmen, like many others, would seek to use that power for their own ends.

The self-serving nature of regulatory schemes is not always apparent. Their purposes are usually concealed behind a lot of public interest fluff generated by the businessmen and politicians proposing them. If, for example, milk producers want a state legislature to create an administrative agency that will restrict competition and raise prices in their industry, they will contend—usually with a straight face—that such an agency is necessary in order to protect the public. They will inform us that certain unethical trade practices in the industry threaten the continued existence of many milk producers, and that if these firms go out of business there will be shortages of milk for children. We are further told that these same unethical practices threaten the healthful quality of milk.

But what are these unethical trade practices of which the milk producers complain? In reading the legislation, one discovers that these conditions amount to nothing more than *low prices.* Some people in the industry are able to produce milk and profitably sell it at a lower price than their competitors, and the less competent businessmen are now before the legislature to put a stop to that. Because producers have a *concentrated* economic interest (i.e., the earnings of any one firm may go up by hundreds of thousands or even millions of dollars if the proposed legislation is enacted), they will show up en masse and be prepared to spend many thousands of dollars to persuade the politicians to support the measure. And because consumers have a *diffused* economic interest (i.e., the legislation may increase the costs of milk by only a few dollars per year per family), they will have little incentive to incur heavy costs to oppose the legislation. No one will likely show up to argue the inherently contradictory nature of a law designed to *raise* milk prices in order to ensure that children will get *more* milk! No one will be there to make the previously mentioned point about the enormous added costs consumers must incur in order to subsidize the legislative schemes of businessmen. And since no one but a Scrooge-like fiend would want to appear willing to deprive young children of an adequate supply of healthful milk, this bill will be whisked through the legislative process in the spirit of smug self-righteousness that attends the projects of all right-thinking people.

The social conflict inherent in such practices should be evident. Because political institutions are allowed to intervene in economic matters, legislative hearing rooms and administrative agencies have become little more than battle-grounds in which producers battle other producers, sellers war with buyers, landlords fight with tenants, one industry encounters another industry, employers brawl with employees, and all with the consumers bearing the brunt of casualties. Even though this racket costs people billions of dollars annually, creates high unemployment rates, stifles innovation, discourages people from entering particular industries, causes other economic hardships and helps secure the blessings of conflict to the political State, it continues. Business and professional groups, labor unions, and other economic interests, continue perpetrating their fraudulent schemes to protect the public from the consequences of free choice!

One of the prevailing myths within our culture is that a distinction exists between *government* and the so-called *free enterprise* system. Though such a distinction can be made *conceptually*, the emergence of the modern corporate State has all but obliterated any meaningful differences between the two systems. Big business and big government in America are so hopelessly intertwined that it is nearly impossible to identify economic behavior that is not dominated—or at least strongly influenced—by political decision-making. To regard the private business system as one in which the wants of buyers and sellers are played out in an environment of free choice and free competition is about as meaningful as treating the practices of medieval theocratic States as expressions of mankind's quest for cosmic and spiritual understanding.

When discussing the behavior of comparatively small business firms, it is relevant to distinguish voluntary market organizations from involuntary political systems. But as such organizations become institutionalized and begin to adopt manipulative and intimidative practices to further their purposes, it becomes increasingly difficult to clearly separate the private-corporate from the public-political. Banks and insurance companies, railroads and power companies, broadcasters and telephone companies, hospitals and national defense contractors are among the more apparent examples of the phenomenon. Government even supplies most of the research and development funding for industry,[8] a fact that not only shifts a major cost of doing business to taxpayers, but channels technological change in directions beneficial to the political State. In the *formal* sense, of course, such a distinction can be made on the theoretical basis that business firms, unlike political agencies, lack the legally-sanctioned power to compel obedience. But when viewed from the real-world perspective of how large corporate enterprises actually organize and influence people in this power-brokered, neo-mercantilistic world, such differences become obscured. The economic life of the world today is dominated by powerful nation-States and powerful multinational corporations whose interests are more symbiotic than adversarial. Officials of IBM, Exxon, and RCA have more in common with the bureaucracy of the federal government than they do with the beleaguered shopkeeper who continues, in an increasingly cartellized environment, his Sisyphian pursuit of what the classical economists romanticized as the fulfillment of the human spirit.

Contrary to prevailing folklore, there has never been a

period in American history in which laissez-faire principles dominated public policy. Even before the Constitution was ratified, government intervention into economic life was a generally accepted premise.[9] It has only been the contrast between the *extent* of government regulation during different time periods that has created the impression of earlier commitments to the maintenance of a completely free environment for economic activity.

The interests that economic and political institutions have in structuring the lives and behavior of people, make the expansion of each area mutually compatible. Political power is, in essence, authority exerted over the economic life of a nation. It is inconceivable that a forceful State domination could exist in an environment in which economic matters had been insulated from political decision-making. It is also doubtful whether the large multinational corporations that reach around the globe *could* or *would* have developed without the powerful arm of a national government to protect their economic positions. While economic analysis would deny the inevitability of a corporate State or other politically-structured economic system, the incentives for seeking a political supervision of production and trade seem to increase with the size of the business organization. When faced with the uncertainties associated with free competition, large nationally-organized industries have shown a decided preference for the protective and stabilizing influences of the political State. It is more than coincidental that the emergence of an omnipotent national government in America was concurrent with the development of large, national industries. Only a powerful national government could coercively structure the domestic economy as well as maintain militarily-backed spheres of influence in foreign markets.

Because government intervention has always played a significant role in economic matters, contemplating the form business institutions would have taken without the anti-

competitive protections and other special State-conferred
privileges becomes rather difficult. Nevertheless, based upon
what we do know, it is worthwhile to speculate whether
giant, highly-structured, heavily-concentrated firms and
industries would likely have developed in the absence of
government support and protection. We know, for example,
that government regulation—far from limiting the size or
domination of firms—actually *promotes* concentration within
industries. Because it is easier for a large firm to spread the
fixed costs of regulation over its larger number of products
than it is for a small firm with a smaller output, regulation
gives larger firms a comparative price advantage vis-a-vis
their smaller competitors. Costly product testing required by
a variety of government agencies, limits much research and
development innovation to the larger, well-financed corporations. At the same time—given their greater political
influence—the larger corporations and the trade associations
they control, have been able to secure the passage of legislation that has been more favorable to their interests than to
that of smaller firms. Although the proposition may contra-
dict our institutionally-sired folklore, government regulation has done far more than market forces have to create the
large, dominant business firms we see today.
    Studies of the merger and consolidation experiences of
business firms suggest that, far from being universally advantageous to the larger firm, increased size may have certain
competitively detrimental effects. Based on the histories of a
number of firms that had undergone mergers, earnings or
market shares have often *declined* following the mergers.
While there is certainly not a consensus among scholars on
this point, there are some who have suggested that the
post-merger declines were due to the problems associated
with a large organization—including lethargy, dissension,
and duplication—as well as the emergence of conservative
attitudes within the firms.[10] Business historian Arthur Dew-

ing has shown that the combined post-consolidation earnings of a number of representative firms had averaged only 65% of their pre-consolidation levels. He attributed such declines to "the difficulties attending the administrative management of a large business," as well as "the difficulties attending the creation of a business organization sufficiently powerful to dominate an industry in the presence of actual or potential competition."[11] Historian Gabriel Kolko's explanations of the post-merger declines experienced by U.S. Steel and International Harvester offer the same doubts as to the presumed advantages of size.[12]

It may prove to be the case that increasing the size of any organization brings with it increased inertia, inflexibility, discord, and instability, factors that make the organization less resilient and less capable of responding to competitive challenges. A free market, in other words, may simply be too volatile, too spontaneous and inconstant, to provide large firms with the security and stability made necessary by their organizational size. Because the political State has the power to redistribute advantages—as well as to compel or restrain behavior—those firms that would benefit from subverting the marketplace through politically-conferred methods have wasted little time in so promoting their interests.

The regulatory process has not protected society's members from the power of economic institutions: it has protected institutional interests from conditions that pose the threat of significant change. If we look beyond the political rhetoric and our PR-induced state of economic illiteracy, we discover that regulation has *standardized*, and thus restricted, the conditions, as well as the products and services, legally available to us in the marketplace. As Harold Laski puts it, "[i]ndustrial standardization seeks to make men live increasingly within the ambit of patterns it finds most economically serviceable."[13] Regulation has also helped to preserve existing technologies from the threats of unhampered innovation. This is particularly so in the public utility industries. Power companies, telephone companies, railroads, the Postal Service, broadcasters, petroleum companies, and others have, with the backing of the political State, steadfastly resisted any entrepreneurial creativity that might make their established technologies obsolete. In order to protect the existing industrial order from the uncertainties attending variation, competition, and other expressions of change, our economic lives have been subjected to rigidity and uniformity. One must, to enter many trades and professions, successfully run through a costly and time-consuming licensing maze designed by others in the business to restrict competition. New products may often not be put onto the market until they have undergone very costly testing procedures, or have been shown to conform to government-enforced standards that discourage product variation. The Horatio Alger success stories have been superseded by the more cynical observation whose origins I do not recall: "build a better mousetrap, and sell enough of them, and Justice Department attorneys will beat a path to your door." In promoting the certainty and stability desired by economic institutions, the regulatory process helps to reinforce within us the belief in the inevitability and necessity of structured social arrangements and, ultimately, "the standardized mind."[14]

Our acceptance of an institutionally-structured economy has caused us to accept a macroeconomic, mercantilist definition of our economic life. We do not think of economic behavior in *personal* or *human* terms, as something over which you and I might have any influence. We take institutional asking prices and wage levels as a given, something to accept or reject, but certainly not to *bargain* about. We tell ourselves that we don't have any bargaining power anyway, and even if we did, we look upon the practice as undignified and beneath us, the sort of thing in which Asian or Arab peasants might engage. We don't regard ourselves as autonomous agents, but as dependent subjects, acted upon by forces over which we have no control. To us, economics is but an abstraction, having to do with such confusing notions as gross national products, unemployment rates, consumer price indexes, and rates of growth. Not being aware that such esoteric concepts are used, in this materialistic age, to maintain our dependencies on those who understand their meanings—just as doctors, lawyers, and priests have employed their secret Latin languages—we have surrendered our economic lives to institutions. We have made our well-being dependent upon their judgments and policies, their organizational systems, and their technology.

We have become so subservient to organizational interests that we regard our economic affluence as something that has been institutionally-bestowed. But our understanding has become inverted. It was not *technology* that improved our lives, but our enhanced *awareness* of the laws of nature and of our own creative capacities. It was the application of human *understanding* that advanced our material well-being by *creating the technology*. The quality of our lives has always depended upon the awareness of our conscious minds. But now look at us. Because we have become institutionalized people, and because institutions have a vested interest in the preservation of their methods, we have learned to believe that our well-being is dependent upon the technology that we have created! Have the scientific and industrial revolutions done no more for us than to replace our feudal masters with technological ones? Was Mary Shelley right? Have we created our own Frankenstein monsters that now threaten the very lives they were designed to enhance?

Our thinking has become so influenced by institutional considerations of pragmatism that many of us are unable or unwilling to be critical of political restraints upon our economic life on any grounds other than practical ones. Many of us seem reluctant, in other words, to endorse human freedom until we have had a demonstration of its practical value. This is particularly evidenced by the increased use of economic analysis by most free market advocates in evaluating government regulatory programs. This tendency may, on the one hand, reflect only a narrowly defined pragmatism that fails to incorporate into cost-benefit analyses the psychic, emotional, and other subjective costs associated with the institutional structuring of, and interference with, the lives of people. But since the perspectives of most economists are institutional in scope, one must question whether their methodologies are capable of assessing such highly personal and intangible matters as psychic human costs. There are real (albeit non-quantifiable) costs involved in the manipulation and victimization of people, or in interfering with the exercise of individual free choice and otherwise eroding the condition of human freedom. The costs of an Auschwitz, or a war, or a system of slavery, or the disruption of neighborhoods by urban renewal, or brutal police tactics go beyond the monetary expenditures associated with such practices. There are costs associated with shackling the human spirit, extinguishing the fire of the human soul, or trampling upon the dignity of even the most wretched of human beings. But how does one account for such factors in a profit and loss statement, or explain them to auditors or institutional investors, or note their contribution to changes in the gross national product? Such costs—like the health hazards occasioned by industrial pollution—tend to become socialized and, as a consequence, obscured. But they operate, nevertheless, to diminish the quality of human life and must be accounted for in any thorough cost-benefit analysis.

It is, of course, helpful to understand the economic consequences of political structuring. But that approach rarely accounts for the effect of such practices upon those subjective, emotional factors that determine the quality of human life. Because they have identified themselves so closely with the business system, free market advocates have tended to be poor spokesmen for unstructured, noninstitutionalized social relationships. It is little wonder that, in an age dominated by a professed desire for human liberation, so few people have become attracted to a system based upon free market principles. So long as the case for a free market appears to be advanced only by defenders of private institutional interests, it will fail to find much support among persons sensitive to the problems associated with the structured and controlled conditioning of human beings. To put the matter bluntly, those desirous of liberating themselves from institutionally-dominant life-styles will not, in the words of an economist friend of mine, be inclined to go to the barricades in defense of lowered transaction costs.

To argue for a system of economic freedom on such practical grounds as efficiency is not unlike arguing against slavery because it results in lower worker productivity. Efficiency is a tool for measuring institutional success. It calculates only that which is of consequence to organizational purposes, taking no notice of those imperceptible and mysterious qualities that separate the poet from the engineer, Walden Pond from The Brave New World. Efficiency is as poor a reason as one could conceive for having a free market, for freeing people's lives and decision-making from the control of the political State. Stated another way, our liberation from institutional restraints is important enough to be undertaken *even if* the economists should inform us that a condition of freedom would be, based upon their analyses, *less* efficient. As was suggested earlier, we may discover that organizational *inefficiency* is the best means for limiting the growth of giant corporate enterprises. In terms of humane values and sentiments, the most compelling argument on behalf of a free market system is that it is premised on personal *autonomy*, on *people being let alone*. A free market means no more than the absence of coercive restraints upon the behavior of people.

To live free from the compulsion, restraints, manipulation, and other institutionally-beneficial burdens imposed by the political State is the *only* significant value of a free market. Only when men and women have put an end to the internally-generated conflicts they experience with others—conflicts they seek to resolve through the exercise of power over others—will they be able to appreciate the importance of free exchange as an indispensable harmonizing influence within society.

10

THE HOLY ALLIANCES

By these ghosts, by these citizens of the air, the affairs of government were administered; all authority to govern came from them. The emperors, kings and potentates all had commissions from these phantoms. Man was not considered as the source of any power whatever. To rebel against the king was to rebel against the ghosts, and nothing less than the blood of the offender could appease the invisible phantom or the visible tyrant. Kneeling was the proper position to be assumed by the multitude. The prostrate were the good. Those who stood erect were infidels and traitors. In the name and by the authority of the ghosts, man was enslaved, crushed, and plundered. The many toiled wearily in the storm and sun that the few favorites of the ghosts might live in idleness. The many lived in huts, and caves, and dens, that the few might dwell in palaces. The many covered themselves with rags, that the few might robe themselves in purple and in gold. The many crept, and cringed, and crawled, that the few might tread upon their flesh with iron feet.
—Robert G. Ingersoll[1]

The basic purpose of any organized religion is the same as that of other institutions: to control people. Throughout history, religions have devoted themselves to subduing the wills of their followers, to persuading, or intimidating, or compelling people to subordinate themselves to church authority and act in a manner consistent with church interests. In the process of doing so, organized religions have left a trail of blood and suffering that continues into the present day. They have sought control of the coercive powers of the State to compel people—under threats of death or the most vicious methods of torture—to obey their edicts. Religions have sacrificed children in order to pacify villainous gods, have mobilized armies to go out and proselytize with the sword, and burned at the stake those who asked questions. The bloody hands of church officials who tortured to death, during the Spanish Inquisition, thousands of innocent persons whose only offense was to have an honest difference of opinion in matters of theology, or the sinister papal intrigues that ran their murderous course through early Italian history, attest to the heinous nature of religious institutions. Apparently dissatisfied with imperfections in the original design of the human character, theocratic despots employed thumb-screws, spikes, dungeon chains, and devices for breaking bones, gouging out eyes, crushing limbs, cutting tongues, skinning, castrating, driving needles into eyes, and for suffocating to death, all for the purpose of refashioning men and women in the image of the established church. In this ecclesiastical tyranny, human character was reshaped by the rack, values were etched with the sting of the whip, and souls were certified by the torch. Those unable to avail themselves of the church's limited facilities for rehabilitation were taught do-it-yourself methods of confession and self-flagellation.

Lest it be thought that such atrocities occurred only in other nations, it is well to recall the seventeenth century American church leaders who had fled to this continent to escape religious persecution, only to set up their own regimes for compelling adherence to church doctrine by hanging witches, torturing heretics, and mutilating blasphemers. In eighteenth century Maryland, for example, it was a criminal offense to deny or profane Christ or members of the Holy Trinity, with punishments ranging from boring the offender's tongue, to burning his forehead with the letter "B," to the infliction of death itself.[2] Such practices confirm H.L. Mencken's characterization of religions as "the chief agents of every sort of suspicion and division, every sort of hatred and enmity that now afflicts the human race."[3] They also remind us of the truth brought to our attention by Pascal: "Men never do evil so completely and cheerfully as when they do it from religious conviction."[4]

Those who might otherwise be inclined to believe that such examples cannot fairly be included in an indictment of contemporary religious practices are encouraged to review recent events. Men, women, and children continue to be terrorized, maimed, and slaughtered in Northern Ireland and the middle east by plastiques-proselytizers of differing religious persuasions. Various religious sects—not the least of which being the Rev. Jim Jones's People's Temple—have turned to gruesome, violent tactics in order to further their purposes. We were reminded—in the sweeping slaughter of Palestinian civilians by Lebanese Christian militiamen in late 1982—of the pious butchery practiced by medieval crusaders, and of the suffering that must always attend "Christian soldiers, marching as to war." The Ku Klux Klan continues to use torches to etch the cross onto a midnight sky, while the Jewish Defense League responds with terror and violence of its own. Nor can any deny the viciousness with which the present government of Iran, under the autocracy of a leading Islamic church official, undertook the systematic execution of men and women for having committed, among other offenses, "crimes against God." The tendency for conflict and violence was made all the more evident when this same leader announced—after a seemingly permanent truce that had lasted some seven hundred years—a unilateral resumption of the holy wars that had set Christians and Muslims at each other's throats. This was accompanied by the persecution of many non-Islamic minorities in Iran, including the hanging of members of the Baha'i religion.

While these examples of savage brutality are not representative of the day-to-day activities at one's neighborhood
church, it is nonetheless true that such violence is occasioned
by an underlying source of conflict that is as inherent in
religious institutions as in any other formal organizations.
Apart from politically-generated conflict, there have probably been, throughout history, no more strongly-held, emo-
tionally-based lines of division among people than those
grounded in religious belief. Many people have been able to
transcend their occupational, geographical, philosophical,
educational—sometimes even political—differences with
one another; but these same people are unable to overcome
their religious barriers. The bitter religious disputes that
have cleaved families have been equally disruptive of the
peace and harmony of entire nations. Much of the tension and
discord caused by theological divisions among people will lie
submerged and dormant. It may, like a volcano, erupt with
massive force and devastating consequences or, like a geyser,
blow off steam on a regular, though subdued, basis. The
intensity of the conflict will vary with both the intensity of
the held belief and the believer's perception of trespasses to
his ego boundaries. To the degree people persist in identifying themselves with certain belief systems, and isolating
themselves from those who do not share in such beliefs, these
systems of thought will continue to exhibit their discordant
tendencies.

While the following chapter elaborates upon the intimidative and manipulative methods employed by churches and
other moralists to gain power over our lives, it should be
noted that the divisiveness that organized religions have
contributed to the world has its origins in the divisions
organized religions have helped us to cultivate within ourselves. Because of their own training, our parents considered
it part of their responsibilities to introduce us to church

doctrine. At young, impressionable ages, we were dragged off to awe-inspiring temples and cathedrals to be advised of what we would never have had occasion to consider on our own: that we were wicked and unworthy beings, doomed to suffer some ill-described "eternal damnation" for our "sin" of having been born. Having been told that our very natures were in conflict with the divine powers that ruled the universe, we were then informed of a special loophole available to us: our fallen souls could be salvaged if only we believed, without question, that everything church officials told us was true; if we would acknowledge our undeserving character and try to overcome it through a life of dedication to the church; if we would condition our deadened minds with catechisms of faith; if we would renounce the evils of selfishness, pleasure, profit, happiness, and other self-centered pursuits, and embrace the virtues of duty, sacrifice, pain, hard work, and other expressions of self-denial. The internal conflict we had learned to experience could be resolved, in other words, only by our living in strict obedience to the very dogmas that generated the conflict! We learned how to confess our guilt to, and beg forgiveness from, these proclaimed insurers of our souls. We became the obverse side of the Faustian coin, sacrificing temporal enjoyment for the eternal values we were certain to lose if we ever dared to question the arrangement.

What judgments are we to make of these institutional protection rackets that shake down men's souls; that glorify themselves as they debase human dignity; that find their enrichment in the impoverishment of the human spirit? What are we to say of adults who prosper by terrifying children?

In spite of the viciousness of organized religions, people do seem to need to inquire into the nature of life, the nature of the order that prevails within the universe, and into other questions that constitute what some might call a need for religious experiences. In this connection, religions appear to be born of the same spirit that stirs scientific pursuits: the human desire to comprehend the patterns and meanings of existence. We are inquisitive beings; learning is quite natural to us. But, as we saw earlier, the need that many people have for answers—or, more precisely, answers with the stamp of certainty—causes many to want to structure and institutionalize their tentative answers or hypotheses. To create one's own explanations for the ways of the universe, and then imagine that such insights have been divinely-inspired, is a masterful exercise in self-delusion.

This tendency for rigid answers is further exacerbated by an element of narcissism within many of us. We delight in seeing our own images reflected in the universe about us. Since the earliest of times, human beings have enjoyed playing Pygmalion—not only with their children, spouses, and friends, but with nature itself. People have paraded upon the human stage a virtual mob of gods, each one fashioned in the likeness of its human creator. We have, in other words, a tendency to project onto the world about us our own definitions, fears, hopes, expectations, prejudices, interests, and tastes, and to confirm in what we see reflected back the universe we *want* to see. It is not surprising, then, that many who have already accepted a pyramidally-structured view of human society would be just as inclined to imagine the cosmos itself to function as a monarchical system of power ruled by divine kings, princes, and lords, and assisted on earth by ministerial authorities.

Unfortunately, what passes for religion in our world is, when it becomes organized, little more than the perpetuation of childhood feelings of domination by and dependencies upon parental authority. Men and women who long ago abandoned the belief that their daily activities were watched over by an Arctic elf nevertheless continue to worship heavenly fathers and holy mothers. The Catholic church is ruled over by an infallible authority whose title, in Italian, is "papa," and who is assisted by a clergy of "fathers." Employing the same conditioning techniques by which people train their pets, these church officials reward with token wafers those obedient supplicants who have learned to sit up and beg. What can be said of the spiritual value of religions that insist on keeping grown adults kneeling and begging forgiveness like fear-ridden, helpless children? How can those who are willing to grovel for morsels of secondhand inspiration learn to stand on their own spiritual feet?

In an earlier chapter we dealt with how our search for *understanding* gets converted into a need for rigid *answers*, and how this, in turn, helps foster institutional structuring. Though we may, by nature, have a need for religious *experiences*, we do not have a need for religious *institutions*. The experiences we seek are, after all, the product of self-searching, of trying to understand ourselves, other people, and the universe about us. Those experiences come only through asking *questions*, not necessarily in getting *answers*. But once a religion becomes institutionalized, searching comes to an end, for to tolerate open-mindedness is to invite the continuing prospect of change that is anathema to all institutions. I know of no religion that says "we are still looking and will let you know if we come up with any other answers." Organized religions prosper only by offering packaged conclusions to men and women who lack the disposition to engage in their own independent inquiries. It is unlikely that such persons would be attracted to a religion that does not profess to have its foundations set firmly in the bedrock of ages. Institutional self-interest, then, is dependent upon churches so structuring the minds of their followers as to develop the contented sense of certainty that comes from settled conclusions. Their answers get carved into stone, and those who do not accept those answers are labeled as sinners or sacrilegious infidels. Those who want to go on asking questions are attacked for blasphemy, heresy, lack of faith or, worse, are put to the torch. In this way, institutionalized religions interfere with and thwart the need people have for religious experiences and understanding.

In discussing organized religions, we ought not confine our inquiries to those beliefs associated with the worship of a divine creator and ruler of the universe. There are many areas, devoid of superhuman deities, in which people accept the validity of certain ideas, and structure their own lives (and try to structure the lives of others) in conformity with those ideas. Marxist ideology has been embraced by untold numbers of true believers with as much unexamined faith and fervor as a Bible Belt fundamentalist's acceptance of Christianity. With the same rockbound faith and vicious zeal that fired the holy crusades of the Dark Ages, Marxist missionaries have gone forth upon the world to convert all of mankind to adherence to an idea. In doing so, they have shown no greater disposition for tolerance of dissenting views than their predecessors. They have demonstrated once again that no man is ever so blind as when his actions are inspired by a vision.

Social or political causes provide other examples of behavior elevated to the level of religious practice. The cause may encompass any of a variety of topics: conservation, feminism, labor unions, political ideology, environmental protection, children's rights, abortion, capital punishment, planned parenthood, monetary reform, mental illness, public education, exercise or weight loss programs, drug use, school-busing, vegetarianism, anti-vivisectionism, or tax reform. This is not to suggest that there is necessarily anything objectionable about the ideas underlying any of these politically-inspired transient creeds. Opposition to capital punishment or abortion, for example, might very well reflect an intense sensitivity to the value of human life. Also, one who was aware that mankind is not *apart* from nature but an *expression* of it would doubtless comprehend how interrelated we are with our environment and seek to live in harmony with it.

But why would one choose to convert such *understanding* into a *cause,* or a *religion?* Why would one seek to anesthetize one's consciousness with social, political, or philosophical orthodoxies? To do so is to worship yesterday's sense of awareness, to paralyze one's intelligence such that, thereafter, one's actions will be firmly embedded in the dried concrete of the past. If a person arrived at certain conclusions through a continuing state of conscious awareness, it should be evident that structuring such conclusions into a formal belief system could only serve the following purposes: (1) to save oneself the effort associated with being continually aware of the present, or, (2) to induce others to accept one's conclusions without, themselves, going through the processes of understanding that led to such conclusions. The practice also forecloses—not only for oneself but for others—the excitement associated with living constantly on the frontier of discovery.

Every religion or cause grows out of a desire either to make one's own life more effortless, or to control and manipulate other people in order to enforce behavior in conformity with the expectations of the true believers. We discussed, in chapter 3, how externally-directed people need to verify their own self-images by impressing them upon others. As the images and world views change, so do the specific causes, but the general practice remains unchanged. The same proselytizing spirit that once sent missionaries into the jungles with Bibles to reform the so-called primitives, now sends lobbyists to Washington with petitions and legislative programs designed to reform modern society. Those who believe that the United States Constitution separated political and religious activity have simply confused form with substance. Religions have become secularized, but their practices remain no more advanced than when the first tribal shaman emerged from a dark cave to terrify his fellow tribesmen with frightmasks and incantations.

Every cause or religion, then, is nothing more than a frozen image of one's past understanding. The process by which this takes place is well-demonstrated in what is known as the "feminist movement." Beginning in the 1960's, many women became increasingly aware that western culture had developed structured role-expectations for women (as well as for men). They began to understand how, for centuries, women had lived their lives in a state of dependency upon men, conforming their lives and their behavior to the expectations of male-dominated institutions. As we saw in an earlier chapter, their initial inquiries tended to reflect a deep sense of awareness of how women had been cooperating in their own subjugation. Many began to speak of effecting their liberation which, at least in the writings of the more perceptive, suggested that women begin to assert control over and become more responsible for their own lives. The spirit was one in which women were encouraged to become introspective, aware of their own natures and capabilities, as well as the restrictive influences upon their behavior. Those who managed to sustain such an energized state of mind discovered a profound dimension to psychological independence that took them far beyond a focus on past grievances.

For many feminists, however, such deeper psychological transformations never occurred. For them, the exploration into what it means to be truly independent took a change of direction toward inflexibility. The nomenclature reflected the nature of this change, as many women abandoned the liberating pursuit of *self*-directed awareness in favor of becoming *other*-directed feminists. The point at which their undertaking became an "ism"—defined by one dictionary as "adherence to a system or a class of principles"[5]—was the instance in which self-*understanding* was transformed into a *religion*, a *cause*. Division was introduced, not only between feminists and men, but between feminists and non-feminist *women*. The excitement of discovering significant truths about oneself gave way to a fervor to convert others, to reinforce, perhaps, one's own weak resolve by changing others. True believers began embracing a new credo and learning their secular catechisms. Like the followers of any religious activity, the true believers began to proselytize others, seeking to persuade them to adopt their point of view. In a missionary spirit, the feminists quickly engaged themselves in efforts to change the ideas, the language, and the behavior of other people. They scrutinized every facet of social life, as members of the faith worked to ferret out heresies and to intimidate others into a conformity with new-sprung litanies. Nothing was spared. With puritanical fanaticism, they disavowed the use of any products associated with sensualism; they descended upon the purveyors of sexist pornography. Everything from nursery rhymes to "girlie" magazines became the object of Carrie Nation-style assaults. Even the English language had to be politicized in order to impress ideological orthodoxy upon speech and mannerisms. Any word containing the letters "m-a-n" in succession had to be exorcised in favor of the more neutral "person." As with all other crusades, one was either "for us" or "against us," and any dissenters within the ranks were quickly purged. Thus a movement, whose origins lay in an awareness of the problems entailed with living in conformity with the expectations of others, ended up in a frenzied effort to get others to live up to *its* expectations. Jacobinism with a pen!

In time, of course, the feminists saw that others were not conforming to the new gospel. Persuasion was not affecting a universal alteration of mankind, and so the feminists took the path followed by all other causes: get hold of the power of the State. Their agenda consisted *not* just of *eliminating* oppressive laws directed at women, but of *using* the State as a weapon for confirming their own life-styles and enforcing their social preferences. In so doing, the feminists, paradoxically, used the same agency of legal force that men had been charged with using to help control and subjugate women! Instead of seeing in their own histories the restraining influences of institutionally-defined expectations, they used their experiences as a justification for the drawing of battle lines between themselves and their perceived oppressors. Instead of renouncing the dehumanizing nature of conflict, the feminists seized upon it as a tool for social change. Out came the political programs: an Equal Rights Amendment to emblazon the feminist *weltanschauung* upon the Constitution; laws to prohibit discrimination on the basis of sex by virtually anyone; laws to redefine fetuses as "non-persons," in order to allow women to rationalize the aborting of their unborn children, and other laws to force the taxpayers to pay the costs of such abortions; laws to provide, again at taxpayer expense, expanded child day-care centers; laws to permit unmarried women who live with a man the same right to an equal share of the man's income as enjoyed by married women; even laws against pornography.

As has already been suggested, it should come as no surprise that the feminist movement would endorse the cause of anti-pornography. It is the nature of causes and religions to be puritanical. The Russian Revolution enforced a very rigid moral code upon the "liberated" prols; the Iranian government of the Ayatollah Khomeini began at once imposing very exacting standards of conduct upon those who had been "liberated" from the Shah, and even passed a law prohibiting anyone from publishing anything deemed insulting to the religious leadership. Similarly, a number of feminists tried to justify anti-pornography legislation with the argument that pornographic publications reflect a hatred of women, and humiliate and degrade the female body. That may well be true, but in such a proposal we see represented the same sentiment for censorship expressed by all other true believers throughout history. Operating from the premise, so well stated by Mark Twain, that "[n]othing so needs reforming as other people's habits,"[6] the devotees of most faiths have shown a willingness to repress—by force of arms, if necessary—the utterance of anything deemed inconsistent with their interests or beliefs.

What truly liberated person could accept this contradiction? What liberated person would want to *institutionalize* liberation, to make his or her happiness and well-being dependent upon the political State, and upon getting every last soul on earth to live up to his or her expectations? What person, having defended the right of a woman to be responsible for her choice of whether to have an abortion, could call upon the State to deny others *their* right to be wrong? What person—having realized for even a fleeting instant, in that state of total awareness, the opportunities for his or her own liberation—would want to control *others*, and thus deny them *their* opportunities for self-discovery and liberation? What, in other words, is the state of mind that differentiates *token* from *total* liberation?

Whether we have found ourselves attracted to feminism, environmentalism, libertarianism, New Age consciousness, or any of a variety of other movements that have developed out of what began as insightful experiences, we should be aware of the tendencies of the human mind to want to structure its discoveries. The danger in this is that the structuring interferes with the spontaneous processes that produced the insights, thus restricting the continuing expansion of our consciousness. Truth does not need to be *defended*, but only *understood*. We require no other confirmation of our understanding than the harmony it produces within ourselves, with one another, and with nature.

In order to understand how institutions structure and control us, one must know how our belief systems limit and guide our behavior. Religions—whether of the cosmic or secular variety—offer some of the clearest examples of the ways in which our attitudes and thoughts can either immobilize our own energies, or redirect them to attack or seek to change others. There are few religions that do not endeavor to find new enemies for their congregations to hate, or new evils—always represented by *other* people—to be exorcised. When we abandon our individual selves and become devoted to an idea, or a group, or a creed, or a cause, or an idealized being, we become the kind of fanatically-structured person whose pathetic character has been so lucidly exposed by Eric Hoffer.[7] Our lives become filled with conflict and contradiction, and we experience dissatisfaction with ourselves. Because of this, we turn to surrogates—whether they be a god, or a messiah, or a guru, or some holy cause—with whom or with which we invest those personal qualities and potentialities we have long since given up hope of discovering within ourselves. As Hoffer has said:

> When our individual interests and prospects do not seem worth living for, we are in desperate need of something apart from us to live for. All forms of dedication, devotion, loyalty, and self-surrender are in essence a desperate clinging to something which might give worth and meaning to our futile, spoiled lives.[8]

If we were consciously aware of what we were doing, we would understand that our ability to conceive and project such attributes is an affirmation of our *own* idealized qualities. That we can identify and embrace perfection demonstrates that we are already the embodiment of godlike characteristics. But to be consciously aware is *not* to be religious. Religions, after all, thrive on faith, on the willingness to believe the allegations of others rather than one's own intellectual judgments. That is why religions have always been at war with the sciences: science represents constant inquiry, the continually questioning mind seeking to understand the universe as it is. Like all other institutions, nothing so frustrates the exploitive ambitions of organized religions as the presence of a child whose "think" is always "why?"

11

MORALITY:
THE GUILT-EDGED
SECURITY

*Moral certainty is always a sign of cultural
inferiority. The more uncivilized the man, the
surer he is that he knows precisely what is right
and what is wrong. All human progress, even
in morals, has been the work of men who have
doubted the current moral values, not of men
who have whooped them up and tried to enforce
them. The truly civilized man is always skeptical and tolerant, in this field as in all others. His
culture is based on "I am not too sure."*
—H.L. Mencken[1]

Closely related to religious structuring is another practice
through which some seek to control the behavior of others:
moral philosophizing. Our sanction of the authority we
allow institutions to exercise over our lives is ultimately
founded in our belief in the propriety of such rule. Accordingly, institutions have found it in their self-interests to
foster such beliefs, and to this end have employed the intimidative, psychologically-aggressive practices associated
with moralizing.

The concept of morality—whatever its specific form—is
particularly suited to the needs of those who covet power
over others. Advocates of any moral philosophic system
share with other exponents of structured human relation-

ships the belief that a totally inner-directed person is a threat to social order, and that people must be conditioned to accept the external direction of their value systems. Moral doctrines not only assume an essentially malevolent human nature in need of institutional restraints; but also, in this secular age, take on many of the functions of religious institutions in searching out a multitude of heresies, blasphemies, and sinful acts.

To reaffirm a point made in the previous chapter, each of us seems to have a need for what might be called religious experiences, a need for a *spiritual* orientation for our lives. It is the essence of consciousness for our minds to try to orient themselves within their perceived universe. We want to understand not only the harmony and order prevailing throughout nature, but also the interrelated quality of life itself, in whatever form it may find expression. We have a need to transcend our temporal, physical nature by discovering our wholeness, our sense of integration with the universe. We also need to understand what it means to be a human being, and what behavior is or is not appropriate in our relationships with one another. Religious and philosophic inquiries often appeal to this sense of curiosity about such matters. As a process of self-exploration, such inquiries can help provide the understanding that is essential to our being integrated and whole. When Socrates declared that "the life which is unexamined is not worth living,"[2] he was affirming this need all of us have to comprehend our being.

There is an important distinction to be made, however, between *understanding* and *thought*, a distinction that is at the core of our problems of conflict. One of the vicious circles in which we have ensnared ourselves is the belief that philosophy could resolve the seemingly eternal dilemma of human conflict and misery. This approach ignores the central role that thought—as distinct from insightful awareness—has played in creating the divisions that have produced conflict.

Western culture has long regarded conscious thought as the only significant approach to human understanding. Only in the formulation of concepts, empirically-based evidence, and sound reasoning, we have been trained to believe, can we comprehend and learn to function within the order that nature exhibits. Understanding, however, is based *not* upon intellectual constructs, but upon the discovery of patterns within our experiences. We perceive these patterns intuitively *before* our conscious minds fashion them into formal concepts. Our understanding, then, precedes the conscious verbalization of that understanding. Furthermore, our conscious thought processes intervene only when our experiences are not attended by an intense, energized awareness. Thought is the product of incomplete experiences, for if our mind is totally involved in our experiences, completely attentive to what is being observed, we do not have the energy for intellectualizing.

The content of our thinking is both past-oriented and the product of limited awareness. As we saw in chapter 5, experiences from our *past*—which were, even at the time they were experienced, incomplete—can never fully inform our *present* thinking. No matter how persistently we try to incorporate our most recent experiences into our thinking, the modified conclusions we reach will be outdated for subsequent experiences. As such, it should be evident to us that thought cannot transcend its limited nature. Being inherently fragmentary, thought must remain divisive and productive of conflict. Thought cannot produce systems of *order* to overcome the *disorder* that thought itself has created, because the new idea will be as fragmented and limited as the old. We delude ourselves if we believe that our thinking suffers only from deficiencies in *content*, and can be improved with better *ideas*. It is the limited *nature* of thought—not the inadequacy of the ideas themselves—that underlies our problems. New and improved ideas will not help us to create social systems free of chaos and violence. Only by being aware of the limitations and propensities of thought, and becoming more sensitive to insightful expressions of a deeper consciousness within us, can we develop the understanding that will allow us to end conflict.

Just as our need for religious *experiences* does not suggest a need for religious *institutions*, our need for philosophic *understanding* does not dictate a need for philosophic *dogmas, doctrines,* or *ideologies.* While religious and philosophic conclusions are always defended as the product of either divine revelation or rational inquiry, in truth the human inquiries that led to such answers have rarely been conducted with impartial detachment. As we have seen, the human mind is a highly energized system that has not been content with its limited role of observation. Our minds have developed self-centered perspectives of the universe. As a result, any conscious explorations of what is or is not appropriate to us as human beings are undertaken by minds that have vested interests in the preservation and reconfirmation of their previously formed self-images. Our minds, in other words, are highly prejudiced, seeking to verify what they already are.

Isn't this the way in which you and I have learned to live? At an early age, our conscious mind declared itself to be in charge, and undertook the management and direction of our existence. Even though our mind is totally incapable of governing and coordinating the multitude of functions carried on quite unconsciously by our various organs, we learned to play the same pyramidal power game with our own body that we learned to employ in our social practices. In both instances, authority flows from the top down; the functions at the top of the pyramid are looked upon as being far superior to the plebeian activities below. This attitude is reflected in our tendency to regard the conscious mind as the very essence of our being while, on the other hand, our excretory functions are virtually synonymous with vulgarity.

Because of its self-centered nature, our mind begins (or, I should say, we begin) to invent thought systems that reflect and reinforce our own self-images. We concoct religions, political theories, moralities, and philosophies, and then delude ourselves into believing that these thought systems have significance, that they represent something *real*. Though we tell ourselves that we are only searching for immortal and universal principles, in truth the processes of philosophic reasoning are an elaboration of our mind's need for intellectual certainty. The examination of values and beliefs that underlies the philosophic search for understanding is not, after all, the dispassionately objective and clinical inquiry we are fond of identifying with the physical and biological sciences. Instead, such explorations are ordinarily undertaken by persons whose particular combinations of experiences, learned attitudes, and genetic predispositions tend to influence their attraction toward some philosophic systems and away from others. The logic of a given philosophic position extends from its basic premises—each of which *assumes* the validity of a value judgment—and will attract those persons whose propensities are already reflected in such basic assumptions.

Although its adherents seek to prove the validity of their position by identifying the consequences to which they lead, the basic premises of any philosophic system remain incurably *subjective*. Try as they have to show that *their* particular philosophy is based upon "God's will," "natural law," "right reason," "the greatest good for the greatest number," "life as the highest standard of value," or the inevitable march of history, no philosophic system has been able to break through the barrier of subjectivity. Every social, political, and ethical philosophy is nothing more than a rationalization of one's preferences, an edifice constructed from the prejudices of its own architects. A philosophy does not provide *direction* to one's life as much as it does a *reflection* of what one already is.

Philosophy helps to satisfy the previously discussed need many people have for certainty, by enshrouding one's beliefs with a metaphysical significance. This provides assurance to the believer that his behavior conforms with "right reason," the "moral imperative," the will of some imagined deity, or the dialectical processes of history. It also helps to persuade others to endorse one's belief system. An examination of most social and political philosophies reveals little more than an effort to legitimize and sanctify certain social arrangements and institutions in order to preserve and expand their influence in human affairs. Unfortunately, the "divine will" is less an expression of the social policies of Jehovah than it is the projection of the attitudes of people who regard themselves as divinely-inspired; the "greatest good for the greatest number" always breaks down into a debate over what is good, while appeals to natural law involve little more than trying to convince others that the forces holding all matter together in the universe are but part of a cosmic design set in motion for the gratification of the speaker's predispositions.

Just as externally-directed people turn to institutional structuring in order to confirm, in the behavior of others, the validity of their own self-images, intellectual structuring— through moral and philosophic systems—helps to validate one's world view. In this way, what may even have begun as a search for understanding quickly becomes lost in an intensive effort to structure and institutionalize particular beliefs into rigidly-codified doctrines to be adhered to by true believers. Learning is replaced by proselytizing, and fellow human beings are compartmentalized into the faithful and the heretics, to be judged by the consistency of their behavior with the established faith. We become judgmental, attributing standards of good and bad to other people (and their belief systems) based upon the extent to which their ideas and the configuration of their ego boundaries conform to our own.

Those who are more concerned with understanding nature than with trying to twist reality in an effort to conform it to their own biases would have no need to structure their conclusions into a philosophic system. Such people would be well aware of how prior experiences can interfere with present understanding. If their present understanding conforms with reality, that is sufficient confirmation. If it does not, they will modify their past understanding to harmonize it with the present. Their attitudes could be expressed as follows: "my conclusions are all tentative. If there is a position more consistent with reality, I want to know about it." A mind that searches with intense energy will give consideration to the philosophic statements of others. But when *inquiry* is replaced by *moral certainty,* and *working hypotheses* are superseded by *eternal truths,* philosophy ceases being a tool for individual understanding. It becomes, instead, nothing more than an intellectual device for attempting to control the lives of other people through such psychic pressures as fear, intimidation, ostracism, and humiliation.

It is no doubt the fate of all philosophic systems to become institutionalized and structured by their followers. As we discovered earlier, there is a degree of insecurity associated with the possibilities of change that attend any open and unbiased inquiry. The externally-directed person—fearful that such inquiries might challenge his present self-image—feels threatened and retreats to the safety of familiar bromides. The unstructured person, on the other hand, is continually open to such potential changes. His or her conclusions are tentative, subject to modification or even reversal when a more complete understanding suggests such a change. The unstructured man or woman feels no need for firmly settled truths, but is able to accept the margin of uncertainty that comes from living with tentative conclusions of unknown life expectancy. The late Jacob Bronowski voiced a related proposition in these words: "[i]n science or outside it, we are not uncertain; our knowledge is merely confined within a certain tolerance."[3]

For those of us who are discomforted by intellectual uncertainty, however, a state of continuing doubt produces anxiety. As we have already seen, our inquiries are motivated by a desire for understanding, and we have allowed ourselves to believe that understanding requires answers. Because we are not aware that understanding comes from *questions* rather than *answers*, our inquiries become very results-oriented. This, in turn, disposes us to the certainty of fixed answers, and away from the tentativeness associated with the processes of constant inquiry.

We have failed to learn what many of the eastern philosophers knew centuries ago, namely, that the closer one comes to an understanding of significant philosophic truths, the more difficult it is to put that awareness into words. Verbalization too often provides only very awkward, incomplete estimates of our understanding and may, in fact, actually interfere with it. The process by which we arrive at such understanding consists not so much of factual accumulation and careful reasoning, as of intuitive insights. As if by spontaneous revelation, we suddenly *know* or *feel* something to be true; we experience what others have called the moment of the "aha!" Of course, such insightful comprehension is not the product of random chance, but of a subconscious mind that has worked over problems and information made available to it through the conscious mind. To quote Louis Pasteur, "chance favours only the prepared mind."[4]

In order to stabilize his own self-image, the externally-directed person will endeavor to formalize the ideas that reinforce that image. Even if this person has, in fact, had a fleeting glimpse of some truth, to structure his understanding into dogmas and creeds is to lock his mind in the past and, in so doing, put an end to the exploration and inquiry that produced the understanding in the first place. As long as philosophy is speculative and pursued with constant inquiry, it remains alive, for it retains the spontaneity and restlessness that is the essence of life. But when we are willing to settle for ideologies, religions, and moral codes, the life goes out, and the human spirit is turned to stone. Consistent with our habits of structuring, this need to verbalize our understanding may only represent our *conscious* mind asserting its dominance over the quiet processes of our *subconscious*. On the other hand, this tendency may reflect the integrating, holistic nature of the brain. We are beginning to understand something of our metaphoric, intuitive "right-brain," and rational, verbal "left-brain" functions—an understanding that is, consistent with our dualistic thinking, premised upon a fragmented, divided brain! Perhaps, as we learn more about brain behavior, we will discover that this need to express our understanding is related to our brain's need for *wholeness*, a purpose that keeps the brain ever busy trying to end the divisions we have created.

Regardless of the origins of the practice, there is little denying our preferences for the certitude of *answers* over the inconstancy of persistent *questions*, even though unfettered inquiry produces a greater awareness of reality. Our tendencies in this regard have been noted in a story attributed to Krishnamurti. The devil and a friend went walking one day. They observed a man bending over to pick up something. The friend said to the devil "you had better be on your guard, for that man over there has picked up a particle of truth." The unconcerned devil smiled and said: "It will make no difference. They will organize and systematize it. There is no cause for worry."[5] We want *understanding*, but we settle for *answers*—usually other people's answers—and invariably end up structuring our own minds. We want to get our conclusions framed, to build altars around them, to enact them into

laws, to develop them into moral codes, doctrines, and philosophies. The institutional order is threatened not so much
by the new idea as by the process of continual inquiry and
doubt.

The compatability of philosophic systems with institutional structuring should be apparent. Like religions, moral
philosophies create divisions within and among people, thus
fostering personal and social conflict. Such doctrines divide
people up into the moral and the immoral, the rational and
the irrational, the righteous and the wicked, the just and the
unjust, the principled and the unprincipled. True believers
join forces with one another—united around bromidic conclusions and unexamined basic premises—and prepare to do
battle in what is truly a moral equivalent of war.

Every ideology is the product of fragmentary thought
processes and the uncertainty of one's understanding. As
such, the existence of any ideology presumes division and
conflict among people. If our awareness was complete, our
understanding would be validated by its consistency with the
world about us. If we really *know* that water freezes at 32
degrees fahrenheit, we have no need to *believe* in the proposition. The truth of the matter has been so clearly demonstrated to us that we feel no need to further validate it
through an ideology, just as modern people do not attach
themselves to belief systems about the law of gravity or the
central position of the sun in our solar system. But it is
because our understanding has *not* been clearly shown to
comport with reality that we embrace an ideology. We
believe that our conclusions represent "eternal truths" because
we are *not certain* that they in fact do. We *believe* because we
are uncomfortable with *doubts,* for doubting—reinforced by
the presence of other men and women who just as firmly
believe in *their* competing ideologies—reminds us of our own
uncertainties and the limited nature of our understanding. As
Kenneth Boulding has suggested, "if an image of the world is

too rational and too consistent it does not become an ideology simply because it does not differentiate the identity of the person holding it from that of anybody else." One could not develop an ideology around the multiplication table, he observes, "for nobody would be against it."⁶ In order to quiet our uncertainties, we intensify our religious, moral, and ideological commitments, thus contributing our energies to the continuing social divisions with which institutions have managed to keep people at each other's throats.

The practice of moral structuring assumes that internally-directed, self-seeking behavior is incompatible with social order, and that some external authority must be invoked to superintend human affairs. In this respect, moral philosophy and political institutions share underlying premises. Just as political structuring presumes an essentially malevolent character of human beings requiring regulation and control through the exercise of coercive State power, so too, the rationale for codes of morality is that human nature cannot be trusted without being subjected to the intimidative restraints of moral pressure. The moralists only propose to substitute fear and psychic intimidation for coercive threats. While the State attacks people's *bodies*, the moralists go after their *minds*. Each, however, is in agreement that complete individual autonomy is inconsistent with social harmony.

When we accept the belief in the necessity for such external direction of our lives, we are telling ourselves that we are untrustworthy and ill-motivated, and that we lack the capacity for responsible, peaceable, cooperative, humane behavior. We tell ourselves that we lack a unifying sense of integrity; that we are fragmented, inconstant, and polarized beings; that we can find harmony and order only by looking outside ourselves. We develop what those who would control us require for their purposes: an increased self-doubt and an increased reliance (if not total dependence) on the judgments of others. We learn to project onto an external authority our individual capacities for good, for responsible and civilized conduct, and for the rational thinking and efficacious actions that combine to provide order in our lives.

We learn, in other words, that standards of goodness lie outside ourselves, and that we can become virtuous only by conforming our actions and our thoughts to these external standards. But whence come these definitions of good behavior? In what corner of the universe do these moral principles reside, and how do they get communicated to us? Is it not clear that those mortals who announce the *discovery* of these transcendental ordinances to the rest of us have developed the principles themselves; that they have made them up? Isn't it apparent that the content of their self-evident propositions is but a faithful reflection of what they find within themselves? It should be obvious to us that the moralists only seek to have us conduct our lives in conformity with their views, and that what they call morality is but a rationalization of their own preferences.

All moral principles, then, are but intellectual devices for social control. The morality arguments presume, as we have seen, the existence of standards residing *beyond* the individual, to which appeal must be had for the justification of one's behavior. As such, they serve as a denial of the wholeness and autonomy of individuals. To have to *justify* one's actions—whether to other persons or their value systems—is to be a controlled, other-directed person. To live with guilt and fear of being castigated as an immoral person, to be dominated by the need for approval and acceptance by one's acknowledged moral superiors is to live the dependency of a child. To structure one's life in obedience to the accepted litanies of a particular philosophic cult is to live *outside* oneself, to be *other than* oneself, to be *another*. To insist—even though the sanctions be psychic—that others conform themselves to your subjectively-determined value-preferences, is to advocate the basic premise of all tyrannies: the right to demand any sacrifice of another human being. The political implications of morality were noted by Bernard de Mandeville: "The first rudiments of morality, broached by skillful politicians, to render men useful to each other as well as tractable, were chiefly contrived that the ambitious might reap the more benefit from and govern vast numbers of them with the greatest ease and security."[7] Nietzsche put the matter more succinctly when he declared that "[w]ith morality it is easiest to lead mankind *by the nose!*"[8]

Morality serves the same function that sanity serves in a narrower, psychiatric setting: not so much to define the *moral* and the *sane* in the community, as the *im*moral and the *in*sane, to the end that the latter persons may be subjected to institutional control and reprogramming. Those who act contrary to the canons of institutionally-accepted behavior are generally considered by the established authorities to be possessed of defective characters or attitudes. With the same self-assurance enjoyed by seventeenth century church officials who sought to exorcise witches possessed by the devil, modern-day psychiatrists and other social engineers undertake the institutionally-serving rehabilitation of nonconformists.

Moral structuring helps to generate the feelings of guilt that are so essential to maintaining control over people. The political State requires voluminous laws for the same reason that churches need a multitude of sins: to keep people laboring to conform their conduct to mandated standards. The underlying assumption of this practice is that "the only way one makes people moral is to keep *telling* them they aren't and that they must be, until, at last, they are shamed into good conduct."[9] The more injunctions there are to obey, the greater the likelihood of transgressions, with accompanying feelings of fear, inadequacy, and blameworthiness on the part of the offender. In the face of being constantly called to account for one's behavior, and experiencing guilt for failing to meet the expectations of others, an individual becomes increasingly neutralized and submissive. One who is guilt-ridden is less inclined to be independent and assertive, and more willing to accept punishment as an atonement for sins. This is a principal reason why the State needs victimless crimes: to universalize feelings of guilt throughout society for those who have engaged in harmless but prohibited conduct. Political and religious institutions seek to prohibit an activity in order to make it more attractive, knowing that the attraction will engender the feelings of guilt that make it easier to control those who have been tempted.

Morality as an instrument of social control is particularly evident in political institutions seeking to regulate the pursuit of pleasure. In our own country, federal, state, and local government officials periodically fall into moralistic fits and attack the vices they perceive as undermining civilized society. They lash out, in tones reserved for those seized by the spirit of righteous indignation, at the evils of alcohol, drugs, sex, pornography, gambling, or other sources of what some people find to be intense pleasure. If the modern day enforcers of prohibition are not blasting away at the distillers of demon rum, they are conducting raids on teenage pot parties, or knocking over bingo casinos, or vowing to clean up neighborhoods inhabited by adult bookstores and adulterous entrepreneurs of the boulevard.

Why does the political State have such an intense concern with people's morals? Are we really to believe that politicians are moved by considerations of highly ethical behavior? The enforcement of moral standards upon people has been so universal among governments all over the world and at all times in history that the practice cannot be regarded as a peculiarly western phenomenon.

The State's interest in enforcing morality involves much more than narrow-minded pettiness on the part of government officials: it goes to the very essence of institutional authority. Not only do moral crusades provide the State with internal enemies against whom it can promise its citizens "protection," they also reinforce the State's fundamental need to control the pursuit of self-serving activities. Organized religions have the same need, thus accounting for their moral attacks upon pleasure-seeking behavior. Institutional success depends upon each of us believing in the legitimacy of their authority over our lives. They can survive only as long as we think it right and proper for their decision-making to preempt our own. The health of institutions, in other words, requires us to become psychologically divided, fragmented persons torn between doing what we *want* and doing what we *ought* to do. In order to get us to play their games, to give up the pursuit of what *we* want in order to promote *their* ends, institutions have had to convince us of the higher value of sacrifice (i.e., the furthering of institutional objectives) and the debased nature of selfishness (i.e., pursuing our own interests).

In order to accomplish this purpose, institutional moralists have employed the inherently absurd doctrine of altruism. Throughout history, humanity has been bombarded with this gospel of sacrifice, the basic assumption of which is that people should put aside their own pursuits and devote themselves to furthering the interests of those other than themselves. Altruism involves more than simply an appeal to human love, generosity, compassion, and cooperation, for such sentiments are natural to us and afford us satisfaction. Altruism means that we should want to do for others that which we really don't want to do. If helping another gave us pleasure, we would then be acting for our own selfish purposes, so we must learn how to want to do something without wanting to do it! Carried to its logical conclusion, altruism would have us fulfilling the ancient Chinese fable in which each person was responsible for doing each other's washing. Altruism is a denial of the self-directed nature of all living things, a rejection of what it means to be alive. That it is impossible for any person to choose to sacrifice his own interests has not detracted from the effectiveness of this concept as a weapon in the institutional wars against human nature.

The implications of this doctrine as a manipulative device for reinforcing attitudes of external direction and fostering expectations of others should be apparent. Activities that give us pleasure, relaxation, material gain, or other significant (and immediate) benefits furnish a greater burden for institutions to overcome in preaching sacrifice. To put the matter in economic terms, pleasurable alternatives increase the costs of our institutional commitments. For such reasons, institutions are inherently puritanical in the sense encompassed by H.L. Mencken's definition of a puritan: "one who lives with the haunting fear that someone, somewhere, may be happy."[10]

The intensity of the State's efforts to control a particular activity seems proportionate to the intensity of pleasure people derive from that activity. For example, the more pleasurable smoking of marijuana is more heavily-regulated than the less pleasurable smoking of cigarettes, even though the former is apparently no more harmful than the latter. Edgar Friedenberg has analyzed official attitudes toward various drugs based upon their relative compatability with institutional interests. Nicotine and caffeine, for example, whose harmful qualities are a matter of record, have effects upon the minds and bodies of employees that help to stimulate and focus their efforts on behalf of their employers. Marijuana, on the other hand, has an intoxicating and relaxing effect that tends to distract employees from their routines.[11] If people were suddenly to discover that chewing on parsley provided an orgastic or euphoric sense of pleasure, the political State would most likely intervene—armed with studies demonstrating its harmful effects—to prohibit its growth, sale, or use. Institutions cannot abide distracting influences.

It could be said that any preoccupation with the pursuit of pleasure—involving, as it usually does, short-lived enjoyment derived from outside ourselves—is only a futile attempt to buy happiness on the installment plan. But whatever we may individually think about such pleasurable pursuits, you and I can afford to take a liberal stance regarding the right of others to seek satisfaction in drugs, sex, alcohol, or other sources. But can the political State, or other institutions, afford to take such a position? What if the unrestrained pursuit of nonvictimizing pleasure were to become more prevalent? Of course, if such activities were susceptible of monopolization by the State, they might be incorporated into an institutionally-serving reward system (not unlike the practice of early religions providing women for the priestly classes). But they are not. Prostitution, gambling, drugs, unorthodox sexual practices, and the like are ordinarily engaged in on an unorganized, decentralized basis by individuals or small groups of persons. Their pursuit does not require large quantities of invested capital, nor do they necessitate highly-structured organizations to distribute or manage the product involved. These activities do not, in other words, require institutions.

The fear institutions have of pleasurable undertakings is the age-old concern of "how 'ya gonna' keep 'em down on the farm, after they've seen Broadway?" What teenager, for instance, asked to choose between a life punctuated by the enjoyment of sex, drugs, or the like, and getting blown in half in service to the State in a war in Lower Ruritania, will opt for the latter? Who would choose to sacrifice himself for the alleged greater glory that is associated with making oneself miserable for the good of some institution? Who would be willing to spend forty years of his life working on a mindlessly dreary assembly line in Detroit when he knew that life had more pleasurable alternatives to offer him? Who would agree to burden himself with the feelings of fear and guilt that accompany the pursuit of one's own interests in a highly-structured world, feelings which, we are told, can only be overcome by renewed dedication to institutional demands?

The pursuit of pleasure is rooted in our self-interest motivated nature. It is in harmony with the belief that each person is a sufficient reason for being, and that there are no higher purposes to which one must subordinate one's life. The intense pleasure we derive from certain activities contrasts with the pain or lack of pleasure we associate with other activities. The pursuit of our own pleasure reminds us of how miserable we have made ourselves by our willingness to be duped into sacrificing our happiness for the glory of organizations. The habit of engaging in behavior that has no other purpose to it than our own enjoyment causes us to question our previously unexamined commitments. We even begin to entertain the notion that life itself has no greater significance than in providing each of us with the opportunity to discover and express our own personhood. It should be clear why institutions have always been so prudish and why morality has been an indispensable element in organizational schemes.

Morality is the wedge that helps to divide us internally and causes us to try to reintegrate ourselves through some institutional identity. Morality diminishes us as it enhances our external authorities. We are more likely to subordinate our own purposes, to suppress our own opportunities for happiness, if we believe that those in authority over us are more important, more virtuous, more worthy than ourselves. Morality keeps us in line; it reinforces the state of mind upon which a consensus for political rule is absolutely dependent. In an excellent article explaining governmental interests in prosecuting acts of obscenity, David Paletz and William Harris state: "[t]hus public authority can be seen as the ostensibly ordered (i.e., rational) and legitimate (i.e., moral) flow of command through the system of language from the commanders to the commanded. Anything undermining public morality in the context of public rationality may therefore result in the decline of public authority." The "public use of four-letter words," they continue, "disrupts the aura in which authority is maintained. It makes for public insecurity in that it challenges the solemnity and respectability associated with the authority or its symbols."[12]

Many people have become aware of the restrictive and conflict-causing nature of institutions, and have offered morally-based arguments on behalf of human freedom. But in doing so, they only help to reinforce institutional control over people. Institutions have thrived because we have accepted the proposition that our freedom is dependent upon our willingness to have our actions limited and restrained by institutional laws and rules. Morality, as we have seen, provides this same self-limiting function. The effort to construct a philosophy of freedom on moral grounds is reminiscent of the tethering system used, in place of cages, to confine the movements of circus animals. With their lengthy chains or ropes, the tethers give the animals the *illusion* of freedom, . . . if only they don't move around too much. The animals' ranges of choice, however, remain circumscribed by external authorities. Those who speak of expanding human freedom, while insisting upon moral restraints on the exercise of that freedom, are advocating nothing more than what the proponents of various political reforms offer: a lengthening of our leg-chains in order to provide us with the illusions of freedom.

12

THE MENTORS
AND TORMENTORS
OF CHILDREN

"But don't, dear children, be alarmed;
Augustus Gloop will not be harmed,
Although, of course, we must admit
He will be altered quite a bit.
He'll be quite changed from what he's been,
When he goes through the fudge machine:
Slowly, the wheels go round and round,
The cogs begin to grind and pound;
A hundred knives go slice, slice, slice;
We add some sugar, cream, and spice;
We boil him for a minute more,
Until we're absolutely sure
That all the greed and all the gall
Is boiled away for once and all.
Then out he comes! And now! By Grace!
A miracle has taken place!"
—From *Charlie and the Chocolate Factory*
by Roald Dahl[1]

Public education has been promoted as a system for universalizing knowledge and skills within society, affording to all the learning that, heretofore, had been reserved for the so-called privileged classes. It is generally regarded as a catalyst for any democratic society, a vehicle for fulfilling

the noble sentiments of opportunity, meritocracy, and
upward mobility that are so firmly ingrained into that hazy
concept known as the American way of life. But when
examined dispassionately, the public school system exhibits a
wholly different purpose. Its *raison d'etre* is *not* to universalize
personally-relevant learning, but *to universalize acceptance of the
idea of an institutionally-structured and directed society*. Schools help
to define and organize society by teaching us to become
subservient to and dependent upon the institutional scheme-
of-things and to accept the certified pecking order. As H.L.
Mencken has put it, the basic purpose of education has always
been

> to manufacture an endless corps of sound Ameri-
> cans. A sound American is simply one who has put
> out of his mind all doubts and questionings, and
> who accepts instantly, and as incontrovertible
> gospel, the whole body of official doctrine of his
> day, whatever it may be and no matter how often
> it may change.[2]

In the words of Ivan Illich, the school system "teaches all
children that economically valuable knowledge is the result
of professional teaching and that social entitlements depend
on the rank achieved in a bureaucratic process."[3] Illich adds:
"[o]nce a man or woman has accepted the need for school, he
or she is easy prey for other institutions. Once young people
have allowed their imaginations to be formed by curricular
instruction, they are conditioned to institutional planning of
every sort."[4]

The public school system has been as essential to the
purposes of the political State and other institutional interests as the parochial school system has been to the Catholic
Church, and for the same ultimate purpose: to condition
people to accept the legitimacy of institutional authority
over their lives. Curricula and teaching methods reflect an
approach to learning that not only accepts, but seeks to

validate existing organizational arrangements and practices. This is true not only for primary and secondary schools, but for professional and other graduate education as well. Medicine, for example, is taught *not* within a framework of how people can remain healthy, but upon the assumption that they will become sick and diseased and require treatment that is highly lucrative for doctors, hospitals, drug manufacturers, insurance companies, and medical schools and research organizations. Legal education accepts, with only sporadic questioning, the prevailing substance and structure of law that legitimizes the established institutional order. Many of my first year law students—not to mention a few of my colleagues—have been noticeably distressed by my questioning the legitimacy of the United States Constitution. Even though this document is unable to withstand a critical examination of its origins—other than as an act of pure usurpation— lawyers accept its primacy as a self-evident proposition.[5] Our tendency to recoil with astonishment when any of our basic assumptions are called into question often reflects the thoroughness with which the education system has conditioned our thinking. In Illich's words, "[s]chool is the advertising agency which makes you believe that you need the society as it is."[6] When the Los Angeles County government declared that children must be taught "that we are all part of one big social system," and "must learn how to participate effectively in the system,"[7] it was asserting the need all institutionalized societies have for gaining public sanction through the systematic indoctrination of children.

How have the schools accomplished this task? To begin with, State legislatures have enacted compulsory school attendance laws—under the guise of promoting the "right" of all children to an education—mandating every child's presence in a State-approved classroom for a period of years. Once in the classroom, the schools begin to teach children as much as they need to know in order to be serviceable to established institutions. One of the first things that is impressed upon each child is the importance of obedience to constituted authority. In the eyes of any school system, a student's highest virtue is to maintain unquestioning subservience to school officials. One school district forcefully expressed such a proposition in a publication for students that declared, in part, that "all pupils shall . . . submit to the authority of the teachers of the schools"; that "every pupil shall . . . conform to the regulations of the school; obey promptly all the directions of his teacher and others in authority." Those who have "wilfully defied the valid authority of supervisors, teachers, or administrators" are subject to suspension by the school, while "pupils who are continually disobedient may be referred to the juvenile court." All of this is necessary, the publication continues, to further the schools' "responsibility of seeking to correct the pupils' maladjustments and/or re-channeling pre-delinquent tendencies . . . ."[8]

The message received by the student is a clear one: those who do not accept a State-mandated subservience to the absolute authority of school officials exhibit "predelinquent tendencies" and need to "make better adjustments." In order to facilitate this "adjustment," the criminal justice system— dressed up in the Orwellian and rehabilitative language of the "juvenile courts"—will be invoked to break the will of the offending student. Those who persist in refusing to submit to the authority of others will, in all likelihood, be forcibly confined within a "juvenile correction facility," *not* for purposes of *punishment*, but for "care" and "treatment!" Ironically, this same publication declares that "any person who willfully causes or permits a child to suffer or who causes mental suffering or inflicts unjustifiable pain or injury on any child is guilty of a misdemeanor." That school officials could include such language without considering its applicability to the public schools themselves is a reflection of a system that has carefully fashioned minds that never exceed the bounds of permissible thoughts.

It is more than just formal rules requiring obedience to authority that impresses upon young minds the importance of learning subservience to established systems. A review of our years spent in the public schools makes quite evident the State processes for subduing the minds of children. The daily pledge of allegiance (have you ever really *thought* about what those words mean?), the ever-present American flag, the patriotic songs, the pictures of U.S. presidents (past and present) hanging on the walls, the red, white, and blue color schemes on bulletin boards to celebrate national holidays, the constant reminders that *others* are in authority and make rules for us to follow (for our alleged benefit), the emphasis on student councils and student courts, the trips to city hall and the state capitol, the periodic visits from police officers to tell us of the virtues of obedience to the law, the civics courses that indoctrinate us with pro-political views, the treatment of history as *political* history and modern problems as conditions to be resolved by political means, the mock presidential elections every four years, the textbooks that repeat without contradiction the importance of patriotism, citizenship, loyalty, democracy, good leadership, and all the other trappings of political authority, the tendency to regard progress as social change and a meaningful career as one involved with political activism or government employment and certainly *not* work in a noninstitutional setting, the importance of voting (reinforced by the common use of the schools as polling places), the assumption that life was chaotic and unpredictable until present legislation was enacted and that it will become even better with more up-to-date laws, . . . these and so many other examples manifest the point I am making. R.D. Laing has described the process this way: "We begin with the children. It is imperative to catch them in time. Without the most thorough and rapid brainwashing their dirty minds would see through our dirty tricks. Children are not yet fools, but we shall turn them into imbeciles like ourselves, with high I.Q.'s if possible.''[9]

The truth of the proposition becomes clearer when one considers the more subtle reinforcements found in the recognized subservience of student to teacher—a teaching methodology that makes the student dependent upon the teacher-authority for knowledge, and fosters the anti-intellectual absurdity that a conclusion cannot even be considered unless it has been previously enunciated by recognized authorities—and classroom activity and rules that remind the student he is there for purposes other than what is of interest to himself.

Through such practices, students learn not only to distrust their own individual judgments, but also to accept for themselves a condition of mental passivity. The teachers (and the school system) determine our intellectual scheduling: they tell us what and when we will study, and limit the scope of our inquiry. We must even get their permission to speak, and dare not talk to our classmates on our own volition. Should any of us be daring enough to voice a dissenting opinion, the teacher may hold us up to the ridicule of our classmates, or punish us with a failing grade. We learn rather early the dangers associated with the expression of thoughts that displease the established order.

The public school system must surely rank as one of the most loathsome schemes ever conducted against human beings. In seizing and twisting the minds of young children, institutions have helped us become half-conscious, fragmented, fearful people. It is because of what we have been trained to become that we fail to see this system as an atrocity against the human spirit.

If you doubt this characterization of the public school system, then think back to your own experiences. Try to recall, as specifically as you can, typical days spent in the classroom, the subject matter that was presented, special activities in which you engaged, the demeanor of your teachers, and the nature of the rules and methods to which you were subjected. If this proves too difficult or uncomfortable a burden, then let me invite you back into my school experiences. My trip begins in a return visit I paid to my old grade school in Lincoln, Nebraska, a few years ago.

It had been twenty-eight years since I had last been a student at Prescott grade school. No Hollywood scriptwriter could have dreamed up a more typical middle-class school in a more typical middle-class community than Prescott. I never did know for whom the school was named, although I have wondered if a school board might have decided to break the pattern of naming schools after politicians and military leaders, by honoring the noted historian William Prescott.

Perhaps out of nostalgic design, my return trip took me along the same path I had walked on my first day in the public school system. How clearly I recalled those feelings of apprehensive self-confidence that accompanied me on my maiden voyage. A Prang watercolor paint set was in the sack I clutched as my mother bid me farewell on our front porch, and I remember having thought: "I don't want to go." Thirty-five years later, my mind raced to other thoughts: of cattle being herded into a meat packing plant; of Jimmy Cagney being led to the electric chair in *Angels With Dirty Faces* (Prescott School does resemble a penitentiary when seen from the east).

Upon entering the school building after a nearly three-decade absence, a strange feeling came over me. It was not, I think, unlike the state of mental discomposure that would accompany an ex-convict on a visitor's day return to prison. I don't know if this strange emotion was brought on by the sense of nostalgia, or whether it was caused by the rather startling perception that nothing had really changed in all that time. The same classrooms, the same hallways, the same odor of chemicals used to clean the floors, it was all there.

Oh, yes, there were new desks, and new teachers, and new blackboards, but I had that strange sensation, as I walked into my old first grade room, that I had but to slap two blackboard erasers together and Miss Albert would immediately appear in a cloud of chalk-dust. While I enjoyed the reminiscing, I had the urge to leave the building at once. I experienced the feeling of being an intruder; I did not belong here; LEAVE! It was almost as if I were window-peeping on my own childhood, fearful that the familiarity of the surroundings might serve as a catalyst for breathing new life into a variety of little Frankenstein monsters long since buried. The thought came over me that psychoanalysts might want to set up their couches in patients' grade school classrooms, and I recalled the theme of a popular song from my youth, ". . . when the movie starts up yonder, at that big picture show in the sky...."

The temptation to leave was overcome, however, by a stronger sense of curiosity: what might I discover about myself? What is there about this place that causes me to feel such discomfort? How strange: to go to school to learn about the world around you, and then to return to help learn something about yourself, and what happened to you on the way. I recalled how my earlier schooling had taught me so much about *other* people: kings, presidents, explorers, inventors, scientists, and writers. Why, I wondered, had it not helped me to know and understand who *I* was?

About this same time, my wife and I, along with our oldest daughter, began visiting a number of grade schools in order to find the best possible learning environment for our daughter. We entered one fifth grade classroom at our neighborhood's public school. The students focused upon us as in one collective Cyclopian gaze. They—one could almost say "it"—were, of course, delighted. I could recall the same feeling of pleasure I had in school whenever our classroom was blessed with a visitor or, better yet, a substitute teacher. The variety, the break in dreary routine, was almost exhilarating: it was a new environment, things were different.

As we sat watching the activities in the classroom, my eyes fell upon a display on the bulletin board just inside the classroom door. It was, in effect, a large organization chart, with the name of the President of the United States (Richard Nixon was then in office) at the very top. This was followed, in descending order, by the name of the governor of the state, the mayor of the city, the superintendent of schools, the principal of this particular school, and then the teacher in this classroom. Beneath this regal hierarchy of the monarchs, lords, and earls who ran the system, and just below the teacher's college baronage that actually ran the classroom, were the names of the resident serfs. There they all were: Robert Ackerman, Debby Steinmiller, Mark Stanton, Alberto Garcia, Cindy Johnson, Ron Washington, Sara Roth, James Cavanaugh, and all the other Bobby's and Jim's and Linda's and Lisa's, . . . there they were, the girls in one column and the boys in another, crammed in between the light switch and the chalkboard for all to see, . . . all in place, . . . *their* places.

If any student forgot his place in society, he had only to look at the bulletin board to get reoriented. There, amidst the other untouchables of his caste, was his name, his assigned place in the social pecking order, and he could look upward into that stratosphere of nobility, all the way up to the very top of the list, . . . the President of the United States. Above that, and slightly to the left, the Gilbert Stuart reproduction, beaming down as though from the heavens (the unfinished portion of the portrait does resemble clouds) a never-tell-a-lie-smile of grandfatherly approval and watchfulness; our original "big daddy," surveying his contemporary offspring. And above it all, the golden-fringed symbol of the entire nation, to which the student recites his daily secular catechism: the pledge of allegiance. Everything is there: his nation, his leaders, himself. Everything is there as a daily

reminder (and reinforcement) of the plight he and his classmates share: thirty little cookie cutter people, the proletariat
of the education collective, struggling for some scrap of
vicarious individuality and identity in a Joe Namath jersey or
a Farrah Fawcett-Majors T-shirt; thirty bored and manipulated prisoners seemingly stranded forever on "Go," while
the peerage lives it up at their expense on Boardwalk. Children learn at an early age the rules of *other* people's games, and
to identify the places *others* have selected for them.

The uncivilized impulse to structure and manipulate the
lives of others is perpetuated in the school system. Like other
traditional institutions, this vestigial appendage from our
more primitive past remains an unchanging, unstimulating
tool of social control. My own childhood experiences are
repeated upon the present generation of education conscripts
with the same faultless, iambic routine as a Marine Corps
bootcamp. In the years that have followed my incarceration
at Prescott School, we have witnessed the development of an
electronic, computerized, space-aged technology capable of
instant xerographic and photographic reproduction, the
transmission of words and pictures to and from any portion
of the globe within a matter of seconds, and the organization,
storage, and recall of such quantities of information as our
conscious minds can hardly conceive. Electron microscopes
allow us to probe the inner lives of atoms. We are even able
to enjoy television pictures of the surfaces of other planets.
Science now permits us to prevent both polio and the heart-
break of psoriasis. But the school system remains virtually
unchanged, grinding out its antiquated catechisms and litanies under a regimented, directed, and rigidly supervised
process that could be transported back into the world of *Jane
Eyre* or *David Copperfield* without any substantial break in the
pattern. A return to Prescott School was, indeed, like a
return to my youth.

It doesn't require too long a visit in a school classroom to discover the system of child manipulation and control that is taking place. It permeates the atmosphere like a suffocating chlorine gas. The most glaring fact is a truth long known by the students: the teacher is in charge . . . *of everything*. If I were to picture a typical classroom from my own childhood, it would show the central figure of the teacher, looming as an omnipresent Orwellian authority. Our entire day was spent under the despotic rule of this State-certified pedagogical duce. We were totally at the disposal of her every whim. We were her cookie cutter people; the blackboards upon which she chalked out her designs; the inflatable Bozo clowns that absorbed her anger and frustrations. We learned to identify the boundary line separating the permitted from the verboten, and learned to conform our behavior to her dispositions and expectations. We learned, in other words, how to survive under the domination of a benevolent dictator.

The manipulation and structuring that goes on in the typical school comes to life in many forms. One sees it in a class of some thirty children marching in a straight line down a corridor—like a flock of ducklings behind their mother— marching to whatever new adventure the teacher has planned for them; marching like obedient little programmed bionic children; marching because they are told to march, and stopping when they are told to stop.

I witnessed a particularly rigid version of this pedantic lockstep system in a modern suburban grade school a few years ago. There were a number of foot-wide lanes set into the terrazzo floors that made up the school hallways, and it appeared that each classroom or grade was assigned a specific path on which to march. A school assembly was about to begin, and I was standing outside the auditorium at a point where two corridors met at a ninety degree angle. Some five to ten minutes before the program was scheduled to start, the procession began. Like generals leading their troops home from the war, a number of jut-jawed teachers paraded their conscripts before me in close order drill. The students were being subjected to a disciplined march. Ever on the lookout for signs that some of the students might be *enjoying* themselves, the teachers were quick to silence any talking—no matter how trivial or quiet—between children, chastised—with the righteous indignation of a Baptist preacher defending church doctrine—any deviation from the assigned pathway, and generally reminded the students of their forceful omnipresence. Had these modern day Miss Dove's been astride cavalry horses, their resemblance to General John J. Pershing leading his armies into Paris would have been complete.

I grew up believing that work and fun were opposites; that work was a duty which, if adequately performed, entitled one to a period of enjoyment and play. This attitude was expressed to me one day by my mother. I recall, quite vividly, her chastizing me for what must have seemed to her a terminal case of laziness on my part. I responded that I had been quite busy at some productive task (which I do not now recall), to which she replied: "that's something you *enjoy* doing; . . . that's not work."

The school system played a major role in the development of this attitude within me (just as I presume it had helped to foster the same belief in my mother). We would, after all, spend some five to six hours a day in the classroom, humoring our teacher's interests, always with the reward of recess and dismissal held out as inducements for our compliant behavior. If we did not get our work done, or if we had misbehaved (i.e., ignored the teacher for one fleeting moment to pursue some matter of interest to *us*), we found the carrot quickly withdrawn: we had to remain inside during recess or stay after school. The practice of requiring a student to remain after school and do schoolwork as a system of punishment is one of the most self-incriminating admissions of the whole education racket, for it acknowledges that children do *not* want to be there; that learning is a form of punishment. It is like the converse practice of some schools in granting time off, or additional free time, to students who have completed their work promptly, a practice no doubt borrowed from adult penitentiaries that allow time off for good behavior.

It is the school system's suppression of the natural desire for *learning*, in favor of the *teaching* of institutionally valued attitudes, ideas, and knowledge, that indicts organized education as a war against human consciousness. Schools have helped us learn that thinking and reasoning and inquiry and critical analysis are insufferable burdens or, at the very least, terribly boring undertakings we are more than happy to leave to experts. Schools have helped us to dull our intellects, to learn to blur distinctions and forego analytical questioning. In place of our own thinking, we have been taught to accept authoritative explanations and to mouth the mindless mantras of contemporary popular wisdom. In this way, schools have produced the pathetic spectacle of men and women who *know* a great deal but *understand* almost nothing. Schools have been the anesthetists that put our minds to sleep so that we may never wake up to question existing institutional arrangements, or consider alternative ways in which to live. Because of this interference with our need for genuine learning, what we call adulthood is, for many of us, little more than the retarded growth of adolescents.

One of the many things we did learn, of course, was that education was an elaborate game, and we learned to identify and play by the rules of that game. Through years of operant conditioning, we became aware of the paramount rule for success in the school system: to be compliant with the mandates of the power structure. We learned, for example, that good (i.e., obedient) behavior would be rewarded in a variety of ways and, conversely, that bad (i.e., disobedient) behavior had its sanctions. Like packs of starved Pavlovian dogs, we learned to slobber our way through mazes designed by others, in the hope of receiving some small morsel of little intrinsic value but which, at least, represented the absence of failure and the discomforts of negative reinforcement.

The most obvious reward/punishment system was the report card. In this, our parents became all-too-willing accomplices of the system, judging us by the expectations of the school officials instead of their own, and meting out a variety of parental disciplines to encourage successful results. I recall my own incentives were to keep from getting bad report cards. A good report card was my passport out of the schoolroom at the regular quitting time, out of the house to play baseball, out of my room at night to listen to *I Love A Mystery*, out of the kitchen at supper time without having to listen to a parental harangue about the virtues of good grades. A bad report card was straight out of one of those World War II "Orient Express" movies, in which the hero has his papers confiscated by a Gestapo officer, thus restricting his movements. I would, in later years, think back upon this entire grading system as really being *failure*-oriented. We strove (if at all) *not* to do *well*, but to keep from doing *badly*. We learned to exhibit the "good citizenship" and "deportment" (i.e., institutional submissiveness) that helped to make up a good report card. We learned *not* how to expand the horizons of our consciousness in order to develop our understanding, but how to master the skills of test taking that would help us better demonstrate our proficiency at playing the game.

Test taking and competitive grading helped reinforce within our minds the institutionally-serving conviction that rivalry and conflict were necessary corollaries of personal success. Through curved grading practices, we discovered that our grade of "90" was enhanced by one classmate's "70" and undermined by another's "100." We also learned that cooperating with and assisting another in his efforts to learn—such as by helping a friend during an examination—

was one of the cardinal sins of the classroom, subjecting both parties to the punishment of failing grades.

The grading system helps to reinforce the attitudes people must have if they are to live a self-repressing, subjugated life in constant subordination to institutional demands. The exhilaration that comes from self-discovery and awareness can, like the use of narcotics, distract men and women from the less pleasurable burdens and duties associated with an organizationally-structured life. The natural joy of learning, therefore, must be suppressed and incorporated into curricula that teach us what institutions want us to know so that we may be serviceable to the duly constituted power structures. Grading systems help us divert our attentions from learning *for its own sake* to learning *as a means to success in an institutionalized world.* Grading helps teach us the importance of competition, to focus *not* on *what* we are learning, but on the externally defined rewards that have replaced our natural incentives for discovery. Most parents continue to be bamboozled into thinking that if their children are getting better grades than other children, or performing at grade levels above the one they are in, and are meeting all the other expectations of school officials, they must be "doing well" in school. The ultimate confirmation of those hopes comes, later, when the child receives a diploma, through which the school system certifies not only the *child's* competency, but its *own.*

Where, in all of this, is there any emphasis upon the child learning what is of interest to him or her? Where is anything more than lip service paid to the student learning how to experience, to know, to become oneself? Where are students encouraged—not just tolerated—to pursue interests of their own that hold out no institutionally worthwhile skill at the other end? Where, except as token gestures, are students permitted to devise their own curricula, or opt for the methods of learning that are best suited to them individually, or to come and go from classes at times of *their* choosing, to learn what and when and by what means *they* want to learn? No one suggests such alternatives to the students. Certainly not the school system itself, which has a vested interest in its present methods; not the institutional hierarchy in society, which also has a vested interest in the school system continuing to turn out institutional conscripts; and not the parents who, themselves, are the well-indoctrinated products of the school system.

There were other—usually more subtle—rewards offered to induce our compliance with the system. One of the principal rewards, as I have already suggested, was to get time off from classroom work. This might take the form of granting the good students a day home from school, or free time in the library. A more common reward used in my day was to assign the good students as hall, playground, cafeteria, or bicycle rack monitors. In later years, the role of school crossing patrol boys and girls was established. In each instance, the good students were singled out from their peers, given badges or armbands of authority over their schoolmates, and assigned to police their respective jurisdictional beats. These functions permitted the students to be absent from the classroom for a short period of time each day.

The hall monitors, for example, got to sit at desks in the corridors (while the rest of us were in classes) and check the extra-classroom movements of any student who happened to be out of his or her assigned compound. In order to leave the classroom, a student had to first obtain a hall pass from the teacher. The hall pass identified the name of the student, the time and date he or she received the pass, and the purpose for which such temporary trusty status had been granted. The hall monitor—so identified by an armband—was not just the Johnny Hansen with whom you went bike riding, he was an official authority, part of the established order. He had been transported, as it were, out of the darkness and into the sunlight. He was up there, at the very fountainhead of power

and authority, able to touch the pump handle. He was, in
every sense of the word, our peer authority, capable of lifting
our passport with the facility of a Richard Conte SS officer.
It was in later years that I learned that the Nazis also made
use of the practice of having concentration camp prisoners
supervise (in exchange for special privileges) the behavior of
their fellow prisoners.

The social implications of these various systems of peer
authority are rather apparent: the student learns that the
exercise of authority over others is a reward for being an
obedient, compliant person. If, in other words, a student
adopts the world view of the school system and its administration, and accepts the designs and schedules others have
arranged for his life, he is likely to be rewarded by having
conferred upon him the institutionally-backed power to
govern his fellow inmates.

My second grade teacher had developed a variation—
with overtones of political symbolism—on the reward system. Each day, following the noontime exercise of the
inmates in the schoolyard, we would put our heads down on
our desks for a short rest period. The window shades were
drawn and the lights were turned off in the classroom. As we
rested, the teacher would circulate through the classroom
and select the two or three students who had been the best at
resting. This meant, of course, that if you were looking
around, or talking to your neighbor, or not cooperating in
some other way, you would not be selected. The selection
process, itself, was unique. You did not receive a kiss on the
cheek or a black mark on a piece of paper—a la the Mafia—
but arose to find, placed on your desk, a six inch high
American flag that the teacher had inserted into a clay stand.
Since this was within the first year of World War II, we
were particularly sensitive to nationalistic and patriotic
appeals. We could not help but feel, in our impressionable "I
wanna' be a four star general when I grow up" eighth year of

our lives, that we were doing something for our country in remaining quiet, and that our sacrifice was rewarded with a miniature symbol of all that "our boys" were fighting for. As we rested in our darkened classroom, each of us sought, in the words of the *Star Spangled Banner*, "proof through the night that our flag was still there," and awoke, as the teacher raised the window shades, to the delight of seeing our prized flag "as it catches the gleam of the morning's first beam."

Upon reflection, my school years were—no doubt like yours—a subtle but effective source of conditioning through which I learned to incorporate into my own personality those ideas and patterns of behavior that served the interests of institutions. Who else but the political State, for example, would have gained from my learning the virtue of obedience to laws, the responsibility of voting and paying taxes, the importance of respecting elected authorities, the glory of killing and dying for the State? But these institutionalizing influences went far beyond training us to become compliant citizens.

I would, in my adult years, be reminded of the striking similarity between the routines of the school system and the business world. I seemed to have traded an 8 to 3:15, five-day-a-week school schedule—each day punctuated by two recesses and a lunch period and the year intermittently blessed by a scattering of holidays as well as a summer vacation—for an 8 to 5, five-day-a-week work schedule—each day punctuated by two coffee breaks and a lunch break and the year intermittently blessed by a scattering of holidays as well as a summer vacation. The teacher, whose moods, expectations, and whims I sought to appease in school, became the employer who demanded my obedience to his authority in adult life. Apart from differences in name, job description, and the type of work involved, the essential ground rules in business were the same as they had been in my schooldays. In each case, work was rarely enjoyed for its own sake, but was regarded as a duty to be performed by "responsible" people in order to fulfill their institutionally-defined obligations. Time off was considered as a reward for my having endured the time spent in performing unpleasant tasks. As adults, we bring home paychecks instead of report cards (although we still compare ourselves with how well others are doing), but instead of heading off to the baseball diamond we now partake of the "happy hour." We join our children in cheering "thank God it's Friday," as we celebrate our brief release from institutionalized captivity. Like young ponies, the promise of periodic respites from our confinements seems enough to induce us to return to our appointed stalls. It is interesting to contemplate, in all of this, the extent to which our negative attitudes toward learning and work are reactions against our childhood experiences with institutionalized structuring.

I must admit, however, that I did not play the school system's game very well. I have no recollection of ever understanding, as a child, *why* I had been sentenced to the school system, although I knew that I was innocent of any wrongdoing; that I had been framed. From a very early age, I had been fully aware that I was not in school for my own satisfaction, but because others wanted me there. I was also aware that the school authorities were not interested in my likes and dislikes, and that I had no control over, or effective means of dissent from, the decision-making of the system. My parents demanded an attendance which I was unable to avoid and, like other lifers, I counted the days until summer vacation and the years until high school graduation. Only as an adult did I come to understand the antithetical relationship between learning and education, and become aware of just how much the school system—with its sophisticated tools for strangling thought and understanding—wars against children and the natural processes of growing up.

13

REDISCOVERING
FREEDOM

*We live in a very low state of the world, and
pay unwilling tribute to governments founded
on force. There is not, among the most religious
and instructed men of the most religious and
civil nations, a reliance on the moral sentiment
and a sufficient belief in the unity of things, to
persuade them that society can be maintained
without artificial restraints, as well as the solar
system; or that the private citizen might be
reasonable and a good neighbor, without the
hint of a jail or a confiscation. . . . I do not call to
mind a single human being who has steadily
denied the authority of the laws, on the simple
ground of his own moral nature. Such designs,
full of genius and full of faith as they are, are not
entertained except avowedly as air-pictures. If
the individual who exhibits them dare to think
them practicable, he disgusts scholars and
churchmen; and men of talent and women of
superior sentiments cannot hide their contempt.*
—Ralph Waldo Emerson[1]

Considering how consistently we have been trained to
accept the institutional organization of our lives, and how
such practices are both dependent upon and productive of
conflict, why are we amazed that we are so violent? Violence
is the keystone of our organizational structures. It is the basic
premise upon which our society operates. We are trained to

be people pushers, to force people to do things our way when they do not otherwise choose to do so. Duress is generally accepted as the ultimate method for securing the participation of others in our purposes. Parents and teachers rely upon it in dealing with children; policemen and bureaucrats retain it as their eventual sanction. Judges issue orders, injunctions, mandates, decrees, and sentences, each with the threat of physical violence to back them up. Psychiatrists accept State-approved force in order to impose treatment upon unwilling patients. Our nation's leading industry, the military, exists for no other purpose than to threaten with wholesale destruction those nations that refuse to act in accordance with American interests. Churches inform us that we live under a violent god who will punish—even by death or consignment to the everlasting torture chambers of hell—those who refuse to obey his whims.

We have been trained, in other words, in the techniques for managing and controlling other people in order to enforce our expectations of them, and to accept violence as an appropriate last resort for securing their obedience to our will. Most teachers do not believe in the efficacy of learning: students must be threatened with bad grades, probation, and expulsion. Ministers and priests do not believe in the power of moral suasion: parishoners must be manipulated with constant reminders of their sinful ways. Ideologists do not believe in reason: true believers must take the revolution to the streets, and man the barricades. Businessmen do not believe in competition and trade: their employees, competitors, and customers must be restrained in the pursuit of their self-interests. Politicians do not believe in a popular consensus: a nation must be ruled with tough laws and an iron hand. Power has become our most intoxicating aphrodisiac because the essence of power lies in its capacity for controlling others through violence and destruction.

Is our power to manipulate and use force upon others the

best of what it means to be human? Are we destined to remain in savage and ruinous discord with one another?

The social history of mankind has been a continuing contest among conflict-ridden people seeking to resolve their self-generated antagonisms at one another's expense. Outward appearances would suggest a struggle between those seeking to establish or extend their control over others, and those who have endeavored to liberate themselves from such restraints. In truth, however, such discord has tended to be mutually conflictive: controllers controlling the controlled, and the controlled seeking to control the controllers. There has probably been, throughout human history, no more than a small handful of truly free men and women. There have been few among the ranks of even the most devoted defenders of human liberty who could be said to be free of the internalized conflict that causes them to fear a totally unfettered mankind.

There have been, of course, significant periods in human history when substantial numbers of people have managed to become liberated from the highly structured, institutionalized restraints theretofore existing. These liberalizing epochs were occasioned, for the most part, by an underlying revolution in human understanding, and provided mankind a greater awareness of the natural order within the universe. The scientific revolution, an outgrowth of the discoveries of a few individuals such as Copernicus, Galileo, Newton, Kepler, and others demonstrated to mankind that nature is governed by forces and processes that are within the capacity of each human being to understand. Having grown up in an age in which such knowledge is simply taken for granted by every schoolchild, we are unable to appreciate the liberating impact of such revelations in helping to destroy the foundations for religion's long held monopoly over men's minds. A comprehension of the fundamental laws of nature was no longer looked upon as God's little secret with the privileged priestly classes. Just as ignorance and fear had kept men in subservience to institutionalized authority, an awareness that each had the personal capacity to understand reality set them free.

The scientific revolution was both influenced by and helped to influence the life-centered revolution known as the Renaissance. People began to inquire into their physical and spiritual natures, and discovered an essential dignity that was to underlie human thought for years to come. Man—not the glorification of his oppressors—became the focus of attention, and with such understanding came a dismantling of the artificially structured and imposed medieval social system.

This expanded awareness gave birth to the industrial revolution, as people began to make use of their understanding of nature's laws to promote their material well-being. The belief in their own sinful natures that had kept human beings huddled in contrite terror at the feet of priests quickly gave way to an appreciation of how the pursuit of one's own interests could serve to benefit oneself as well as others. Seventeenth and eighteenth century liberal philosophers expressed their understanding of the broader social implications in all this, suggesting that mankind both *was* by nature and *ought* to be politically free. The classical economists furthered the general proposition by demonstrating the value of a self-disciplining, politically uncontrolled economy. At the same time, the romanticists explored the human spirit and discovered man's basic unity with the rest of nature. As a consequence, human beings learned—contrary to the railings of the established institutions—that mankind has the capacity for creativity, understanding, and peaceful and humane relationships, and that all of this was possible not in spite of human nature, but because of it.

The effect of all this was to weaken—at least temporarily—the institutional absolutism under which church and State had traditionally exploited mankind and tyrannized the human spirit. Feudalism, which had kept mankind politically and economically at the base of a divinely inspired pyramidal power structure, went the way of the pragmatic Syrian steelmaker. Martin Luther and other reformation cultists arose to challenge the premise that the established church had a monopoly on eternal salvation, thus helping to free the human mind and spirit from the structure of official dogma. People began to conceive of living for their *own* purposes, free of externally imposed restraints. They began to question the authority by which others claimed the right to rule them, and even offered the heretofore treasonous proposition that human society was subject to no higher will than that of the people who lived within it.

In spite of such liberating influences, however, mankind has not managed to *remain* free of institutional domination. The liberalism of the eighteenth century has been replaced by the Statism of the twentieth, as nations are brought increasingly under the absolutist rule of a variety of fascistic, socialistic, communistic, militaristic, theocratic, or corporate-State tyrannies. Why has this been so? Once having discovered the advantages of living free of imposed restraints, how could we have been willing to allow the continuation of institutional despotism over our lives?

The answer to this question lies in understanding freedom. To begin with, we must understand that most organizations are disposed both to making themselves permanent, and to structuring their members into subservient behavior in order to accomplish such permanence. These tendencies can be neutralized only by a *constant awareness* on our part, not only of such inclinations, but of the *spontaneous* and *autonomous* implications of what it means to be human. The essence of life consists of spontaneity, and spontaneity implies freedom. Like life itself, freedom should be considered a *verb*, not a noun. Freedom is not so much a *physical* state (as we are accustomed to regarding it in the west), as it is a state of *mind*, the expression of a continuing process of attentive, self-directed living.

Freedom, in other words, is a reflection of our living in a state of highly energized consciousness, living in a manner that is harmonious with our natures. We cannot rely on our past understanding to keep us free, any more than we can satisfy today's hunger by recalling yesterday's meal. It is only in being continuously aware that we can maintain our autonomy. In the words of a familiar phrase, eternal vigilance is the price of liberty. The man or woman who is consciously aware is a self-controlling, self-responsible being. Again, this is not a matter of philosophic preference or acquired habit: it is but a recognition that each of us is constituted, by nature, to be the only one capable of making the decisions upon which our actions are based.

For reasons we have already examined, however, many people do not want to maintain such a continuous state of awareness. Many of us prefer to structure our lives on the basis of our past understanding. Having discovered the value of a condition of freedom, we believe that we can make that condition *permanent*, so that we may pursue our other interests without being interrupted by concerns for the loss of what we have already acquired. We create constitutions, or statements of principles, or other litanies, and assume that our adherence to such *words* is the embracing of *freedom* itself.

We have allowed ourselves to believe, in other words, that our *future* freedom could be assured by what we did *today*, that we could give ambitious people power over our lives and then control the exercise of that power by the scribbling of words on paper. Not only have we accepted the contradiction that our freedom *could* be structured, but we have also gone so far as to believe that only in so structuring it could we preserve it! Believing in the absurdity that *we* control the political State, we have placed our freedom in the hands of the very political institutions that have always been the greatest threat to our liberty, and have directed them to *protect* it! We have forgotten to be distrusting of power, preferring to believe the promises of those who have told us they will only use power for *our* benefit.

Because we have not chosen to remain aware, we have come to experience division and conflict within ourselves. Because we have learned to distrust and fear others (as well as ourselves), we have been hesitant about dismantling institutional structures. We fear a condition of freedom for *others* and responsibility for *ourselves*, and demand a degree of control that correlates with such fears.

Even our efforts to liberate ourselves from perceived restraints tend to foster conflict and a desire to regulate and direct others. If we identify others as our oppressors, we polarize *our* interests and *theirs*, and insist upon altering or restraining *them* as a necessary condition for accomplishing our own liberation. Although we may try to convince ourselves that such controls over others are but a temporary expedient, we only end up rigidifying the conflicts upon which institutionalization becomes a permanent feature of our social life.

We must come to an understanding that breaking away from the restraints of *others* does not free us from our *own*. Nor can we become liberated by seeking power over other people. One who has power over another may enjoy certain advantages, but independence is not one of them. The slave master, the tyrant, the guru, or other leader is as dependent upon those he rules as they are upon him. Just as ego boundary attachments produce a continuing requirement for enemies, the practice of trying to control others makes our well-being dependent upon those we seek to govern. When the behavior of others is essential to our own interests, we experience a loss of personal control over our lives. We become less than complete human beings, unable to express the self-sufficiency that provides the unifying sense of integrity, of wholeness, in our lives. Like two men handcuffed together, having expectations of others necessarily diminishes the control over our lives that is essential to our own freedom. This is not simply to suggest that the loss of *your* freedom poses a threat to *mine*, but to recognize that freedom in a social setting consists of any relationship in which two or more persons respect the autonomy of one another. We cannot be free, ourselves, until we understand this reciprocal nature of freedom: *I* am not free as long as I insist upon *your* being restrained.

Our lack of constant awareness has also permitted us to accept definitions of freedom that are not necessarily consistent with the actuality of being free. Because we have learned to confuse the *word* with the *reality* the word seeks to describe, our vocabulary has become riddled with distorted and contradictory meanings smuggled into the language. George Orwell and Lewis Carroll have, perhaps more so than any other writers, demonstrated to us how the corruption of language is a prerequisite for tyrannical rule. As long as we are willing to allow Humpty Dumpty his proposition that "[w]hen *I* use a word, it means just what I choose it to mean—neither more nor less,"[2] we leave ourselves open to ambitious, disingenuous persons seeking to convince us that "freedom is slavery" and "war is peace."

Far too many men and women know of no greater principle in life than that of obedience to authority. What is even more pathetic, most of these people would doubtless contend that adherence to such a principle was the essence of freedom. To avoid jail, in other words, is to be free! But how different are their views from those of us who speak of the necessity of "freedom under law," or "freedom within limits?" Freedom within boundaries is no freedom at all, but only a State-licensed privilege. We are not free if we must ask permission of those we have allowed to circumscribe the limits of our choices. Institutionalizing freedom is like trying to plan spontaneity, or program creativity: it is an oxymoronic contradiction in terms.

Another of the many concepts we have accepted in the name of fostering human freedom but which, on closer examination, proves to be totally incompatible with liberty, is *equality*. At first blush, this concept has a seductive ring of elemental fairness to it which, at least in one sense, is unobjectionable. That has to do with the constitutional notion of "equal protection of the laws," whose underlying premise is that if a law is to have universal application, there is less likelihood of the lawmaking process becoming oppressive. Equal protection, in assuming that everyone has the same status in law, was theoretically designed as a barrier to prevent the political State from destroying the rights of individuals.

Given the existence of political institutions, there is little quarrel with the idea that every person subject to State authority should be treated without arbitrary distinction. The notion of different legal standards for whites and blacks, or rich and poor, or rural and urban residents, or religious and nonreligious persons is an ethically indefensible position. The problem, however, is that this notion of equality assumes the legitimacy of the political State itself. It is premised, in other words, upon the exercise of coercive State power as a given. The issue becomes *not* whether people should be *free* from State direction and control, but how the exercise of such power can be made more reasonable by being made more generally applicable. We focus our inquiries upon such questions as whether statutes or governmental agencies are discriminating in their treatment of citizens, and ignore the fact that *all* laws—no matter how carefully drafted or enforced—compel or restrain with *un*equal force. But as long as we are willing to believe the absurd proposition that freedom is assured as long as tyranny is suffered by all, the State will be able to increase its restraints upon our lives while we bask in the illusions of freedom.

If accepting the existence of the political State was all that was implicit in the concept of equality, the negative impact upon human freedom would be much less severe. Unfortunately, the concept itself has been enlarged upon to embrace not only the idea of equal protection of the laws, but also a more pervasive demand for economic and social equality. According to this elaborated view of equality, people have a fundamental right to be undifferentiated from other people. This idea feeds upon the sentiments of envy and comparison, and has been a major contributor to social conflict. Who we are, and what we have, and how well we are doing become considered in relation to the successes or failures of others. We learn to take careful account of our likenesses and differences with one another. No matter how pleased we are to accomplish some result, our sense of satisfaction can turn to resentment when we discover that our neighbor was even more successful. We imagine the good fortunes of others to have been at our expense, and appeal to self-serving notions of "fairness" to reorder our differences and thus redress our grievances.

The doctrine of equality also helps reinforce the mutual opposition of interests that fuels all political systems. In the name of pursuing equality, various groups have turned to the political State demanding that legalized force be used to prevent private individuals from discriminating, or to take privately owned property and distribute it to those who do not have it, or to rearrange the lives of people—or society itself—in order to minimize any distinctions among people. A concept that we have been taught to regard as a limitation on the power of the political State has been employed, by the State itself, as a rationale for extended governmental interference in the lives of all of us, . . . and all in the name of promoting a free society!

Many of us are no doubt attracted to the notion of egalitarianism for the same reasons that others, throughout history, have contributed to the social pressures for other types of conformity: the need to validate and reinforce one's self-image. We saw, earlier, how externally-directed men and women want others to reflect their world view. Whether one feels a sense of guilt for having succeeded while others failed, or a sense of inadequacy for having failed while others succeeded; or whether one feels a need to verify one's religious or ideological commitments by compelling others to conform their behavior to such doctrines, the explanations for egalitarian political and social programs are deep within the minds of those advocating them. It is not self*less*ness that motivates the egalitarian, but the rankest form of self-centeredness: the forcible remolding of men and women into patterns that reflect the egalitarian's own self-image.

It may be that popular sentiments for equality can be partially explained as the product of our contradictory social practices.[3] We are *social* beings who need the companionship and cooperation of one another, and yet we have learned to value the institutionally-defined *distances* we keep from one another. The more we distinguish ourselves by reference to our attachments, the more we foster the social division that denies us our sense of community. Perhaps the passion for equality—like the drive that unites disparate individuals into all-consuming, faceless crowds—is but a reaction against such an artificially-structured society. If we can reorder our relationships and redistribute our material possessions, it may be sensed, we may be able to eliminate our differences and rediscover our social union. But if equality is to become permanent, it must be institutionalized, with the political State forever rearranging and readjusting our lives, and stripping each of us of the autonomy that is the essence of our personhood.

We ought to have learned from George Orwell something of the tyrannies inherent in notions of equality. E.E. Cummings' statement that "equality is what does not exist among equals,"[4] expresses a sense of the innate dignity of each person that is totally lost in the perniciousness of a system of State-enforced uniformity ruled over by a privileged elite of "Handicapper-Generals."[5] It is difficult to imagine a more flagrant denial of the principle of equality than that found in the underlying premise of all political systems, namely, that some persons will enjoy the privilege of exercising power over the lives of others. As long as we are willing to allow those who would rule over us to corrupt freedom into such contradictory absurdities as the Rousseauean notion that we could be "forced to be free,"[6] we shall never comprehend what it means to live as self-controlling and self-directed beings.

The doctrine of equality, along with the practice of dividing ourselves into collective ego identities, has also been responsible for the increased tendency to regard human rights and the enjoyment of freedom as *group*—rather than *personal*—attributes. It has become more and more popular to speak of "minority rights," a phrase implying the *group*, the *collective*, as the "one" whose freedom is to be protected. Our rhetoric speaks of "women's rights," "children's rights," "Indian rights," or the rights of "the poor," "the handicapped," "blacks," or some other designated group. Rather than treating human rights and freedom as something universal and indivisible, applicable to all by virtue of their very being, the emphasis on group rights suggests the enjoyment of special State-conferred privileges. If women, for example, have rights qua women, then presumably men have some different category of rights, a condition bound to create conflict between persons of different groups.

As paradoxical as it might otherwise appear, the current emphasis on minority rights makes it quite unfashionable to speak of the rights of the smallest minority of all: the individual person. But as long as our attention is upon the rights of the *group*, the individuals who comprise society will continue to be the objects of group sacrifice. As long as we are convinced that in fostering *group* rights we are advancing *human* rights, we will see no contradiction in the universal thwarting of personal wills that is characteristic of all State action. If we are content to lose ourselves in group identities, we will not only experience a diminished personal freedom, but we shall also be denying the reality of our being and our nature as self-controlling individuals. It is not in Popular Front visions of a faceless, soulless, lockstep equality that any of us will discover what it means to be truly liberated. Those who "cannot acknowledge any human identity smaller than 'the proletariat,'"[7] will be unable to comprehend that the essence of our humanity is to be found in our commonly-held need for forms of social cooperation that respect the essential dignity and autonomy of each of us.

To endorse the doctrine of individualism leads to equally disruptive results. Because individualism developed, like much of the concept of equality, as a countervailing influence to the power of the State, it has been more a philosophic reaction against the State than an expression of mankind's natural social relationships. As a political doctrine, individualism has served—like any concept of "human rights"—as a claim to immunity from State coercion. As such, it is a doctrine that not only acknowledges the legitimacy of the State—i.e., by *limiting* rather than *ending* State power over people—but also regards our individual interests as being essentially in conflict with our social needs. Unfortunately, in assuming that each person lives within a zone of buffered isolation from all others, that human society is a constant struggle of each against all, this doctrine has also helped to contribute to division and conflict in society, all to the benefit of the political and legal institutions that promise to moderate such differences.

To regard ourselves as unique, isolated beings is to not

only overindulge our egos, but to ignore our common biological origins. If we were to trace our individual genealogies
back just two thousand years—a fraction of the millions of
years we humans have been in existence—each of us would
account for 147,573,952,589,676,412,928 direct ancestors, a
figure that is ten to twelve *billion* times the estimated number
of humans who have ever lived on this planet! Mathematics
alone demonstrates that those of us now living are individual
expressions of a shared gene pool, enjoying with many total
strangers a crisscrossing of common ancestors. Furthermore,
each of us manifests, in our personal development from
conceptualization through infancy, the evolutionary history
of all of mankind. We begin as one-celled life forms, divide
into more elaborate systems, and then pass through succes-
sive stages in which we resemble fish, then amphibians, and
then reptiles. Even after birth, our behavior tends to resemble that of our so-called lesser primate cousins. Then, at an
age of from ten to twelve months, we get off all fours and,
like our evolutionary forebearers, learn to stand erect and
walk.

Each of us is, quite literally, the history of humanity alive
in the present. It is not just that we are the *product* of evolution: we are the living *process* of evolution, a process that
continues within us. In a matter of months, you and I went
through the same evolutionary stages that it took our ancestors millions of years to accomplish. It should be clear to us
just how much we are a part of one another, *not* just *philosophi-
cally*, or as an expression of trendy, gooey sentimentality, but
actually. It should be equally evident that embracing the idea
of individual separateness denies the millions of years of our
common biological history that has produced us all. Like
blossoms on a tree in an orchard, each of us reflects a shared
ancestry.

Perhaps if we were to superimpose the sentiments that
underlie the otherwise seemingly contradictory notions of

equality and individualism, we would discover what is closer to the truth: that in being individually *unique*, we are all the *same*. The search for human liberty is not one in which every individual is arrayed against the presumed collective of all others, or of one group struggling against another group, but is a pursuit that should serve to *unite* us on the basis of our common desire for the autonomy we require if we are to experience the self-fulfilling transcendence of our continuing evolution. If we can learn how to end the practice of making distinctions among ourselves, and of judging one another by standards that are spun out of our imaginations, we may be able to terminate our wars of each against the other. When we no longer have self-induced needs for categorizing one another, we shall also have ended our needs for comparison with one another and, with it, our attachments to such conflict-ridden notions as equality and individualism.

Unfortunately, the concept of human freedom—like such abstractions as "justice," "morality," "democracy," and "the common good"—helps comprise that body of social bromides and unexamined images upon which the health of institutionalized society depends. These words have value to institutions only because they have no definite, concrete meaning to the rest of us. We regard the content of such concepts as self-evident propositions, and look askance at those who wish to dig beneath their superficial glitter. We believe that we are free because we have embraced institutional slogans that *tell* us we are free. Freedom, in other words, has come to represent a commitment to what, upon close examination, proves to be only the established institutional order. Without any apparent discomfort, men and women are able to equate the world's most powerful and pervasive State apparatus with a free society, and are even able to treat the forced conscription of young people in service to the military machine as necessary for the preservation of freedom itself!

To reduce freedom to meaningless phraseology is to fail to understand the self-controlling, self-fulfilling implications of the concept. Freedom is neither an accident of human history, nor only an expression of ideological preferences. Freedom is a natural human condition, the denial of which places mankind in as artificial and constrained an environment as zoo and circus animals.

Our willingness to submit to institutional control has been reinforced by our external attachments. Fear of losing something we value motivates us, in part, to participate in the purposes of the political State. We know that the State has the power to forcibly deprive us of our money, our property, our liberty to move about, our freedom to engage in various pursuits, or our status and reputation. Because we value such external attachments and fear being deprived of them, we are inclined to obedience in the face of State threats.

But though our *attachments* can be taken from us by force, our *free will* cannot. Since our will is wholly within us and subject only to our direction, others are unable to forcibly control our volition or judgments. We, alone, make the choice to allow others to command us. We may, of course, have become so accustomed to obeying authorities as to give the appearance of being under their control. Our conditioning may, in fact, be so complete that we are truly unaware of any alternative mode of behavior. Nevertheless, it is *our* conditioning, *our* refusal—for whatever reason—to reclaim the authority to direct our own lives, that underlies our obedience. We fear any questioning of such authorities because we want to protect our external attachments more than our own sense of autonomous being. When asked if the tyrant does not threaten us by attacking the "external things" in our lives, Epictetus replied: "Not at all, if I feel that these things are nothing to me: but if I fear any of them, he does threaten me. Who is there left for me to fear, and over what has he control? Over what is in my power? No one controls that.''[8] Viktor Frankl discovered this same truth while a prisoner in Nazi concentration camps. What "makes life meaningful and purposeful," said Frankl, is a sense of "spiritual freedom," which he describes as "the last of the human freedoms—to choose one's attitude in any given set of circumstances, to choose one's own way.''[9]

Because our attachments increase the likelihood that we will cooperate with those who would control us, it should be evident that only our *attachments* can enslave us. We are free only when we are complete within ourselves. Only when we value something outside ourselves more than we value the inviolability of our will do we make ourselves vulnerable to the loss of our freedom. Because we cannot lose our free will but can only choose to relinquish it, we have nothing to fear from others. The realization of that fact *is* freedom.

Liberation, then, develops out of understanding. As we have seen, understanding is, itself, the product *not* of *certainty* but of *doubt*. It reflects *not* that psychological immaturity we associate with nihilistic delusions and reactions against worldly imperfections, but the maturity of a healthy, inquiring skepticism. Understanding arises from a state of mind that accepts the possibility that *everything* one has learned may be wrong and must continually be reexamined and reverified. Liberation comes only when one is willing to live on that edge of constant uncertainty, refusing to allow oneself to remain entangled in attachments or mired in the concrete of prior understanding.

The self-awareness and consciousness raising activities of recent years have helped many people to become conscious of the fact that they are living controlled lives, structured to conform to the expectations of others. The interest in liberating oneself from institutional and societal restraints reflects, at least in many, a deeper understanding of the necessary relationship between a condition of human freedom and the opportunities for self-fulfilling, growth oriented behavior. The essence of consciousness raising or self-actualization, or even the effort to make a less significant improvement in one's well-being, presupposes a condition of *change*, in which free-functioning individuals are able to alter their behavior in response to their enhanced understanding. Just as variation is a necessary condition for our continuing physical evolution, psychological and social transformation will occur only if we are free to pursue a diversity of alternatives. Pluralism and dissimilarity are the catalysts for personal and social evolution, however disruptive they may be to institutional needs for uniformity and stability. If we are to put aside our violent ways, we must fundamentally change. But change cannot occur unless one is free *to* change; change implies the absence of restrictions. To quote Harold Laski once again:

> nothing ultimately matters save maintenance of the conditions which make for the emancipation of personality. Our business, if we desire to live a life not utterly devoid of meaning and significance, is to accept nothing which contradicts our basic experience merely because it comes to us from tradition or convention or authority. . . . That is why the condition of freedom in any state is always a widespread and consistent skepticism of the canons upon which power insists.[10]

Institutional structuring interferes with the processes of change and growth upon which the full expression of our personalities depend. Institutionalism imposes conservative, status quo maintaining influences upon people, and thus impedes the development of new ideas, new technology, alternate modes of behavior, or any other changes deemed threatening to existing institutional interests or arrangements. Those who seek to preserve existing relationships or impose new ones upon others by erecting a network of barriers, rules, laws, moral codes, and other restrictions do more than simply protect their positions or advance their self-interest: they interfere with the efforts of others to improve *their* lives. The result is to frustrate the dreams, hopes, and expectations of those seeking their own personal fulfillment.

How then, in the face of institutional restraints, do we manage to become free? Many of us are so accustomed to the processes of political decision-making that we conclude that the recovery of *our* freedom depends upon a majority of our fellow humans supporting our position. According to this view, *others* hold the key that will free us, and it is the attitudes of these others that must be changed if we are ever to regain our liberty. Freedom, in other words, becomes something to be *organized* and *voted upon,* to be restored by the very processes through which we gave it up in the first place!

Neither you nor I will recover our freedom through petitions, elections, or legislation: if we have to ask the politicians to make us free, we are only confirming the extent of our dependency. We will become free *not* when our *neighbors* understand what it means to be free, but when *you* and *I* do. We will not become free when the State goes away; rather, the State will go away when we become free. We have no saviours—be they religious, political, ideological, or technological—to whom we can turn for salvation: the passion to live as free men and women will either arise within *us*, or we shall not experience it at all. Since freedom is a condition natural to us as human beings, we need do no more to reclaim it than resolve to exercise full control over our individual selves.

You and I will become free, in other words, only when we realize that we are our *own* captors. To be aware of that fact *is* to be free, for we are no longer imprisoned by our own illusions. In the words of a sign that hung above the road at a school in Colorado at which I once taught: "the man who knows what freedom means will find a way to be free."[11]

Our freedom will not be attained by *political* revolutions, but only by a *spiritual* revolution within each of us. The only change that will really matter must involve a fundamental revolution within our consciousness. Such a profound change will occur within us only if we are aware of how our organized practices war with our very nature, and place us in a state of permanent conflict with one another. But that awareness will come about *only* if we choose for it to, only if we are willing to step back and observe our behavior and the thinking that has produced it.

Once we have freed *ourselves* by dismantling the pyramidal power structures within our minds, we can begin living in total freedom with others. Society, after all, is nothing more than individuals associating and cooperating with one another. Once you and I have freed our lives of all conflict, we will be able to enjoy harmonious, conflict-free relationships with others. Having no expectations of others, we are less likely to be perceived by our neighbors as a threat to their well-being.

Albert Schweitzer has identified what is surely an essential premise for any truly humane and peaceful society. "Humaneness," he tells us, "consists in never sacrificing a human being to a purpose."[12] Would it be possible for persons who have come to experience a deeper understanding of the interrelated and continually transforming nature of *all* life to ever again be prepared to sacrifice the interests or the lives of others in order to advance their own? If freedom implies being in control of one's own life, would any person who has begun to experience the elation of his or her own liberation be inclined to suppress and restrain others? By what strange and distorted definition could one be regarded as humane who would restrict and control the decision-making of other human beings over their own lives, or impose external direction upon others and thus deny them the opportunity to create for themselves the diversity of experiences upon which personal development and self-actualization depend?

How could one be said to have a great *love* for those whom they do not *respect* enough to permit them to exercise authority over themselves or determine their own purposes, or define their own conditions for happiness, or establish their own relationships with others, or be what *they* want to be? What feelings of human distrust, disrespect, and elitist contempt must motivate those who regard others so little as to deny them their own opportunities for discovery and expression? What love of mankind is to be found in those who, under the guise of altruism, are prepared to use and exploit their alleged beneficiaries in order to accomplish their own purposes? What civilized man would presume to supervise the lives of others, to be the keeper of other men's dreams? What, in the final analysis, can be said of any human being who would deny to others the fundamental freedom to *be*?

14

THE NEUTRALITY

OF NATURE

> *. . . in nature there are neither rewards nor punishments—there are consequences.*
> —Robert Ingersoll[1]

A consequence of our institutionalization has been the development of a problem oriented outlook on life. As we have seen, the political State thrives on conflict. It seeks to convince us of the presence of threats to our well-being from which it, alone, can protect us. If we allow ourselves to believe in the existence of such threats, we find ourselves besieged by problems, be they foreign governments, pollution, drugs, the shortage of energy, cancer-causing foods, discrimination, unemployment, pornographic books, or anything else. Business institutions try to convince us that unrestricted competition, free trade with foreign nations, or low prices, are threats to our economic security, and ask us to help do something about such problems. Schools define nonconforming youngsters as hyperactive, and try to persuade their parents to provide treatment for this problem, so that the children may become more institutionally malleable. Religions talk about the problems of sin, or low church attendance, or the emergence of so-called cults that threaten to attract people away from more traditional, established religious institutions. We could go on, but the point should be evident: institutions require, for their success, people with an externalized, other-directed perspective, people whose point of reference is away from themselves and toward others. A conflict-ridden, problem oriented world is a reflection of the externalized, other-directed, institutionalized outlook of people.

Contrary to the self-serving fear mongering of institutions, I find myself drawn increasingly to the realization that there are no true *problems* in the world: there are only *conditions* we have chosen to regard as problems. Nature is unswervingly, incorruptibly, unsympathetically, unemotionally, unintentionally *neutral*. Nature plays out its paradoxical patterns, at one moment working its seemingly inexorable logic from apparent cause to effect, with matter and energy embraced in an endless synthetic dance. At another moment, nature appears to be spontaneous and whimsical, exhibiting the unpredictability that we associate with free will. We exist within a universe of boundless conditions: birth and death; growth and decay; darkness and light; heat and cold; matter and anti–matter; large and small; land and sea; sickness and health; predators and prey; dry and wet; fast and slow . . . all in a continuum of varying gradations and in a context of time and space that differ relative to our individual perspectives. Nature does not juxtapose order and disorder, or act to deliberately confuse its constituency. What we call chaos is only our lack of understanding of the processes that created a condition. Nature is neither good nor evil: it simply *is*, indifferent to the consequences of its processes, neither caring for our sufferings nor joyous of our pleasures. It is neither masculine nor feminine in gender; does not speak English; does not back the United States of America in time of war, or side with the proletariat in the march of history; does not vote a Republican ticket or embrace any religion; maintains no portfolio of investments; and is not out to help or hinder any of us. It comes in all sizes, shapes, and colors, but does not discriminate. It neither knocks us down nor helps us up. It is apolitical and aphilosophical; it is neither malicious nor altruistic. It is, in a word, *apathetic*, not giving a damn for any of us because it hasn't a damn to give.

To declare that problems do not have an objective existence is not to suggest that the *conditions* we call problems are
not real, nor is it simply to play cute word games. Wars,
famines, bigotry, pollution, tyranny, urban crowding, crime,
drug use, disease, unemployment, drought, earthquakes,
plane crashes, weather, death, halitosis, baldness, taxation,
auto accidents, venereal disease, noisy motorcyclists, and
"ring around the collar": these and many other conditions do
have a measurable, identifiable reality to them. The man
who has been mugged by a drug-crazed teenager has, in fact,
been mugged by a drug-crazed teenager. The woman and the
homosexual who were refused employment because the personnel director had a bias against women and homosexuals
were refused employment. The dog litter on New York City
sidewalks, or the industrial wastes in the Ohio River, or the
oil spills that wash up on Gulf coast beaches are *what* they are
and they are *where* they are. But acknowledging the *reality* of a
condition does not create the *problem*. We create our own
problems by *choosing to react* to various conditions. Whether
and how we individually choose to respond to the world
about us—including other people—determines whether and
to what extent we will experience problems in our lives. In
words whose origins I do not recall, we are as happy or as
unhappy as we think we are. This is not meant to suggest that
we ought or ought not be concerned about any particular
conditions. The statement is intended, rather, only as a
value-free recognition of the essential distinction between an
objective condition, and our *subjective reaction* to that condition we
have learned to call a problem.

That a problem arises *not* from a condition itself, but from
our *reaction* to a condition, can be illustrated by two separate
news stories that appeared one week on a television news
program. One involved some residents of an area near
Kennedy International Airport in New York City who were
protesting jet noise in general, and the proposed landing of a

supersonic transport in particular. Equipped with sensitive sound-measuring devices to document the precise degree of their collective righteous indignation, these people let it be known that the presence of noisy jet aircraft in their neighborhood was a problem not to be tolerated. At about the same time, a news story out of Beirut, Lebanon, told of repairs having been made to the war damaged airport there. For the first time in many months, airplanes were able to take off and land. The story went on to relate the joyous responses of Lebanese residents to the sounds of jets flying over their city. To the victims of the bloody civil war which had all but consumed that city, the noise of jet aircraft meant the opportunity to escape to safer parts of the world.

What, then, can we say of the problem of jet aircraft noise over heavily populated areas? To whom is such a condition a problem? Only to those who choose to so regard it. Does this mean that the residents of Beirut were right and the New Yorkers were wrong? Of course not. After all, it could be argued that the Lebanese had not identified noisy jets as a problem because too many of them were busy fighting *other* self-generated problems: people of different religious affiliation. Once peace returned to Beirut, we might well discover these same Lebanese focusing their attentions upon the problems of jet noise, too. But if we want to learn more about ourselves, and want to understand the underlying causes of the conflict we experience, we need to become more aware of how our attitudes contribute to the disorder we create. We need to understand that there is nothing inherent in any condition that dictates a particular response on our part. If—perhaps because of our increased expectations—we find ourselves more intolerant of a given condition, it is *our reaction* that creates the problem for us: *the problem does not induce our reaction*. We choose, for a variety of reasons quite personal to each of us, to have certain conditions be bothersome to us.

A hypothetical situation can further demonstrate the

point. Imagine two adjoining homeowners—call them Smith and Jones—each with a beautiful lawn. A neighbor boy decides to take a shortcut across these lawns, and is witnessed doing so by both Smith and Jones. Smith reacts to this trespass with rage: he screams his indignation at the fleeing boy, and chases him down the street with a garden rake. Smith returns home, his blood pressure highly elevated, calls the boy's parents and threatens both criminal and civil prosecution if he ever repeats his misadventure. Jones, on the other hand, chooses to ignore the incident, noting that no damage had been done and recalling how, in his youth, he had done much the same thing.

The trespasses upon the properties of Smith and Jones by this boy were objective and real. The conditions were nearly identical for each property owner, and yet Smith was the only one who experienced a problem. This does not mean that Jones was right to ignore the boy's trespasses, or that Smith was wrong to want to maintain the inviolability of his property. It means only that each man had it within *his* exclusive power to *choose* whether to treat the condition as a problem. Smith's problem was not *caused* by the boy's trespass: if it was, then why didn't it also cause Jones to react? Smith's problem was caused, instead, by Smith choosing to react to the trespass.

The subjective nature of our so-called problems was brought home to me one afternoon while flying from New York City back home to Los Angeles. I remember thinking, as I crossed an entire continent in the short span that intervened between lunch and dinner, of my own grandfather who had come west from Pennsylvania in a covered wagon. I could imagine the conditions he faced: bad weather, muddy roads, sickness, the discomfort of being bounced around in a dirty wagon. While thinking about this, I noticed a fellow passenger on my flight complaining bitterly to one of the stewardesses about an anticipated fifteen minute delay getting into Los Angeles. Although I had no way of knowing, I had the feeling that my grandfather would have better endured the announcement of a fifteen minute (or even fifteen hour) delay following weeks of uncomfortable travel across open country, than was my fellow traveller. My grandfather would likely have regarded a six hour trip across the continent (even with the extra fifteen minutes thrown in) as something on the order of a miracle. But not this disgruntled airline passenger: he had a problem; he had been "wronged" and "unjustly treated," and he intended to do something about it, too!

It should be rather clear where our so-called problems come from. Though we may be inclined to believe otherwise, the conditions we face are certainly no worse—and, on the whole, are probably better—than those existing in prior generations. By comparison with the nineteenth century, the physical conditions in which we live—our standard of living, medical care, sanitation facilities, means of transportation and communication, the quality of food, clothing, and housing—have improved exponentially. So, where have our problems originated? Does nature hide them someplace and spring them upon us when we least expect them? Have our fellow humans become infested with an increasingly malicious and troublesome nature? Or, are our problems the products of our own unique problem generators: our minds?

The neutrality of nature encompasses, of course, our dealings with other people. Although we have been carefully taught to distrust one another's motives and behavior, each of us acts to further our own interests, *not* to cause harm to others. But because we may each desire the same exclusive thing, or may prefer something which is incompatible with someone else's wishes, we tend to interpret other people's motives as malicious. Because the actions of others may interfere with what we want, we jump to the conclusion that they are a threat to us, a problem to be overcome. In an earlier chapter, we discussed the institutional exploitation of the ancient practice of scapegoating. Our tendencies to regard other people (or conditions) as the causes of our problems, inevitably lead us to conclude that our well-being can be advanced only by changing or controlling other people (or conditions). This becomes simply a variant of scapegoating.

Another closely related practice is the tendency many of us have for seeking redress for so-called injustices. I do not recall who it was who defined justice as "the redistribution of violence," but that is the effect of our angrily striking out at, and demanding the punishment of, those who have victimized us. We are outraged that this person has harmed us, or our friends, or even complete strangers. We assume a posture of righteous indignation, and call upon the political State in the most morally compelling language and tone we can muster: "we demand justice!" The refrain "you done me wrong" echoes throughout popular music; the desire for justice permeates our literature, social philosophy, legal dicta, and political oratory, while different generations of youths have grown up with a variety of hero-figures with a common calling in life: "the relentless pursuit of justice."

There is no question that some people have, in pursuing their own interests, been the source of great harm to others. The regimes of Adolph Hitler and Joseph Stalin did cause death and injury and suffering to uncounted millions of persons, while the butcheries of the Charles Mansons and the Charles Starkweathers have added their less ambitious totals to the record of death and suffering. Of course, as we have seen, injury to others is one of the consequences of dividing ourselves off from others, of identifying ourselves apart from others. The conflict generated by institutions is no different, in nature or in its origins, from that perpetrated by unsanctioned criminals. We may think that we become emotionally irate and issue demands for the satisfaction of our sense of justice because others have caused injury to us or to our friends. But if that is so, why do we not also react angrily at the diseases or natural disasters that cause far more suffering than do the murderers, rapists, burglars, and muggers running loose? We feel sadness, compassion, and regret at our losses to the forces of nature, but we rarely take to the streets to demand retribution against the San Andreas fault or a tornado. If we can isolate the virus responsible for our illness, we may try to kill it, but we do so clinically, as a rational act for our survival. We do not take the virus-killing drug with the same vengeful passion that we demand the ritualized killing of a mass-murderer who has victimized total strangers. Though we may suffer far greater injury at the hands of nature than from our fellow humans, we do not react against nature as though we were the victim of a grave injustice. Instead, we treat these nonhumanly caused threats and injuries as part of the normal risks associated with living.

Why, then, do we react when other people cause us harm? Why do we not simply take it in stride, seeking to avoid such harm as much as possible, but without becoming morally incensed should we suffer some loss or injury? Some might say that the act of the criminal was *intentional* and could have been prevented had the wrongdoer chosen to behave noninjuriously. That may well tell us why the crime occurred, but it does not explain why we choose to explode in a great moral outrage at someone else's wrongful conduct. The act of the wrongdoer has obviously triggered something within us that causes us to become angry. It is not, however, that *he* has made *us* angry by his actions. Rather, because of his actions, *we choose* to become angry at *him*. Each of us controls our own energies; each of us, alone, can cause ourselves to become happy or angry. If we become excited about something—whether the noise of a jetliner, the trespass of a neighbor boy, or the exploits of a murderer—it is because *we* work *ourselves* into a state of frenzied excitement: nobody else can work our glands for us. So, again, why do we choose to react?

It is neither my purpose to play word games nor to devote an entire chapter of this book to an explanation of the obvious. When we stop and think about it, it may indeed be quite apparent that each of us is in total control of our emotional responses. It is equally clear, however, that we do *not* always "stop and think about it," particularly when we are busy reacting to someone else's behavior. We continue responding to the actions of others with "he made me angry" explanations that are no more valid than the childlike "he made me do it" excuses.

Our tendencies to react with anger and demand justice when others have done us harm are occasioned, I believe, by the same factors underlying all human conflict. Once again, it is our willingness to separate ourselves from others, to divide ourselves up into mutually exclusive groupings, that contributes to our sense of righteous anger. The mudslide and the burglar may both be causing damage to our property, but it is the *burglar* we regard as the trespasser. It is in order to distinguish ourselves from him, and from all other persons unlike ourselves, that we have established ego boundaries and put ourselves at war with others. It is the trespass of our *ego* boundaries, the refusal of the burglar to respect the divisions we have created, more than a violation of the *physical* boundaries of the property itself, that is the source of our felt sense of anger. A wild animal may come onto our property and we are inclined to treat it with a sense of curiosity, but let the neighbor's dog (which we identify with our neighbor) wander into our yard and we are outraged, particularly if the dog should urinate on our property (the means by which canines establish their own territorial boundaries). The dog is no longer just an *animal*, but an extension of a member of our own species from whom we have separated. The violation of our ego boundaries can be accomplished only by someone *we* have defined as an outsider. It is our self-image—fashioned within our own minds out of the material of our own expectations—that accounts for so much of how we think and feel about other people.

Perhaps the biological sciences can provide some insight into how our reactions cause our problems. As Lewis Thomas has written, the diseases that threaten our lives are more often the product *not* of harmful bacteria, but of an overreaction by our body's defense mechanism to the presence of such bacteria. Thomas suggests that such overreaction is caused by what can be likened to "paranoid delusions, . . . explainable in part by our need for enemies," noting that most bacterial invasions are of minor significance. In Thomas' words, "[d]isease usually results from inconclusive negotiations for symbiosis, an overstepping of the line by one side or the other, a biologic misinterpretation of borders." He then adds:

> The microorganisms that seem to have it in for us in the worst way—the ones that really appear to wish us ill—turn out on close examination to be rather more likely bystanders, strays, strangers in from the cold. They will invade and replicate if given the chance, . . . but it is our response to their presence that makes the disease. Our arsenals for fighting off bacteria are so powerful, and involve so many different defense mechanisms, that we are in more danger from them than from the invaders.[2]

What a perfect analogy to the organized conflict and violence that now threatens our collective existence as a species. Our institutional "defense mechanisms" with their "need for enemies" have spawned wars, religious and ideological bloodbaths, torture and murder by despotic police states, and the continuing threat of nuclear extermination. We defend the borders of our institutional ego boundaries with a hair trigger paranoia that is prepared to react with deadly force to any appearance of a trespass. We imagine our fellow humans or nature itself to be hostile to our interests, and extrude a seemingly endless flow of problems and threats to be resolved by institutions. We are, in short, at war with the nightmarish inventions of our conscious minds, and now find our survival imperiled by well-organized responses to the threats we have created ourselves!

There is another factor that helps to explain our anger at being victimized by others. Most of our anger, I believe, is *self-directed*. When we become angry at other people or conditions we are, to a large extent, expressing disapproval or dissatisfaction with something about ourselves. This includes much of the anger we feel when we are demanding the correction of a felt injustice. Let me emphasize, once again, that I am not addressing the relative merits of the complaining party's case, but only seeking to identify one of the causes of our anger. It seems that when we angrily react against someone else, we may only be expressing an anger or sense of uncertainty we really feel toward ourselves. We are not condemning our *victimizer* as much as we are damning ourselves for being *vulnerable*, for having allowed ourselves to be victimized. It is discomforting to us to realize that because of our poor judgment, or failure to take adequate precautions, we are subject to attack, capable of being harmed by others.

Much of the anger that arises within us when someone trespasses our ego boundaries can be characterized as self-directed. When we define others as being *apart from* us, as being beyond our ego boundaries, we expect them to honor the lines of division we have established. In fact, we look upon it as our responsibility to defend our boundary lines, to preserve and protect our interests. Under such circumstances, we would expect one who has attached so much importance to creating and defending his exclusive ego boundaries to regard a transgression by another as a personal failure. A successful trespass of what we regard as ours confirms to us that we have been inadequate, incapable of preserving our identity by maintaining the inviolability of our borders. Such an action is an affront to the image we have of ourselves.

As a consequence of all this, the victim of a wrongful act—rather than admitting that shortcomings of his own might have contributed to his loss—might well prefer making the wrongdoer the object of the anger he really feels toward himself. After all, the criminal *did* commit the act; he *is* responsible for what he did; he *is* blameworthy. Why not allow the criminal to become the scapegoat, *not* for his *act*, but for the emotional reactions of those who have been reminded of their own weaknesses and vulnerability, and the failure of their expectations?

Along these lines, I have wondered if much of the anger felt by many World War II veterans against the Viet Nam era "draft dodgers" was not, in fact, directed against themselves. That such open defiance of State authority represents a denial of the validity of their own self-image, an attack upon their ego boundaries, no doubt accounts for the greater part of the reaction by such veterans (and others identifying themselves with the State). But beyond that, the example of young men being able to successfully avoid war or postwar punishment by moving to Canada must have made the youths from the 1940's painfully aware of the options they chose not to exercise. The presence of young men refusing to back down to the monstrous power of the federal government must have been an unpleasant reminder that most men who go off to war are not brave: they only lack the courage to deny the State's authority to send them into combat. Would not the awareness of such matters be terribly demeaning to one's heroic self-image? And to what extent are young blacks today, in voicing their righteous indignation at the nineteenth century institution of slavery, really directing their anger at their own ancestors for having cooperated with this system? It is no doubt troubling to dig back into one's roots and find great-great-grandparents who were willing to be subservient and grovelling, so opposite of the proud and self-respecting qualities young blacks seek for themselves and their children today, as they fashion new self-images.

*   *   *   *

It is, perhaps, from our ancestral ties to a frontier spirit that we learned to view nature as a hostile force to be controlled or conquered. The image of the pioneer plainsman, the mountain man, or the dust bowl farmer, each standing firm against nature's implacable elements and seeking to wrest from a fickle earth the means for human survival, looms as an expression of mankind's nobility. But such a view isolates us from nature, and puts us in conflict with our home. We can, of course, continue with this divisive attitude. Perhaps it will be the crowning achievement of our intellect to isolate ourselves from the rest of nature, thus developing with the universe itself the same relationships of exclusion, conflict, anger, disorder, and war that we have been able to so effectively manage with our fellow humans!

Scientists such as David Bohm and Karl Pribram have theorized that the universe may be a hologram, or may be analogized to a hologram. Holography is a photographic system in which light waves are recorded and then reconstructed, with the use of laser beams, into three-dimensional images. What is remarkable is that any portion of the hologram contains the entire image (i.e., one can remove a piece of a holographic photo of a tree, enlarge it, and obtain a picture of the *entire* tree). Bohm and Pribram have suggested that the universe may be holographic in nature; that what we have learned to mistake for separate entities and processes may only be manifestations of an integrated, whole system.

Like the hologram, they postulate, the universe may consist of a system in which each part reflects the whole, and the whole is expressed in each part.[3]

If the universe is a holographic system, a unified reality, what are the consequences of us humans deciding to separate ourselves into antagonistic groupings? It should be apparent that such divisions substitute *fragmentation* for *harmony*, and disrupt the order that is common to the rest of the universe. What we must learn—if we indeed choose to end our contrived, organized miseries—is that mankind can never realize a transcendent harmony with the rest of nature so long as we insist upon our divisive, artificial systems of order that mask and feed upon the disorder they necessarily engender.

Some may sense despair in these words, and ask that the prognosis for mankind be tempered with hope. But it has not been my purpose to foster *hope*, only *understanding*. To have hope without understanding is but to worship another person's insights: therein lies the fatal flaw of every organized religion. To insist upon a groundless optimism is only to indulge in the childish luxury of evading the harsher side of reality.

Still, there is some basis for being optimistic about the future of mankind. In recent years, a number of men and women have begun to perceive the life-threatening consequences of our one-sided war with nature. The increased power and sophistication of our weaponry against our environment has, paradoxically, increased the likelihood that we will *lose* that war and, perhaps, sooner than we might have expected. As a result, our traditional attitudes toward nature are slowly being replaced by an awareness that mankind is *part of* nature, rather than an occupying army; that nature does not need to be *conquered*, but only *understood*.

As this emerging view gains prominence, human beings may also understand the life-destroying implications of our varied wars with one another. When we have become more sensitive to the movement of life that flows through the entire earth, when we are able to appreciate the compatibility and harmony that prevails throughout nature, when we are able to see ourselves as inseparable and coequal participants in nature's continuing experiment on this planet, we may then be able to look upon the face of any human being without ever again seeing an enemy, a competitor, or other threat.

15

ON MOTIVES AND GOOD INTENTIONS

*Those who have given themselves the most
concern about the happiness of peoples have
made their neighbours very miserable.*
—From *The Crime of Sylvester Bonnard*
by Anatole France[1]

There is a tendency for both the defenders and the critics
of any particular institution to focus on the motives of those
who comprise it. Debates on the relative merits of the
political State, for example, tend to oppose "altruistic,
public-spirited" with "self-seeking, power-hungry" explanations for political behavior. The practice assumes that the
purposes of those who control institutions are of greater
significance than the *nature* and *consequences* of their actions.

This motive-seeking inclination is equally apparent in
assessments people make of the business system. Those who
consider themselves as anti-business see capitalists as greedy,
grasping, insensitive and unprincipled beings. Try to think of
a movie or a television program with a business theme to it
that did not consist of a bleak portrayal of the motives and
characters of businessmen. Dickens told us nothing of the
business competency of either Ebeneezer Scrooge or Bob
Cratchett. Nor did he tell us anything of the economic or
social impact of Scrooge's business decision making. It
seemed to be enough for us to be told that Scrooge was the
epitome of greed. For all that we know, Scrooge's firm may
have been lending money to finance research directed

toward the discovery of a drug to combat the plague, . . . or Tiny Tim's illness. But that he did so in order to get *rich* was apparently enough to bring him into moral disrepute.

Those who defend private capitalism tend to play the same game, regarding businessmen as noble and creative benefactors of mankind. One cannot read Ayn Rand, for example, without seeing the mirror image of Dickens, leading us to not only accept, but to see the virtue of Scrooge's selfishness. Those who share this view likewise tend to overlook the nature of the business activity involved. How noble were those businessmen who devoted themselves to the manufacture of napalm that was dropped on screaming children in southeast Asia? How virtuous were the previously mentioned officials of I.G. Farben who, during the Nazi regime in Germany, seized the opportunity to employ slave labor as a way of promoting their selfish interests? How exemplary are those banking and industrial leaders who continue to promote the American government's support of fascist police states in Central and South America, South Africa, South Korea, the Philippines, and other totalitarian regimes that promise to make their instruments of torture and murder available to provide businessmen with political and social stability and security?[2] At this point, of course, the debate between the pro- and anti-capitalist simply generates into a heated discussion over whether human nature is inherently "good" or "evil."

If we wish to understand institutions and how they affect our lives, it should be apparent that making value judgments about the motives or the personality traits of the people involved will not advance that understanding. For example, at a time when we are asked to choose between an unregulated and a regulated economy, between private capitalism and State socialism, it is in our interests to inquire into the nature of these systems in order to comprehend the impact that either would have on our lives. When we make such an inquiry calmly and without a sense of conflict-creating partisanship, it should become evident that the *motives* of those involved are totally irrelevant. And even if they were relevant, it should be clear to us that businessmen are no better motivated or moral than are bureaucrats or commissars. As we saw earlier, rarely are the formulators or supporters of institutional policies motivated by a malicious delight in the suffering of others. No matter how inhumane or savage the consequences, organizational practices are generally carried out with the best of intentions by men and women who believe in the propriety of what they are doing. Years of inattention—punctuated by a conditioning in contradictory beliefs—can produce a state of mind in which the individual is consciously unaware of the nature and consequences of the behavior he is sanctioning. Nevertheless, our contradictory premises play themselves out in our unconscious minds, generating much of the *personal* conflict that is the foundation for our *social* antagonisms.

Focusing on people's motives reflects an intellectually shallow, relatively effortless approach to the understanding of given conditions. To emphasize the personal intentions of institutional actors is to avoid the more difficult work of identifying the causes and consequences of specific problems, clarifying issues, and engaging in the comprehensive, critical analysis that is necessary for intelligent understanding. This superficial trend is particularly noticeable among journalists, political activists, and ideologues, and shows an increasing presence within academic institutions. It is common for the advocates or critics of various political, social, or economic policies—whether of the left or right—to be greeted by charges of trying to make names for themselves, or promoting book sales, or stirring up trouble, or being ideological polemicists. Even if such charges are true, what relevance does that have to what they are saying? What if a Marxist is *right* about western cold war policies? How would we know?

What if a free market economist is *correct* in his assessment that minimum wage laws are most harmful to the poor? How would we find out? Concentrating on a person's motives allows us to dismiss what he is saying without having to think about or analyze his statements. Understanding the cause of a given problem is often difficult—particularly when the consequences of an action are not immediate, and the time lag between a cause and an effect is interspersed with many variables (and apparent variables) of unknown significance. When faced with the intellectually demanding task of sorting out and weighing such factors, it is likely that many will opt for the less burdensome approach of questioning a speaker's intentions.

In an earlier chapter, we saw how government regulation of economic activity serves to institutionalize and restrict exchanges among people. The practice not only has the effect of limiting human freedom and denying to each of us the authority to direct our own lives, but it also makes for a less efficient use of economic resources. That businessmen have been the principal promoters of such regulatory schemes, in order to further their interests, may help us to understand the origins of these laws; but is that as important as understanding the human consequences involved in such practices? Even if we do not like the motives of some (or even all) businessmen, even if we regard them as greedy or disreputable characters, as long as they do not have the backing of political institutions to force us to trade with them, or to legally keep competitors out of their market, or to legally compel higher prices, they are in no position to cause us harm. The government official, on the other hand, even if we believe him to be motivated by the noblest and most humane of sentiments, is in a position to do untold harm to millions of people. This is so not because he *wants* to cause injury—he may, in fact, truly wish to benefit mankind—but because he has the legal power to compel our obedience to his decisions.

These decisions will always be based upon a lack of complete information, and when this is combined with the universal applicability of political actions, one can be assured that both widespread *mistakes* and *interference* with the personal preferences of individuals will occur. Thus we are left with the seeming paradox: greedy men who lack institutional power over us are in less of a position to cause us harm than are unselfish and generous men armed with such power. It is the nature of the *institutions* and the *effects* of the decisions themselves, and not the *motives* of those who make the decisions, that should attract our attention.

This point was never more clearly demonstrated to me than on a tour my wife, one of my daughters, and I took of a beautiful old hotel in California. The hotel had been carefully planned and built by a businessman and his wife, and they travelled the world to find art objects with which to fill its massive rooms and corridors.

Following their deaths, the hotel eventually came into the ownership of a group of businessmen whose sense of aesthetics was not the same as the couple who had built it. These subsequent owners, motivated by pragmatic considerations, began to make changes. They sold many of the paintings and antiques in order to get operating capital for the hotel; they took down the beautiful draperies that graced the ceilings and replaced them with acoustical ceiling tile; they broke the impressive effect of large, open hallways and stairways by installing government-mandated glass firewalls; they even spray-painted some gold-leafed carvings in order to save operating costs.

The tour of the hotel ended in a chapel built around an immense and beautiful gold altarpiece. Even non-religious viewers had to be impressed with both the grandeur and the detail of numerous carved saints and other religious bric-a-brac, some of which was covered with a two inch thickness of gold. Our tour guide informed us that the man who had built the hotel bought this altarpiece in a foreign nation. He went on to tell us how rebel groups in other countries would often overrun local churches to get their gold religious and art objects, melting them down in order to help finance their revolutionary causes. We were left with the impression that the original owner of this hotel had purchased the altarpiece in order to save it from destruction by such groups.

As we walked out of the hotel, I was struck by a sense of irony. Here was a building, many of whose art works had been taken out and sold by its subsequent owners for purely pragmatic reasons. Within the walls of this hotel stood one of the most beautiful works I had ever seen, saved from the hands of rebels who might otherwise have destroyed it in order to further their self-proclaimed idealistic purposes. One building, in other words, had been stripped of its art work for *practical* reasons, while others had suffered the same fate for *idealistic* reasons, and yet the consequences were *identical*. The reasons given by each group for their actions were only that, . . . *reasons*, . . . *rationalizations* designed to justify doing what they wanted to do.

Why do we involve ourselves with questions about the motives of those who exercise institutional power over us? Do the bombs that blow children apart acquire a decency in wars of "national honor" that they do not in wars fought to advance political or economic ambitions? Is the grief suffered by a family over the shooting death of one of its members made more bearable by the knowledge that the killer was motivated by mistaken belief instead of a malicious disposition? Were the executions of witches carried out by the Salem theocracy made holy by the fact that their stated purposes were to *save* rather than *persecute* human souls? Is the violence and misery any less real because it is conducted by men who believe in what they are doing? In a world that cries with the pain of institutionalized suffering, why do we busy ourselves with the purposes of those who so persistently exploit other human beings? Why do we not question *our-selves*, instead, in order to understand why we are willing to subject ourselves to institutional authority? Neither institutions nor their leaders are the source of our problems: *we* are. But as long as we are focusing on the motives or the character of those who inflict harm upon us through the exercise of organizational authority, we are failing to consider our personal involvement and participation in the processes of our own victimization. We question other people's motives because we do not understand our own responsibility for the disorder in which we find ourselves. We have become so well-trained to look outside ourselves for both the source of our problems and our well-being, that we look for scapegoats to take the blame for institutional wrongs. That is more comforting to us than questioning our own reverence for and obedience to institutional authority. It is more assuring to believe in the corruption of corporation officials than in the corruption of the corporate-State political system that spawns influence-peddling, bribery, and monopolistic practices. It is less distressing to condemn a Richard Nixon for the lies and deceptions of Watergate, than to confront the greater deceit and dishonesty of government itself. Superficial criticisms of the *personalities* involved allows us never to have to question those commitments we made without question, and saves us from the discomforting self-examination that might reveal our role as silent coconspirators in our own suffering.

It has always been in the interest of institutions to discourage such inquiries. Our independent judgments have been neutralized with assertions that life is too complicated and incomprehensible for us to have any meaningful opinions that differed from established orthodoxy. The medieval God who spoke only to popes and kings, and whose mysterious and seemingly capricious ways could not be fathomed by ordinary men and women, has been translated, in this secular age, into the politically-directed society whose problems are "too complex" to permit any "easy answers." While this proposition has never dissuaded institutions from insisting upon *their* easy answers, it has been useful in characterizing opposition to institutional policies as products of uninformed, simplistic minds. On the other hand, for those of us who struggle vainly to reconcile the conflicting institutional demands upon our lives, there *are* no easy answers. As long as we persist in efforts to *accommodate* our contradictions—instead of *identifying* and *ending* them, as long as we believe that it is the mark of intelligence and maturity to learn to internalize the discordant pressures upon our lives and to moderate them into middle-of-the-road policies of managed confusion, we will continue to dismiss as hopelessly romantic and impractical those who suggest to us an uncomplicated life of peace, order, and clarity.

Institutions have helped train us to be weak, and have then exploited that weakness to maintain their power over us. But this could never have occurred without our willing participation. One of the consequences of institutionalization has been our acceptance of the belief that *others*—certainly not *ourselves*—have caused our problems. If we wish to understand how institutions have affected our lives, we must begin by understanding how our attitudes and reactions have been influenced by our involvement with organizations. We must be willing to stand back and observe what we have become, and resist the temptation to do what institutions have trained us to do: look beyond ourselves for answers. Once we have become aware of our own complicity, we will be in a better position to understand the consequences of institutional forms of behavior.

I used to introduce my students to the study of law with a lifeboat situation taken from the classic case of *United States v. Holmes.*[3] Following a shipwreck forty-one passengers and crew members got into a lifeboat which, unfortunately, was not large enough to hold that many persons. In an effort to save as many lives as possible, crew members threw sixteen persons overboard. The longboat survivors were eventually rescued and, upon their return to the United States, one of the crew members was tried and convicted of the crime of manslaughter.

In rendering its opinion in the case, the court was faced with the same conflict as my students. There were no easy outs for either the court or the members of my class. The crew members, after all, had not been evil men; they had not acted out of any malicious motives. They did not torture their victims or take fiendish delight in their deeds. On the contrary, the evidence undeniably showed a reluctance by the crew to do what they had done. These men—including the defendant—were motivated solely by the normal human desire for survival. Like Dorothy in *The Wonderful Wizard of Oz*, these men were only trying to get back home. In the final analysis, the court condemned the defendant *not* for having acted to save his own life and the lives of as many others as possible under the circumstances, but for his having assumed the arbitrary authority to decide which of the persons would have to go overboard to a certain death. No one, the court reasoned, had any such rightful authority, even when exercised for the sole purpose of saving one's own life.

The point I hoped my students would draw from the discussion of this case is that we are not unlike those persons in the lifeboat. We can, perhaps, analogize ourselves as passengers on a giant lifeboat hurtling its way through a sea of space. We are not evil or malicious persons. We are, rather, somewhat scared and uncertain beings, trying to be courageous and assertive, seeking only to make it in this world, seeking to survive, trying to find our way home. We do not intend harm to others, nor do we delight in human suffering: quite the contrary. We want to reach out to others, to comfort and be comforted, to love and be loved, to develop a true sense of friendship, cooperation, and community with others.

Even though our motives may be good, we have the capacity to cause harm and suffering to other people because we have learned to reject our own natures. We have become other-directed persons. We live *outside* ourselves, alienated from our very selves, living as metaphysically externalized beings. We identify all that is good and all that is bad as being out there someplace. We regard others as the source of truth, understanding, and values and, at the same time, look upon other people and external conditions as the causes of our problems. We have learned to distrust our own capabilities and motives, and have created make-believe worlds of witches and fairy godmothers, whose respective magic, we believe, plagues and protects us. In the process, we have become so alienated from ourselves that we seem willing to accept the Skinnerian proposition that we are, indeed, subject to the influence of everything and everyone but our own free wills.

We have abdicated control over and responsibility for our own lives, and learned to accept direction from those who have not hesitated to take control of what we have abandoned. We have helped to subdivide mankind into mutually exclusive groupings, the "we's" and the "they's," and thus helped to solidify the foundation for conflict in human society. We have come to fear and distrust others—as we fear and distrust ourselves—and have demanded structured, institutionalized machinery to control others and provide the order in our lives that we can no longer find within ourselves. We have helped to set up institutions that thwart our wills, deny our natures, demand our unquestioning obedience, and impose decisions upon us, with a resulting frustration, anger, and violence, and a deepening alienation from ourselves and others. If institutions have become strong and powerful, is it, perhaps, because we have allowed ourselves to become weak and powerless?

Is it so surprising, then, that we observe mankind—ourselves included—in a state of continual conflict? Should we be amazed to discover violence and disorder attending our efforts to deny and refashion our own natures? Isn't it evident that we experience conflict with *others* because we are at war within *ourselves*? We have spent so much energy trying to drive the spirit of life out of ourselves; to replace our free will with the rigid structure of artificial, store-bought instincts; to burden ourselves with institutionally-derived contradictory value systems that breed guilt and confusion within us; to suppress our emotions, to deny our tendencies for creation, understanding, love, peace, and happiness; and to embrace any belief that offers us escape from ourselves, and avoidance of the reality of what we have become. We are fighting *ourselves*: do you expect us to not fight *others* as well? We fear and dislike what *we* are: do you expect us to be any more considerate of others? Isn't the cause of human conflict painfully and abundantly clear? It should be equally apparent that inquiring into the motives of those who wield institutional power only prolongs the underlying conditions for conflict. The *solution* is to be found in the same place where the *problem* began: within you and me.

16

GETTING OUT OF

OUR OWN WAY

It is impossible for that which is free by nature
to be disturbed by anything but itself. It is a
man's own judgments which disturb him.

* * *

When therefore, we are hindered, or disturbed,
or grieved, let us never impute it to others, but to
ourselves, that is, to our own views.

—Epictetus[1]

It should be evident, by now, that the conflict we experience as a result of merging our individual selves into collective, institutional identities is of our own doing. It is part of our problem that we have learned to seek comfort in identifying *other* persons as the causes of our difficulties. Until we are prepared to acknowledge, to ourselves, that the demands and pressures from others can exert influence upon us only if we allow them to and that institutional demands can get in our way only if we help to construct the barricades, we shall go on playing the same old game with only minor variations of the rules. Only when we understand that our complicity in institutional behavior is a denial of our nature and our capacity for living as self-directed, self-controlling, self-responsible persons, will we liberate ourselves and take ourselves out of conditions of conflict.

An interesting phenomenon, reported in kidnap and hostage cases, attests to our willingness to cooperate in our own victimization. That has to do with the tendency of many kidnap victims—especially after prolonged confinement—

to come to identify with their captors and to interfere with the efforts of their rescuers. Even in cases in which the parties had been total strangers, those who have been held hostage under an immediate threat to their very lives will often end up siding with their captors. This tendency goes far beyond those strategic acts of feigned cooperation designed purely for the hostage's own self-defense. Something more in the nature of a psychological transformation takes place, with the original victim taking on a commitment to the cause of the man who has incarcerated him under a threat of murder. So commonplace is this practice that police who are trained to respond to terrorist practices are reluctant to inform the hostages of their rescue plans.

This phenomenon may tell us something about what we have become. It is, perhaps, a reflection of the degree to which our minds have become institutionalized that we should come to identify with those who use fear and the threat of force to exercise authority over us. After all, we do identify ourselves with the political State, which coerces us into participating in far deadlier military undertakings. If we have become conditioned to identify ourselves with agencies that demand power over us, it should not be surprising that we would dutifully respond to the hostage-taker whose methods, for all practical purposes, are indistinguishable from those of the State. Hostage interference with the efforts of rescuers differs little from our own inclinations to embrace the power-seekers who encourage and exploit our weaknesses, and to damn the voices of liberation who urge us to break free. We have become like cattle which, upon entering the slaughterhouse, lick the hands of the butcher, contenting ourselves with the security that comes from confinement and the certainty that comes from death itself.

It is a relatively simple matter to escape the prisons others create for us. It is far more difficult to escape from the ones we have created for ourselves. Many of us end up serving self-imposed life sentences for crimes we have not committed, or have locked ourselves up for preventive detention, fearful of where the free expression of our natures may lead. We have denied ourselves adequate counsel in our defense, have refused to confront or examine the witnesses against us, have plea-bargained away our claims of innocence, and have inflicted upon ourselves cruel and unusual punishments that the United States Supreme Court would not countenance against the most vicious of fiends. I once knew a man who had lived most of his adult life in prison and who, upon getting out, committed a crime in order to get caught and sent back to the only predictable and certain environment he had ever known. How different was this man from those of us who insist upon our *own* institutional confinements? We are prisoners in cells of our own making, fearful of turning the key that would expose us to the responsibility for our own lives.

There is nothing in our nature that compels us to lock ourselves into a subservient dependency upon others. This is a form of behavior we have learned through a lifetime of careful conditioning on the part of those who would exercise power over us. As we discover what we have become, and how our cooperation has been indispensable to the processes of our own subordination, and as we become aware of the consequences of our being externalized and other-directed, we will come to abandon our old habits. When we confront and resolve our own fears and feelings of inadequacy, when we begin to understand what it means to live without having expectations of others, when we can face those discomforting qualities within ourselves and stop projecting them onto others, when we can *be* without having to identify with anything whatsoever, then, perhaps, we can begin to assume full responsibility and control over our lives.

Many people, today, have apparently sensed that their own lives are too greatly affected by demands and pressures generated by social institutions. It is now fashionable to seek to counteract these influences by pursuing one's own liberation. In the process of doing so, many have come to identify themselves with any of a variety of group classifications. Such groups may be based upon race, religion, sex, nationality, age, physical or mental condition, ideology, sexual preferences, or other categories. The consequence has been to produce a social fabric based upon a patchwork division of hyphenated people. In the name of liberation, people have organized themselves into squadrons designated as "feminist" and "gay," "black," "white," and "gray." The list—as we have already seen—goes on and on. In a manner consistent with Perls' ego boundaries, it is now popular for people to compartmentalize their identities, to divide and separate themselves from those faceless others who are known only by their absence of insignia, be it a button, a style of dress, a bumper sticker, a slogan, an astrological sign, or a rigid adherence to a litany of words.

It should be clear that such an approach to liberation has only served to further divide people and generate more conflict and that a greater amount of tension now exists between and among members of these mutually-exclusive groupings than before such subdivisions became popular. If there is any doubt of this, try reading the public statements of individuals claiming to represent various group interests. Do their words reflect a sense of inner peace and social affinity, or are they characterized more by a righteous resentment of perceived iniquities, and demands upon other people? Have those involved with such groups really found liberation, a freeing of the human spirit, or have they only taken on new sets of expectations, new structures of attitudes and beliefs, new leaderships and chains of command? Have the liberated been able to conceive, as yet, of their liberation from their liberators?

Such superficial, trendy approaches miss the very essence

of liberation. To be liberated is, after all, nothing more than being in control of and responsible for one's life, to be aware of one's nature and capabilities and of the influences upon one's behavior. True liberation comes from *within oneself*, not from changing other people. To the degree people have been living in a state of dependency upon or subjugation to others, they have been active participants in the affair. On the other hand, it is less troublesome to our egos to persuade ourselves that the persons upon whom we have made ourselves dependent are to blame for our having been held back. However gratifying this might otherwise be to our psyches, the truth is that others cause us far less harm than we like to believe. Most of our problems are occasioned by our unwillingness to live self-directed, self-controlling lives. We have learned to be dependent upon others, and content ourselves with letting other people make decisions for us, protect us, assume responsibility for us, provide us security, and shape our attitudes. It takes a genuine and continuing effort to understand ourselves and the nature of the influences upon our lives and to be autonomous and responsible individuals. There are no shortcut methods to avoid the introspection necessary for any meaningful liberation. Adopting a new dogma, or mouthing new slogans, or rallying 'round new flags, or adhering to the pronouncements of new leaders only reinforces the already existing processes of externalization, division, and group identification that created our problems in the first place.

True liberation is not a process of pulling away from others; it is not learning to react to the statements or behavior of other people; it is not seeking one's identity in other people, or accepting the primitive herd premise of "four legs good, two legs bad"; it is not endeavoring to change other people's attitudes and behavior, or redesigning institutional structures. Liberation, in short, is not an *outward*-oriented process through which one tries to become something else in relation to other people. It is an *inward* process: learning to understand oneself and, in recognizing one's own self-imposed limitations, acknowledging control over and responsibility for one's actions and life. As we become more self-directed, as we become more of ourselves and less the reflection of others, we shall discover a meaning to liberation that is far removed from the institutionalized and structured definitions implicit in contemporary society. Liberation will not be found in groups, or newsletters, or legislative proposals, or ritualistic slogans, or picket lines, or constitutional amendments, or boycotts, or in supervising the speech or the thoughts or the actions or the reading habits or the mannerisms of others. Liberation does not, in other words, consist of *reforming* or *destroying* prisons, but of learning to *walk away* from them. It is not a process of making *other* people get out of your way, but of getting *yourself* out of your way.

Such changes will occur *only* if we are prepared to undertake a radical transformation of our consciousness. We must make a choice to live *not* by our habits, but by continuous awareness of the present. What we need are totally new ways of thinking about things, and this will not take place as long as we regard the present as only a bridge that links our dependencies and habits of the past, and our fears and expectations of the future. We must, in other words, learn to live by our *intelligence*. We must be willing to grow into adulthood, which means that we must give up our childish ways. We must stop kidding ourselves and stop faking reality and stop responding to the uncertainties in life by pulling our institutional blankets up over our heads.

We have seen how, in order to maintain their domination over people, institutions have always had to war against human consciousness. An uninhibited awareness of reality would quickly expose to men and women the absurdity of institutionally-generated conflict, as well as the insanity of their continued participation in it. For this reason, religions have stressed the importance of faith in the pronouncements of church leaders, and denigrated doubt and reason. Schools have been principally concerned with indoctrinating minds with institutionally-serving ideas, not with the unfettered development of mental capacities. Businesses have endeavored to keep our minds focused on the pursuit of material values, and have helped us learn to regard the non-material as immaterial. Governments have made a habit of lying to and deceiving their own citizens; have censored communications among free minds; have punished the expression of unpopular ideas as treason, sedition, pornography, and espionage; and have employed witch-hunting clerics and psychosis-seeking psychiatrists to identify and remove from society those men and women whose views diverged too greatly from established norms. Institutions have combined to keep people weak, frightened, confused, ignorant, and apprehensive, because clear-thinking, rational, totally conscious minds would be a threat to the continuation of their vicious games. I suspect that much of the pressure directed against the use of drugs in our society reflects a fear, on the part of institutions, that narcotics and hallucinogens may help to make people aware of altered states of consciousness. When men and women begin to explore their mental processes and undeveloped capacities for understanding, institutionalism may well be doomed. Having experienced an enhanced state of consciousness, and the joy of discovery that accompanies it, men and women are likely to go on and examine the nature and the consequences of their institutional commitments. Such an awareness, it is no doubt feared, may help to free people from the inhibitions and restraints of their institutionally-structured learning, and help them to see reality clearly, without the blinders or the distorted lenses provided by their trainers. The established order has a vested interest in the continuation of our present mind-set, and rigorously resists anything—whether in the form of ideas, life-styles, or chemical substances—that might fundamentally transform our consciousness.

But drugs will not free our minds from their present confinements. To think that is to remain externally-dependent, looking outside ourselves for a magic potion or sacred doctrine which we need only swallow in order to find salvation. Total awareness can occur only within our own minds, and requires conscious effort on our part. It is through our consciousness becoming aware of and examining itself—which is not unlike the experience of viewing infinity by looking into one of two mirrors that face one another—that our mind begins the process of understanding itself.

What it means to be truly liberated was demonstrated, at least allegorically, in an incident in Orange County, California, in early 1978. A hippopotamus named Bubbles had escaped from a local wilderness park and hid out, for nearly three weeks, in a small lake nearby. Bubbles was a daily news feature, nothing more than a so-called change of pace story to the news media, as park officials and county sheriff's officers endeavored to capture her and return her to the park. We shall never know, with certainty, what her plans were, for after repeated futile attempts to recapture her, Bubbles was finally gunned-down with one of those so-called harmless tranquilizer bullets and later died.

One could only wonder whether, with so many murderers, rapists, robbers, burglars, and muggers running loose in the Los Angeles area, local officials might have misconceived their priorities. On the other hand, Bubbles did represent a threat to the established order and had to be subdued. Think, if you will, of the implications of a heavy, slow-footed, dumb animal breaking loose from the institutional role others had established for her. While we humans content ourselves with the illusions of freedom—getting to vote for the warden of our choice or passing resolutions demanding larger cages— Bubbles decided to go over the hill. She made a choice to live as her nature demanded—free and self-directed—not as a penned-up object of curiosity serving institutional needs.

Here was a woman who renounced zoo-sponsored women's conferences and recognized that she, alone, could accomplish her liberation. While her female colleagues were satisfied to pass resolutions to change the name of the "Manchurian tiger" to the "Personchurian tiger," Bubbles was hotfooting it to open country. For almost three weeks Bubbles was free of institutional confinement. She enjoyed her freedom without causing any injury to others, in spite of her having homesteaded in a metropolitan area populated by millions of human beings. She was a living denial of the basic premise of all institutions, namely, that the processes of living must be planned-for and coordinated, and that the exercise of freedom must be controlled and supervised.

Think of the symbolism in all of this. What if Bubbles had made it? What if we well-trained, obedient humans—who have confused a long leg-chain with freedom, and who go into our Pavlovian slobbering on cue (altogether convinced that we are expressing our free will in so doing)—were to have the benefit of such a quadrupedal role model living outside its appointed institution? What if we became aware of the possibility of living according to our own natures, and for our own purposes, instead of to satisfy organizational demands? What child would be content to return to those children's zoos known as public schools? How many adults might start giving serious consideration to saying "no" to all those institutional demands, and take back the control and responsibility for their own lives? Such sentiments were no doubt stimulated within those of us who identified with Bubbles and cheered her on.

This four-legged threat to western civilization was abated, however, done in by persons who will likely go through life without even dreaming of so daring an exploit. The tragedy was not just that Bubbles died, but that she was only able to pull it off for nineteen days. It was too bad for her that she wasn't the "Hillside Strangler": they would never have caught her!

But Bubbles did give the rest of us hope. We all have a tendency to get ourselves so deeply involved in the detailed, concrete appearances of what we call daily living, so tied up with trying to resolve the problems we have created for ourselves, that we become alienated from the life processes of which we are a part. None of us—including Bubbles—was born to live as structured, regimented, or controlled beings. Institutions have, with our well-conditioned participation in the matter, managed to create environments for all of us which are not in harmony with our natures. More often than not, we confuse these artificial environments with reality, just as the owners of the wilderness park in which Bubbles had been confined sought to recreate an African wilderness within a major metropolitan area. Perhaps Bubbles—though having never been to Africa—sensed the difference between her institutionalized surroundings and the reality to which her nature was suited. Perhaps she broke out in search of an environment more natural to her. We will never know, of course. But what lesson does this incident hold for the rest of us?

Most of us tend to go through life without ever really understanding ourselves or the orderly processes of nature. We have become so alienated from our involvement in these life forces that we are totally unaware of how institutional practices interfere with living. It was evident that none of the persons involved in trying to recapture Bubbles wanted her dead. But, as we have seen, people's motives are rarely the source of problems. Most of us go about doing what we do with the noblest of intentions, and yet we end up doing harm to ourselves and others because we really do not understand the full implications of what we are doing.

One news reporter, admittedly saddened by the whole

affair, offered a typically institutional explanation for Bubbles' death, saying that she had died because "her heavy internal organs, about 500 pounds, pressed against her diaphragm, cutting off breathing." Was this so, or did she die because her choice to live free, according to her own nature, was unacceptable to those who were determined not to allow her the exercise of that choice? Didn't she die because well-meaning people failed to understand the necessity for life to pursue its own natural expression and fulfillment? Perhaps in the public outpouring of tears and sadness following the news of Bubbles' death, there was a sensing of this fact. Perhaps people experienced their own involvement with life and came to empathize with the suffering of a creature not so much unlike themselves.

Can we, like Bubbles, overcome our institutional dependency? Can we go beyond our cage-rattling form of make-believe liberation and *really* break out of our self-imposed confinement? Can we learn to stop living *outside* ourselves, to abandon our dependency on all external authorities, to take back the total control and responsibility for our lives, to live *not* as institutional authorities direct, but in conformity with our natures as free, self-directed persons?

For many of us, liberation is only a *game*, an *idea* to be talked about and played with in groups whose members are united by common buzzwords. But to actually *abandon* our dependencies and attachments is something else again, and so we do not change. We may be willing to consider alternative social practices, but only if such changes do not upset existing institutional arrangements. If someone suggests to us that we abandon institutionalism altogether, we dismiss them as romantic utopians. We tell ourselves that their visions are too unrealistic to ever work, failing to see that it is the fantasy of institutionalized order that is unworkable. Though institutions chew us up and devour us, we condition our consideration of alternative practices *not* upon a demonstration of relative superiority, but upon assurances that such alternatives will be absolutely failure-proof—a standard we refuse to apply to existing systems. We continue to endure the constant disorder of politically-generated chaos, violence, economic disruption, wars, and the threat of nuclear devastation, but insist of those who speak of discontinuing political practices to prove that a Stateless society will provide for flawless order. We use every excuse we can muster to avoid the self-examination that will cause us to confront our organizational dependencies and bring about a fundamental change in our systematic madness. We are content to remain as psychological cripples, willing to consider the prospects of total freedom and responsibility only upon assurances of the kind of security that comes from a dependent state of mind. We will consider the frightening possibilities of adulthood, in other words, only if we can bring along our security blankets and teddy bears for comfort.

If we are to get out of our own way, to free ourselves from our self-imposed dependency on external direction and control, we must begin to understand how we create division and conflict within ourselves. If we have allowed ourselves to become fragmented and self-alienated beings, we must learn how to become reintegrated. But how do we go about doing this? We could, of course, employ the methods of the so-called human potential movement and undertake our rehabilitation as a self-managed behavior modification project. We could, in other words, turn to such methods as biofeedback, sensitivity training, self-actualization, or any of a variety of other human development programs, and retrain ourselves to become more self-directed. But such an approach would be premised on the very notions of division, control, supervision, and direction we were trying to overcome. We would simply end up replacing one externally-derived, structured authority with the new one we would program into ourselves at the direction of our psychological guru. The popularity of biofeedback methods—many of which involve the imposition of pain or other discomforts upon ourselves—attests to how well we have learned to be motivated by externally-imposed punishments. In some instances, these methods could be characterized as the scientific age's version of self-flagellation!

Even if we were able to develop our own standards of behavior, wouldn't we simply be substituting a structure of *internal* origins for the *externally*-based one being jettisoned? If we did that, we would only be continuing the processes of internal division. We would find ourselves right where we began: polarized into a good self and a bad self, with the former judging and seeking to control the latter. No longer would institutional authorities be programming our lives and making decisions for us: *we* would be running our lives and fashioning ourselves into being what *we* want *us* to become. *They* would no longer be in charge of structuring our lives and mandating expectations of us, *we* would. We would become both the regulator and the regulated, the leader and the follower, the manager and the managed. We would play the role of both reformer and sinner, as we plunged with missionary zeal into the task of our own salvation.

It should be evident that any effort to *change* ourselves necessarily implies a division between the one to be changed and the one to do the changing. Since, as we have seen, *thought* has produced the divisions within us, and division produces conflict, the consequences of such an approach ought to be predictable. If you doubt this, ask yourself what is likely to occur when your conservative self—clinging to the fears, prejudices, guilt, and experiences accumulated over a lifetime—is confronted by your newly-enlightened, progressive self. Will you not experience discord and disunity, as your split selves dispute their respective claims to your allegiance? Will the clash of competing interests you have set up not simply produce more of the conflict, confu-

sion, and dissatisfaction, and the feelings of guilt and inadequacy, that led you to try to change yourself in the first
place?

How, then, *do* we learn to get out of our own way, except
by becoming *aware* of the processes and attitudes within us?
But can we become aware without *judging* ourselves? Can we
learn to *observe* (and to be aware that *we* are observing
ourselves) without evaluating or criticizing or being embar-
rassed by what we see? Can we learn how to watch our minds
and the whole movement of thought taking place within
them without any intentions or desires or expectations? Can
we, in other words, relax the endless chattering of our
conscious minds long enough to observe the reality of what
we have become, without allowing our ideas and our judgments to divert our attentions toward the petty conflicts we
have learned to mistake for reality?

17

REDISCOVERING
THE COMMUNITY

*The problem is to find a form of association
which will defend and protect with the whole
common force the person and goods of each
associate, and in which each, while uniting
himself with all, may still obey himself alone,
and remain as free as before.*
　　　　　　　　—Jean Jacques Rousseau[1]

As we have discovered, nature is characterized by a sense
of orderliness. Human society, itself a part of nature, embod-
ies its own systems of order serving, quite spontaneously and
without conscious human direction, to provide social harmony and stability. Institutional rhetoric would, of course,
leave us with the impression that *institutions* are the fountainhead of social order, that *they* are responsible for bringing us
together and uniting our discordant tendencies into a harmonious and peaceful whole, and that *they* have civilized us
and made life bearable. By now, however, it should be clear
that institutions have been disastrous to the well-being of
mankind. The political State has not established order; religions have not made us more moral; education has not blessed
us with wisdom; the mass-marketed affluence of our industrial system has not provided us with security; our ideologies
have not advanced our understanding. In fact, as we look
more closely at these agencies, we discover that they produce
the opposite of their proclaimed benefits; that they have been
the principal cause of human conflict and disorder; that
institutions have weakened the natural bonds that otherwise

unite us in a spirit of cooperation, neighborliness, love, and mutual respect; that institutions have helped to divide us and set us against one another in wars, disputes, rivalries, competition, and other forms of conflict.

Institutions have not established social order: quite the contrary. They have—but only with our willing complicity in the matter—introduced division, separation, otherness among people. They have staked out institutional boundaries and induced us to identify our very souls with their mischievous purposes. They have helped us to appreciate the distinctions of another person's race, language, nationality, education, religious or philosophic views, political affiliations, occupation, or place of employment, applying institutional pressures in order to reinforce such distinctions. To paraphrase the song from the musical *South Pacific*, we have been carefully taught how to hate those who do not fall within the ego boundaries for which we have so much love. In doing these things, institutions have defined and managed our conflicts, condemning virtually all of us to that condition of "perpetual war" that assures the "perpetual peace" of certainty and permanency to institutions.[2] With our help, institutions have managed to weaken the systems of natural order within society, and have taught us to view the resulting chaos and confusion as mandates for their social engineers to construct and impose upon us all even more of their self-serving structures of artificial order.

One of the genuine tragedies of American life in recent decades has been that we have become thoroughly institutionalized people and, in the process, have lost the sense of community and of society that is natural to us as human beings. In identifying ourselves with institutions—whether they be the political State, an organized religion, the corporation for which we work, a labor union, an ideology or a cause—we have mistakenly assumed that we are fulfilling our social nature. What appears to be a sense of community in our organized system of living proves, upon examination, to be little more than our collective participation in fostering the private interests of institutions, as well as those who profit from them.

Institutions have their *own* purposes, their *own* needs. To the degree we devote ourselves to organizational purposes, we are not pursuing our own natural social need: to cooperate with one another in order to realize our *personal* needs. Society, in other words, is not a herd grouping of people sacrificing their individual interests and their lives for the good of the group. If it was, slave labor camps would not so offend our sensibilities. Society represents more than just the anonymous organized mob it has become under institutional domination. It is a more humane set of relationships than that premised upon the cannibalistic exploitation of some for the good of others. Society is held together *not* by a burdensome and spiritually debilitating sense of duty and self-denial, but by genuine feelings of love and cooperation that flow from an understanding of what we have in common with one another.

Society, then, consists of our coming together for our mutual benefit and includes our working together, sharing our experiences, happiness, and grief, and helping one another discover the joys of nature. In other words, simply *being with* one another. Such purposes, it is rather clear to see, are far removed from the manipulative, conflict-ridden, exploitive activities of institutions.

Human beings are both *individual* and *social* animals. Society is as natural to us as it is to the dolphin, the elephant, or the lion. Other social mammals are able to maintain their societies without the use of institutional apparatuses; they socialize without imposing formalized authority, regimentation, or organized supervision upon one another. They neither legislate nor moralize; they maintain no courts, prisons, or bureaucracies. They do not assign one another identification numbers or license one another's behavior. Other animals may defend territory, but they do not appear to develop machinery of war or establish vast empires. They do not punish or systematically torture or sacrifice one another. Some of them make limited use of tools to produce goods, but without busying themselves with board of directors meetings or punching time clocks. They often help one another to learn, but build no formal schools of indoctrination and award no degrees. Even the dolphin—one of the earth's most intelligent creatures—is able to maintain a joyous, loving, and cooperative social life without being burdened by religions, ideologies, or moral imperatives. It may be answered, of course, that none of these other animals have our highly developed intellectual capacities. But this is a distinction of questionable merit since we humans alone have the intelligence that permits us to terrorize and victimize and enslave one another, and even threaten the extinction not only of our *own* species, but of life itself! Perhaps we shall one day discover that the dolphin began to exhibit its characteristic mocking smile only after it had discovered man!

Institutions help to isolate us within our individual selves and interfere with the full expression of our social needs. They have helped us to become, again in Riesman's words, a lonely crowd. Institutions have, in effect, nationalized our social relationships. They have taken society from us by eminent domain. So complete has their domination been that, when we hear such words as "community" or "society," most of us tend to think not of *people*, but of depersonalized *abstractions* and of pervasive *institutions*. The nation, for example, has been conquered and subjugated by the political State; the face-to-face processes of production and exchange have been merged into faceless multinational corporations; our need for spiritual fellowship has ascended into the hierarchies of large churches; the city has annexed the neighborhoods, and city hall has subdued the city; the labor unions have turned brotherhood into a weapon to repress individuals and glorify the herd; schools have substituted for the mutual joy of learning, a vicious competitive routine in which institutional certification, not understanding, becomes the objective.

Society, that sense of community in which we can realize the fulfillment of both our individual and social natures, has been taken over and held hostage by institutional interests. Institutions no more equate with society than school buildings do with learning. Nor is the former a prerequisite for the latter. The needs we have for personal closeness to others, for mutual support, cooperation, affection, and assistance, have become lost in organization charts, committee resolutions, corporate charters, faculty meetings, power struggles, public hearings, amendments to bylaws, and two-thirds votes of those members in attendance. What sense of community is to be found in a congressional hearing room or city council chamber? What school administrator is truly fired by a zeal to help others learn? What hospital truly comforts the sick or the dying? What religious leader is able to relate to the spiritual needs of individual persons? What national labor union official, accustomed to White House dinners, is really able to identify with workers earning one-tenth his salary and accustomed to frozen TV dinners? What corporation knows its customers as anything other than computer entries, or can sympathize with the frustration of vainly trying to get a business firm to correct a defect in one of its products? What police department is really motivated by a desire to protect innocent, helpless people?

Our social life is not one in which people generally cooperate, assist, exchange, and share with one another. Our lives have become increasingly numbered, cataloged, and computerized by the depersonalized numbering, cataloging, and computerizing practices of faceless institutions. We are like the cookie cutter people, shaped and decorated by master bakers, but bearing only an outward resemblance to human beings. Our closeness to others is, all too often, only a matter of the relative positions in which we have been placed on the organizational cookie tray.

There is always a temptation among social commentators to analogize conflict and social disorder to a jungle. It would be a slur upon the rest of nature, however, as well as an undeserved tribute to human organizations, to so character- ize the consequences of an institutional environment. The most ferocious of four-legged predators could not begin to match a lowly platoon leader's capacity for inflicting death and destruction upon his own kind. The least-experienced camper could more easily find his way out of an uncharted region of the Amazon jungle than he could work his way through the Internal Revenue Code or understand an insur- ance contract. No jungle mother would enroll *her* offspring in a zoo, or regard the sacrifice of its life as a patriotic virtue. Neither would her mate find purpose in becoming an at- tachment to an assembly line, nor would she insist upon an equal right to such a fate as a necessary condition for her own fulfillment. To the best of our knowledge, other animals manage to live without the promise of heaven or the fear of hell hanging over their heads; they build no temples and worship no gods; and none have been observed tearing out the hearts of their fellows upon altars, or butchering one another in order to resolve their theological differences. And again, let it be remembered that it was institutionalized humans—not the so-called lesser primates—that ritualisti- cally slaughtered one another in the name of "love" in the jungles of Jonestown, Guyana!

Perhaps we humans have allowed our consciousness to wander too far afield of our natures. Perhaps we can learn something of ourselves by observing other forms of life which, though less intelligent than ourselves, have appar- ently managed to live quite well without the benefit of institutionalized insanities. Few of the other life forms share our fancy for organized conflict or structured behavior. The contrast has been most poignantly noted by E. E. Cummings:

> when serpents bargain for the right to squirm
> and the sun strikes to gain a living wage—
> when thorns regard their roses with alarm
> and rainbows are insured against old age
>
> when every thrush may sing no new moon in
> if all screech-owls have not okayed his voice
> —and any wave signs on the dotted line
> or else an ocean is compelled to close
>
> when the oak begs permission of the birch
> to make an acorn—valleys accuse their
> mountains of having altitude—and march
> denounces april as a saboteur
>
> then we'll believe in that incredible
> unanimal mankind (and not until)[3]

The question remains: is it possible for us to reestablish a sense of community, a society with one another? Can we walk away from institutions and abandon their contrived methods of social control? Can we rediscover the social order that is natural to us as human beings, and learn to live in a free and unfettered association with other people? Can we liberate ourselves, *not* from other people, but from the institutional barriers we have erected that keep us *in* and keep others *out*? Can we free ourselves from that most confining influence: the expectations we have of others? Can we, in other words, free ourselves from our institutional detention and regain society from those who hold it behind hallowed walls?

If we are to undertake the deinstitutionalization of society as a stated purpose, a cause around which we will organize ourselves to rearrange other people's lives, then the answer to these questions is "no." As long as we regard *any* social change as important to our well-being, we shall simply continue playing the very institutional games we are trying to abandon. Such methods, premised upon the propriety of *some* people changing the behavior of *others*, fosters division among people and pulls us further apart. We can hardly expect people to be drawn back together by manipulative and inherently divisive tactics.

When we are living externalized, institutionally-oriented lives—pursuing wealth, power, and status—we put ourselves in competition with others who, we perceive, are after the same things we want. How much cooperation is exhibited by rivals who struggle over institutional bones? By contrast, the self-directed, internalized person—because he derives satisfaction from within himself—can afford to be cooperative: others are not a competitive threat to him. A person who does not set himself apart from others through ego boundary identifications is less likely to make distinctions between himself and other human beings and, as a consequence, is more likely to experience a genuine compassion for the problems of other persons.

We are so accustomed to equating the political system with social order that we overlook the spontaneous, non-mandated patterns of behavior by which we humans manage to harmonize our interests. To believe that social order is the product of externally-imposed sanctions restraining a malevolent and disruptive human nature is to overlook a basic fact: we would not be so universally attracted to institutional promises to provide social peace and harmony unless the need for such order was already within us. Just as our ability to create gods confirms our own godlike qualities, our formulation of such concepts as peace, cooperation, and harmony demonstrates that *we* are the source of the order that is necessary to our lives.

We humans not only want social order, but we are often able to provide it for ourselves *in spite of* institutional disruptions! The market place (as distinguished from the present politically-supervised system of production, pricing, and distribution), customs and manners, children's play groups, neighborhood cooperation and assistance (in both urban and rural areas), and cooperation within the family are among the more apparent examples of natural social order. Upon reflection, the idea of society functioning without the supervised direction of institutions is no more improbable than that our bodies should operate in an orderly, well-coordinated fashion without the benefit of our conscious direction and oversight.

Our willingness to cooperate with one another—even when we are total strangers—is often most clearly seen in catastrophes or natural disasters. We sometimes hear of people rendering assistance to stalled motorists or the victims of auto accidents; the willingness of farm families to open their homes to travelers caught in a blizzard; the common practice of friends and neighbors harvesting the crops of an ailing farmer, or helping load or unload the furnishings of one who is moving to a new home; or the tendency of people to provide financial help for an unemployed or hospitalized neighbor.

One of the more impressive examples of spontaneous, nondirected social order I have witnessed occurred in the spring of 1975, while I was living in Omaha, Nebraska. A portion of the city had been hit by a very destructive tornado, and for those whose only information about this tragedy came from television network newscasts, it might have appeared that political institutions had been responsible for extracating Omahans from this tragedy. The mayor and the governor issued press releases; the National Guard was called out; a command center was set up to allow government officials to talk with one another and to the press; consistent with their elevated status, politicians by the planeloads flew over to survey the damage (by contrast, when *other* people sought to view the aftermath of the storm, these same government officials were quick to label them as "morbid sightseers"!); the federal government declared the damaged region a "disaster area." All of this combined to give at least the outward appearance of federal, state, and local governments reestablishing order within a broken community.

Such, however, was not the case. Even as we listened to local radio stations describing the path of the storm as it continued through Omaha, we began to hear accounts of people coming out of their homes to begin searching through the rubble of their neighbors' homes for survivors. The police, trained like fundamentalist preachers to believe in the malevolence of human beings, immediately began to report this activity as looting (even though no one was arrested for looting). Within minutes, local motels began announcing, through the radio stations, that they would make their vacant rooms available, without charge, to persons whose homes had been destroyed. Truck rental firms offered, again without charge, the use of their vehicles to persons who wanted to move their belongings to safety. Local warehouses offered free storage space for such belongings. Local churches and civic groups announced that they would serve as collection centers for persons who wished to contribute food, clothing, blankets, or money to help storm victims.

All of this was *spontaneous*, arising within minutes after the tornado hit, while the political dignitaries were still arranging for their first press conferences and trying to figure out how to exploit the situation for the maximum media exposure. Because telephone service was nonexistent for a long time, a local radio station spent the entire evening serving as a communications center, . . . *not* for the mayor and the governor to talk with the press, but to permit friends and relatives from outside the storm area to make contact with storm victims. And while all this was going on—and continuing for many days thereafter—thousands of volunteers descended upon the damaged area with power saws, axes, trucks, shovels, tractors, and other tools to help clean up the undescribable mess. So many volunteer workers showed up, in fact, that many were requested to return home in order to reduce congestion in the area.

The spontaneous, nondirected, well-coordinated system that had sprung up to solve an immediate problem disappeared as soon as things got back to normal. To my knowledge, there was no effort made to institutionalize this impromptu organization, or to elect officers, or to set up an organization chart. There were no bylaws or corporate charters to guide the efforts of these many thousands of people, or to plan for the handling of any future disasters. Having served its immediate purpose, the organization simply ceased to be; its members returned home. The politicians and bureaucrats, on the other hand, stayed around. As late as one year after this disaster, officials from the federal government were in Omaha to hold a press conference to advise the public of how much the local politicians had done to organize the cleanup and recovery from the storm. But those who lived through it all knew better.

We *do* have a need for a sense of community, for cooperation with one another, not as acts of *sacrifice* or *duty* but of human *fulfillment*. Unfortunately, institutions—particularly political ones—have tried to take away our opportunities to experience working together. The State has told us that *it* will provide for relief, *it* will come to the aid of those in need, *it* will pick up the broken pieces. As a consequence, the State has institutionalized poverty and adversity, and kept the recipients of welfare benefits in demeaning states of economic and psychological dependency. While such practices assure permanence to the bureaucracies they have spawned, this has come at the expense of dehumanizing the poor as well as fostering a growing cynicism about helping them. We have allowed the State, in other words, to wedge itself in between ourselves and others, thus interfering with our natural needs to come together and help one another. Having acknowledged the propriety of the State regulating, bureaucratizing, and depersonalizing our needs for social cooperation, should we be surprised to discover that we have become alienated from each other; that we are, indeed, mutually lonesome souls reaching out for one another but unable to touch?

I remember reading, a number of years ago, about a particular species of gulls that lived together on a very crowded island. Like many other forms of life, these gulls maintained territorial boundaries but, because of their close proximity, numerous trespasses occurred. In order to keep such constant trespasses from escalating into deadly battles which might ultimately threaten the survival of the species itself, these gulls had evolved a nonviolent behavior pattern. When a trespass was threatened, the two competing gulls would stand on their respective plots of ground and tear up grass with their beaks. How like these gulls have we humans become? We are crowded together, wanting so much to reach out but, because we have isolated ourselves within our respective confines, we are unable to do much more than tear up grass. Are we not able to see the gull-like behavior in our habit of talking to one another but saying nothing? Have we, perhaps, like the gulls, discovered that saying nothing is a way to preserve social peace within our lonely crowd?

Is there an alternative to our social loneliness? Is it possible for us to rediscover the sense of community and the spirit of cooperation that has characterized less highly-structured societies? Can we learn to *come* together, rather than be *herded* together in that divisive corruption of society known as the political State, to associate freely and willingly in a spirit of peace, love, mutual respect, and common purpose? Can we learn, in other words, that society can be something more than just a euphemism for organized exploitation, manipulation, and sacrifice? Can we learn that we are social beings for whom social order is as natural as our other needs for self-expression and fulfillment? If we are to rediscover the truly *social* meaning of society, it must be in those forms in which we can *be ourselves with one another*; in which our relationships with one another are based upon our personal, intrinsic qualities and *not* upon institutional certification and status; in which we can realize that ultimate personal benefit of social living envisioned by Ivan Illich, to be "spontaneous, independent, yet related to each other...."[4] Human society need not take the form of either a regimented, spiritless anthill, or a confederation of hermits. If we are to avoid our collective self-extermination, we must understand that *imposed* order inevitably produces conflict, violence, and chaos; that only in spontaneous, nondirected order can mankind experience social harmony.

The previously-discussed holistic theories that are emerging in the physical sciences reinforce the view that *freedom* and *spontaneity* are essential to order. Social systems require no more external planning and direction than do other autonomous systems in nature. Erich Jantsch, drawing upon the work of Nobel Prize-winning chemist Ilya Prigogine, has observed that "non-equilibrium" states in nature "may be a source of order." Jantsch describes such states as open, continuously renewing, spontaneous, and dynamic, reflecting what he calls "order through fluctuation." Then, suggesting the application of this principle to human society, he concludes "[t]he more freedom in self-organization, the more order!"[5]

We need to become conscious of the fact that the type of social environment in which institutions will thrive is incompatible with the nature of individual human beings. Organizational entities are inherently conservative, needing to not only inhibit disturbing practices, but to dominate the people and conditions that can affect their interests. There is a tendency not only for inertia and inflexibility, but instability, within most organizations, a fact that makes their well-being vulnerable to the processes of change. In order to keep such unsettling influences under control and within boundaries that do not threaten their existences, institutions have had to resort to structured and restrictive practices. Because human nature is characterized by spontaneity, resiliency, and autonomy, institutional efforts to manipulate people into stable environments and rigid patterns of behavior necessarily produce conflicts between people and social organizations. Considering our present paradox of an established order that suffers from so much chaos and violence, we must give serious attention to discovering alternative ways of living that do not put us in a state of war with ourselves and one another. If life is most fully experienced in self-directed spontaneity and exploration, we must strip away, within our own minds, all that causes us to shackle that life force. When we begin to understand that order and harmony are natural to all life—and not something imposed upon a flawed species by external authorities—we shall begin *abandoning* the institutions and *dismantling* the organizational structures through which we have denied the order within life.

If we go about the task of trying to *establish* natural order, we shall—as we have seen—only end up where we now are: seeking to impose the constructs of our past-oriented, partial-understanding mind upon the present. If we wish to rediscover the free and unstructured social community natural to human beings, we must look for it where we lost it: within our own understanding. We must become fully aware of our own natures, and come to understand the complementary—though seemingly contradictory—truth that, while each of us is a unique individual, we are also indistinguishable from one another. When we understand that in being *different* we are all the *same*; that our individual uniqueness is what makes us all alike; that we are brought together *not* by the *suppression* of our individuality, but for the *fulfillment* of it, the barriers of fear that keep us hidden behind institutional walls will begin to erode. When we arrive at that understanding— and *only* when we do so—we will find ourselves adopting, with quiet spontaneity, patterns of living with one another that are more peaceful, trusting, and loving. Only then shall we be living in harmony with ourselves, one another, and nature, . . . as complete human beings.

18

EXPLORATIONS
OF A
NON-INSTITUTIONAL
WORLD

Sanderson: If you'll begin by taking a coopera-
tive attitude—that's half the battle. We all
have to face reality, Dowd—sooner or later.

Elwood: Doctor, I wrestled with reality for
forty years, and I am happy to state that I
finally won out over it.
>   —From the play *Harvey*
>   by Mary Chase[1]

Institutionalized society has imposed upon mankind an artificial reality not unlike that of the rat maze. Our world is very neatly defined for us by the walls and barriers that surround us, and we quickly learn to measure the worth of our lives in terms of our proficiency at running the maze. We spend our lives scurrying about in pursuit of token rewards (or avoiding punishments) held out to us by our institutional keepers. Like laboratory rats who have known no other environment, we are unable to conceive of the possibility of our world existing in any other form, or of our lives involved in anything more significant than established maze-running.

Is it possible for us to break out of our highly-structured

network of rat mazes and discover what a *real* society would be like among autonomous, responsible, self-directed men and women? Can we learn how to organize ourselves into groups without creating our own social Frankensteins; how to work and play and help one another *without* institutions, *without* politics, organizational hierarchies, "hot" and "cold" wars, manipulation, moral imperatives, indoctrination, exploitation, rules and regulations, conflict, and all the other trappings of what we are fond of calling modern civilization? Is a life without institutions truly possible, or are we—like utopian visionaries—only indulging ourselves in the kinds of intellectual distractions that comprise the "leisure of the theory class"? And if we *are* able to walk away from our organizational confinements, where will it all lead? What new forms of association will we adopt, and will they—to invoke the litmus-test question of our institutionalized world—really work?

The contemplation of any fundamental change understandably provokes such pragmatically-based inquiries, a process by which our minds endeavor to harmonize *present* understanding with *past* knowledge. As we have already discovered, our tendencies for structuring are generated by the past-oriented nature of our accumulated knowledge. Thus, when we confront the prospect of living our lives free of the self-structuring premises by which we have been taught to live, we do so through our conscious minds, which have a vested interest in the maintenance of their own structured forms. Because of their conservative orientation, our minds tend to regard with disfavor any proposition incompatible with the status quo. Our efforts to get beyond the confines of our limited understanding are not unlike trying to convince the established order of the legitimacy of the revolution, or slaves of the value of abandoning the plantation in favor of a condition of freedom.

When one understands the full significance of personal

liberation, the meaninglessness of preliminary inquiries into the practicality of freedom becomes apparent. In the first place, to condition the exercise of one's autonomy upon assurances from others is to never experience liberation. It is a reflection of our own structuring that we are so hesitant about the unknown, and demand warranties that cover all possible consequences of our actions. If we insist on carrying about on our backs the shells of security fashioned in our past, we will remain confined by our psychological dependencies. Only if we can learn to appreciate the uncertainty, the sense of variety and surprise that gives excitement to life, only if we can learn how to *think* and *act* with *thoughtful spontaneity*, will we experience the kind of liberation that goes beyond the babbling of bromides. To condition our freedom is to strip away the natural and unprompted qualities that provide its very essence. It is not the certainty of success that frees us from our acquired habits, but our willingness to act in the face of uncertainty. It is the *necessity* of freedom, not its *practicality*, that should be of interest to us.

It must also be remembered that the pluralistic premises of a free society presume no artificial limits to the possible life-styles or organizational forms that autonomous, self-directed people will adopt for themselves. For this reason, it would be highly presumptuous of anyone to try to predict how free men and women will choose to live their lives. It is sufficient to observe that people would be making such decisions for themselves—without binding others—and that a variety of personal and social practices is likely to result. Because we are social beings, however, it is probable that a continuing experimentation with noninstitutional forms will produce other patterns of association. It is also very likely— based upon what we have learned of human behavior—that many of the new and unstructured forms of organization will, themselves, eventually become institutionalized. There are no guarantees that any of us might not grow weary of the tempo of continuing awareness and opt for the passive comforts of settled truths and certified behavior.

With all of these thoughts in mind, and without presuming to suggest the specific forms of association that liberated men and women *will* develop for themselves, it might be worthwhile to explore—in a purely hypothetical fashion—a number of *possible* alternatives to present institutionally-structured practices. I have no idea how a society composed of tens of millions of autonomous men and women would differ from our present one, other than to be reasonably assured that it would not have a uniform appearance. As I have already suggested, it is not my purpose to lay out the blueprints for a utopian society. Those who are unwilling to set sail upon a new course without other men's maps might feel more secure traveling in the company of gurus and ideologues. But as free, self-directed human beings, we will be creating our personal working definitions of a desirable world as we develop our own preferences for living. I have no confidence in my ability to predict how you might choose to live your life (a personal shortcoming that makes me inadequate to govern others), but I have complete confidence in your ability to make such decisions for yourself. One need not know, in advance, what an eventual cure for cancer might be in order to be convinced of the legitimacy of the scientific process as the means for discovering such a cure.

The purpose of this chapter, then, is only to show some of the ways in which men and women might be able to *cooperate* with one another for their mutual self-interest (as distinct from being *sacrificed* for collective institutional interests). In doing so, we need not rely on crystal balls, but draw upon a variety of experiences of many people who have, for a number of years now, been seeking alternatives to institutionalized forms of living.

During the 1960's and 1970's, and continuing into the 1980's, increasing numbers of men and women became attracted to life-styles, approaches to self-understanding, and patterns of social organization that were premised on voluntary, nonmanipulative, self-directed, personally-meaningful, unstructured, and decentralized ways of living. Call it "self-awareness," "self-actualization," or "consciousness-raising," more and more people are questioning the traditional, institutionally-serving attitudes and life-styles by which they have heretofore been content to live their lives. Out of such inquiries have come untold experiments in both personal and group behavior, including efforts to expand the capacities of the human mind; increased attraction of people to more natural ways of living—including childbirth, the raising of children, healing, the provision of food and shelter, and even dying; the growing popularity of alternative, unstructured methods of learning—for both children and adults—premised upon what the public school system would regard as the heretical view that learning is both a natural and enjoyable activity; an increasing insistence by people for more meaningful, challenging, and self-controlling work environments; and a greater interest in the creative processes—whether in music, painting, technology, crafts, or any other human activity.[2]

Many people have, in other words, been moving away from the institutionalized methods of doing things. They have become increasingly aware that their essential unity with one another and with nature itself makes petty and totally irrelevant the parochial institutional bickering that surrounds them. Many have abandoned the traditional organized religions in favor of newly emerging philosophic and religious movements offering a less-structured and decentralized format. Others have established schools that provide children an alternative to the prevailing system of State-certified ignorance and illiteracy, or so-called "free universities" that offer adults courses of instruction in subjects that are of interest to students, but fail to meet rigid university curriculum requirements. Many others have discovered, through various writings typified by the late E.F. Schumacher's *Small Is Beautiful*, that technology can take forms that *serve* rather than *subdue* human beings and that material pursuits can benefit mankind without dominating the human spirit. A growing disillusionment with government and politics that began at least as early as the 1950's, erupted into the 1960's opposition to the Vietnam War, and has expanded since the 1970's into a broader disenchantment with the entire political process.[3]

A continuing examination of our personal and social behavior is likely to generate a variety of additional alternatives to institutional structuring. Such changes could be reflected in any of the following heretofore institutionalized areas:

1. *Political behavior.* As men and women become more autonomous and self-directed, and are able to end the divisions within themselves that cause conflict, we should witness the decline of politics. There has already been a widespread questioning of political authority during the last two decades. Anti-war and anti-draft demonstrations, tax protest movements, organized opposition to mandatory school-busing, declines both in voting and respect for politicians, and resentment toward bureaucracy and general discontent with the size and scope of government have been dominant themes in American politics in recent years. There appears to be a growing sense of awareness that the political State is more of a *disruptive* than a *moderating* influence, and that it *thwarts* more than it *serves* the wills of its citizens. Such sentiments have even begun to fuel revolts in totalitarian regimes, including the iron curtain nations.

People who have undertaken serious explorations of the nature of human relationships soon discover the conflict-ridden, inhumane nature of State action. The political organization of society is premised on coercive and manipulative practices and, as such, is totally incompatible with peaceful and liberated forms of association. A conflict-free society would be characterized by cooperation, not coercion; by mutuality, not manipulation; by personal autonomy, not collective authority. A conflict-free society, in other words, would be a Stateless society.

In a noninstitutional society, alternatives to present political power-structures could be found not only in such forms of neighborhood and community association as were discussed in the previous chapter, but in a variety of profit and non-profit organizations. We have, perhaps, become so awed by the power and majesty of the political State that we tend to forget that virtually every service provided by it is or has been provided through voluntary organizations. Volunteer and privately owned fire departments provide protection in thousands of communities. The early fire companies were precisely that, "companies" that offered fire protection to subscribers in much the same sense that insurance companies protect individual customers. Volunteer and privately owned security services flourish in most major cities in spite of the presence of enormous government police departments. Private arbitration is emerging as an ever-more-popular alternative to the overcrowded and sluggish government courts system. Privately run schools have long been available as options for parents dissatisfied with public education. Private parcel delivery firms compete quite favorably with the U.S. Postal Service. Privately owned toll roads and bridges have existed in this country for centuries; real estate developers have built residential streets and parks; and private foundations and corporations have built untold numbers of museums, zoos, amusement parks, libraries, hospitals, airports, and colleges and universities. Private charities were providing for the poor and the needy long before government welfare programs became politically popular, and they will no doubt continue to do so long after state and federal government agencies have gone bankrupt. Weather forecasting, conservation programs, and land use planning have been engaged in by airlines, lumber companies, real estate developers, farmers, and untold numbers of other private sources outside the walls of government. Those of us who truly wish to contribute to the order and well-being of our communities— instead of clamoring for government programs to absolve us of our felt responsibilities—will have unlimited opportunities to do so in a Stateless society.

If you or I want a particular service performed, we are fully capable of providing for it ourselves, whether individually or by joining with others to do so. As we have seen, the agents of the political State are blessed with no wizardry or other superhuman talents: they are only people who enjoy the legal power to compel the rest of us to do what we do *not* want to do, or to prevent us from doing what we *do* want to do. When we are able to understand that the only power possessed by political institutions is that which we have relinquished over ourselves, we will also be in a position to devise our own means of providing the services heretofore supplied by governments.

There is, on the other hand, one governmental function that a Stateless society would have to do without: the conduct of war. While no sane, life-valuing man or woman would look upon this activity as a service worth preserving anyway, most of us have been indoctrinated in the ideology that the defense of a nation is dependent upon the warmaking capacity of the State. Such herd-organizing propositions obscure the fact that the subordination of our lives to collective political authority makes us *more* vulnerable—not less— to foreign aggression. The political State provides us not a *shield* but a *jugular vein*, a central point upon which a foreign State can focus an attack upon an entire nation. A nation without political authorities could only be conquered by invading troops going door to door in a virtually hopeless— and dangerous—undertaking to persuade people to surrender their accustomed liberties and submit to domination. But because we have already submitted to political rule, any would-be invader would only need to conquer our present rulers who could surrender—or perhaps "quitclaim"—the entire nation to their authority. Contrary to one of the basic tenets of our social orthodoxy, in *unity* there is *vulnerability*, not strength.

Of even greater significance, however, is the fact that the war system itself poses a far more dangerous threat to all of us than do all of the alleged enemies by which the State has maintained its power over us. In the vernacular of contemporary world politics, it is neither communism nor capitalism nor fascism that represents the greatest menace to mankind, but "ism" itself, the belief in the necessity for the political organization of human society. In a world in which the very existence of life is threatened by thermonuclear, neutron, and laser weapons—not to mention our more conventional tools of slaughter—we may yet have time to discover that *dis*organization is not only our *best*, but perhaps our *only* method of defense. The most effective defense against tyranny—foreign or domestic—is a state of mind that insists upon its autonomy and refuses to submit to the authority of others. Nothing so distresses the aspirations of tyrants as the presence of men and women who will not allow themselves to be dominated by others.

2. *Economic behavior.* As we saw in chapter 9, the highly-structured, industrially-centralized nature of economic life in our modern corporate-State society is largely the product of business-supported political programs. In a Stateless society, business firms would be deprived of the artificial supports, restraints, and other devices that raise prices, inhibit the development of new products and the entry of new competitors, close markets, promote monopolies and industrial concentration, standardize costs and product designs, and otherwise limit the free play of economic

decision-making that might pose a threat to established positions in the market.

For the reasons previously discussed, it would be very difficult—although by no means impossible—for large, established firms to steadfastly maintain the competitive resiliency, the entrepreneurial incisiveness, and the organizational flexibility necessary to preserve their market positions. Managers would have to become more innovative and creative, more sensitive to the wants of both customers and employees, and more aware of the *human* costs—not just the material costs—of doing business. Labor unions—stripped of their government-created monopoly status over all employees in a bargaining unit, and having to seek support from among freely-choosing workers—would have to become more responsive to the individual needs of those they would represent. To prevent the seemingly inevitable ossification brought on by bureaucratization would require of an organization composed of tens of thousands of individual decision-makers the exercise of a continuing collective awareness. It is one thing for an individual to practice constant awareness: it may be too much to expect of large, corporate enterprises.

For such reasons, the deinstitutionalization of our lives would likely result in more decentralized, individualized or small-group oriented, forms of economic activity. Various writers have addressed, in one form or another, the need for transforming existing organizational structures into systems in which the interests of individuals, not institutions, are paramount. From Schumacher's appeals for the development of intermediate technologies, to Toffler's predictions of a return to such dissipated systems of production as the "electronic cottage," to Scott and Hart's and Kirkpatrick Sale's more generalized proposals for organizational reform, there is a growing recognition that institutional demands are exacting too high a price when calculated in human terms.[4]

The movement away from highly-structured, centralized

systems of economic activity has already been observed in the increasing popularity of personalized computers and communications technologies; in the interest in designing homes and other buildings as self-sufficient units, with individualized power sources (e.g., solar, wind power, privately owned generators) and recycled energy and other resources;[5] in a return to smaller, personally owned specialty stores (e.g., health food stores, meat markets, produce stores, boutiques) as alternatives to the standardized wares of chain and discount stores; and in the emergence of barter and other manifestations of an underground economy as an alternative to the highly-regulated, taxed, computerized, social-security-numbered, central-bank-controlled, credit-card-transacted, institutionalized "official" economy. Just as the industrial revolution helped to liberate men and women from the highly-structured feudal system, we may be on the verge of a *new* economic revolution. As previously noted, however, whether such a revolution reaches fruition in our lives depends upon whether we are able to adopt the new technology without accepting the life-structuring logic of the old order. Can we, in other words, use the emerging technology to help facilitate our personal autonomy, or will we simply sit back and wait for the existing institutional order to figure out how to retain their monopolies over us? The new technologies will *not* liberate us: we must do that for ourselves, by questioning our own attitudes and understanding. But they can facilitate our emancipation from institutional controls once we determine to be free.

One of the more important benefits men and women will doubtless derive from an abandonment of institutional methods of economic behavior is a rediscovery of the *joy*, rather than the *burden*, of work. Because institutions have insisted upon the paramountcy of their interests over ours, we have become accustomed to regarding work as an onerous duty, a sacrifice we are expected to make in exchange for a life-supporting income. It would not be an exaggeration to suggest that most people who work within institutions do not derive genuine pleasure from the work they do, a truth that represents one of the sadder of human costs. Once we begin to live for our *own* purposes, however, we will likely discover the truth of Maria Montessori's observation that "the secret of a happy life is congenial work,"[6] that the most pleasurable rewards from human labor are to be found not in money, but in the satisfaction obtained from the work itself.

Finally, as we continue to discover more about the self-ordering nature of the universe, we may understand that an economy is not just some collective abstraction detached from our personal lives, nor is it confined to the processes of producing and exchanging goods and services, with the pursuit of monetary advantage as the only motivation. Such fragmentary thinking has contributed to the conflict in our lives. As we become more conscious of the functioning of holistic systems, we may come to understand the economy as a spontaneous, self-adjusting, living network that expresses, reconciles, and disciplines—all without compelling—the varied interests of men and women. Economics involves much more than buying and selling things and making money: it is an expression of how we cooperate, make choices, and trade with one another in everything that we do. An economy is the most substantial manifestation of a holistic, living society. When political institutions regulate economic activity, they are imposing a structured, artificial order upon a natural, self-ordering system. The regulation of an *economy* is the regulation of the lives of *people*. The control of production, exchanges, prices, wages, and product quality, is the control of the choices that people make for themselves.

3. *Religious and philosophic behavior.* Because men and women have needs for what can be called cosmic understanding, questions of a religious and philosophic nature will continue

to occupy human attentions. Such pursuits are not, however, synonymous with institutionalized religion and philosophy. In order to avoid the continuing effort associated with actual understanding, many of us have settled for established dogmas, doctrines, and ideologies that offer the superficial appearance of such understanding. Churches and moral philosophies have provided us with instant morality, settled truths without the burden of examination or comprehension, and answers without questions.

Those who have been unwilling to content themselves with such shortcut approaches have expanded their searches for understanding. The increasing popularity of eastern philosophy, personally-oriented religions, so-called trans-humanistic philosophy, and generalist and interdisciplinary approaches to learning (premised on the *integration*, rather than the traditional academic *segregation*, of knowledge), reflect a dissatisfaction with doctrinal, institutionally-centered bodies of beliefs. Men and women are becoming more insistent that religions be personally relevant, that they help provide an enhanced sense of spiritual understanding. There is a growing impatience with those highly-structured religions that emphasize catechismal consistency, or seek to impose ritualized behavior, thinking, and life-styles upon church officials and members alike. Demands for liberalization, for a retreat from centuries-old traditions, are commonplace. As people move away from institutions, they will no doubt continue these trends, abandoning the established religions and moral philosophies, the ideologies, and the systems of thought, in favor of inquiries that draw upon a wide range of philosophic and religious ideas, but only for purposes of *examination*, not *attachment*. Such inquiries would reflect the searching, spiritual nature of human beings that the established religions have long forgotten.

As we continue to alter our perceptions of the universe, we are likely to discover how organized religions have alien-

ated us from the rest of nature. We may even discover that
the alleged irreconcilable differences between the sciences
and religions exist only when established religions seek to
inhibit open inquiry; that the need for religious experiences
and the need for scientific truths both have their origins in
our need to comprehend the cosmos.

What if scientists and philosophers began to see similar
patterns at work within the universe? What if, in other
words, they each began to perceive the cosmos *not* as bits and
pieces of differentiated matter and energy, but as a giant
organism, of which planets, stars, molecules, and microbes,
are the constituent parts? These people might even agree to
abandon the traditional demarcation between "living" and
"non-living" things, and to identify all energy as an expression of *life*. When we consider the intelligence exhibited not
only by other animals—particularly the sophisticated intelligence of whales and dolphins—but by plants, and when
quantum physicists report that subatomic particles behave
almost as though they were acting with intention, would it
be so lacking in scientific basis to suppose that the universe
itself might be evolving from energy to matter to life to
consciousness? Considering our own amoebic and reptilian
ancestries, is it so far-fetched to imagine that the cosmos
might be evolving a central nervous system, through which
networks of information and awareness would permit the
same kind of integrative communication among the galaxies
themselves that we now take for granted within our biological systems?

One can see at once how such a perception of the universe
would stand traditional religions on their heads, for most
have been premised upon the existence of an alienated being
of universal intelligence whom we have heretofore chosen to
call "God." But what if this cosmic intelligence did not
precede creation, but will *evolve* out of creation, just as our
intelligent minds evolved out of crude life forms? What if, in

other words, consciousness is universalizing itself through us, so that the cosmos will be able to comprehend itself? This is not to say that there is any clear evidence for this proposition, or that any of us ought to be so silly as to *believe* in it: that way lies the trap of the traditional religions. It is to suggest, however, that such a perception of the universe would reveal a totally different pattern of cosmic intelligence than we see in the vain, petty, spiteful, jealous, vicious, and retributive gods of our ancestors. It suggests, as well, our need to abandon the traditional pyramidal power structure view of the universe, in which all power is centralized in some cosmic monarch who rules with undeniable authority. In its place, perhaps, would emerge the view that the locus of this universal understanding is *everywhere*—not in some omniscient elite—with power decentralized among decision-makers who are both autonomous and interrelated.

All of this is purely conjecture, of course, but it does seem clear that the philosophic and religious inquiries now being undertaken by intelligent, thoughtful, and unstructured minds will lead them closer to this alternative view of the universe than it will the Old Testament understanding of the cosmos dominated by a neurotic and vindictive tyrant.

4. *Learning.* Parents who understand the importance of autonomous, self-directed learning in the development of their children have, in recent decades, been turning to unstructured, student-centered schools as alternatives to traditional structured methods of formal education. The kind of learning that is important to such parents is not so much the *information* absorption and *skill* certification that characterizes traditional education, but the development of self-motivated approaches to learning, along with the thinking, reasoning, and analytical skills that make autonomous learning possible. Consistent with the fundamental self-awareness and life-centered attitudes that have emerged since the early 1960's, more and more parents have been demanding school envi-

ronments that regard learning as an indivisible part of the flowering of the mind, body, and personality of the child.

As men and women become more aware of their own institutionally-restrained patterns of living, they will no doubt become more sensitive to both the *methods* and the *substance* of their own children's learning. They will search out the schools that offer self-centered learning, rather than social or religious indoctrination; that treat learning as a natural and enjoyable activity, rather than a burdensome duty; and that help the child to develop his or her own harmonious sense of intellectual order, rather than imposing a rigid hickory stick conditioning upon the mind. They will evaluate the quality of their children's learning *not* in terms of the testing and grading standards by which schools have traditionally certified students to other institutions, but by the ability of their own children to deal effectively and independently with the world around them. Recognizing that learning is both natural and pleasurable to all of us, these parents will have little difficulty understanding that the institutionally-mandated system of compulsory learning makes about as much sense as a system of compulsory fun.

The schools that will survive in a noninstitutional world will, in other words, be those that most effectively help children learn *how to learn*, and for the children's own purposes, rather than schools that emphasize the administration of programs, and the supervision and certification of students. Learning as a means of developing individual understanding may become as central to the purpose of schools as institutionally-serving skill and attitude training is today. Should that occur, we may discover that learning is not just something one does in *preparation* for living, but is a continuing activity throughout a lifetime. Schools themselves would then have to choose whether or not to abandon their rigidly-structured, traditional methods and join with their students to face the excitement of uncertainty and spontaneity that accompanies genuine learning.

Since uniformity is not likely within a free society, there will unquestionably be a variety of learning systems. In addition to the more familiar schoolrooms, we are likely to see more use made of emerging technologies. Home computers may provide us with instant access to libraries and other information sources throughout the world; video tapes and laser discs can afford students the opportunity to view lectures and films when the student is prepared to do so; closed-circuit television—in which students have the means of asking questions of teachers and of each other—will continue to make the home an expanded classroom (thus reducing the enormous capital costs that help make education a luxury beyond the incomes of many families); microfiche cards (with readers in the home) can provide books and other learning materials at a fraction of the cost of present methods of printing and reproduction; and technologies yet-to-be created can further expand our individualized, noninstitutional capacities for learning.

No matter which of the above organizational areas we are considering, it is important to distinguish the *substantial* from the *superficial* form of change. As we have seen, the divisions that exist within our minds generate conflict in our understanding, as we try to reconcile our new awareness of truth with our carefully-organized accumulations of prior learning. Just as we may be tempted to structure our understanding of the need for an *un*structured consciousness—creating new belief systems and dogmas which we hope will reduce the effort we must make for our future awareness—so, too, institutions may be inclined to exploit the current popularity of "expanded awareness" and "human potential" experiences. That such efforts usually amount to little more than institution-serving gimmicks—a "new and improved" package that masks the same dreary product—is evident from an examination. A number of highly-organized religious and philosophic movements have incorporated into their rigidly-defined doctrines, practices and rhetoric made popular by the "consciousness raising" of the 1960's and 1970's. Many business firms and governmental agencies have picked up the "self-actualization" concepts of Abraham Maslow[7] and the related ideas of other management theorists, and employed them in efforts to motivate their employees to more closely identify themselves with organizational goals. Even the military has taken advantage of some of these ideas, using various "human potential" techniques to not only alter the self-image of soldiers, but apparently to change the public's perception of the military from aggressive and warmaking to "peace*making*" organizations. Some militarists have even proposed redesigning the military into a global force that "protects" the life of the earth the way our bodies' defense systems protect our health! But underlying such fanciful proposals is the same steel-fisted power and authority to compel obedience that typifies all political systems. A Marine in a park ranger's uniform remains an agent of State violence.[8]

Schools, of course, have made superficial efforts to provide token, make-believe unstructured learning within otherwise structured environments. I was once in a traditional, teacher-centered public school classroom when, all of a sudden, the teacher announced to her students: "all right, class, it's time for the self-directed study period." The inherent contradiction in a program of scheduled spontaneity was so apparent that I had a difficult time holding back my laughter. The gimmicky nature of such programs—in whatever institution they arise—is revealed by a common underlying quality: they are invariably designed to promote greater efficiency for, or dedication to, institutional interests, by trying to create the impression that there is really no conflict between individual and organizational purposes. However much we may be attracted to the rhetoric or the ritual of such seemingly "bold" and "original" programs, beneath their surface lurks the same premise of institutional primacy that has plagued mankind throughout history. The employee, or the student, or the church-member, or the citizen who takes literally the words that speak of the congruence of individual and group goals will very quickly realize who is in charge should he attempt to redirect the organization in pursuit of his objectives. No significant revolution in human consciousness will arise from activities to be engaged in only so long as they prove serviceable to institutional purposes.

*   *   *   *

There is a subtle quest for power over the lives of other people in trying to predict the course of the future. If we can convince others that our visions of tomorrow accurately represent what will transpire, we may help influence them to adopt life-styles and attitudes that comport with our speculations and preferences. Men and women who value being fashionable find an attraction in being first on the bandwagon, first to mount the crest of a "new wave." As the history of religions and ideologies has shown, there is a tremendous manipulative power in prophecy.

But there is no scientific way to view the future, and the explorations into which this chapter has gone ought not be regarded as social prophesying. It is sometimes difficult enough for me to figure out where I have *been*—in spite of all the hard data provided by experience—without being so presumptuous as to suggest what even *I*—much less you and four billion other people—will be doing in some undefined tomorrow. It does seem rather certain that western civilization has about run its course, and that we are living in the dawning years of a culture totally foreign to that into which you and I were born. Whether our society is on the verge of a peaceful and exhilarating New Age, or an ever-more-destructive and repressive neo-Dark Ages, will depend on whether we face the changes with *intelligence* or *reaction*. The significant changes in consciousness that have already occurred within tens of thousands of men and women, offer tremendous optimism concerning our future. If we choose to live as we have in the past—as highly-organized, externalized, structured, reactive, conflict-ridden people—the organizational forms that we adopt as tools for our madness will be totally irrelevant to any humanely-inspired inquiry. If, on the other hand, we are able to liberate ourselves from our self-imposed servitude to institutions, . . . who is to say how millions of free men and women will choose to express their autonomy? It is enough, for our purposes here, to suggest that liberated, self-directed people will likely discover a variety of alternatives to present forms of social organization. It is enough, I believe, to note that free men and women will find their *own* ways to be free.

19

ANOTHER BEGINNING

If the human race is to survive it will have to change more in its ways of thinking in the next twenty-five years than it has done in the last twenty-five thousand.
    —Kenneth E. Boulding [1]

Politicians, business and religious leaders, educators, and television and newspaper commentators—the principal spokesmen of institutional interests—periodically arise to voice concern over the decreasing willingness of people to sacrifice themselves for the sake of institutions. Former President Carter expressed this attitude when he spoke of the "crisis of the American spirit," which he defined as "a growing disrespect for government, for the churches, schools, the news media and other institutions."[2] When organizational missionaries mount the pulpit to evangelize about the subordination of our individual interests to those of institutions, they reveal the nature of the game being played. If it were true that institutions did only reflect and promote our personal interests, there could be no real objection to our deciding upon alternatives to present institutional practices. Those who moralize against such changes are telling us, at least implicitly, that organizational purposes ought to preempt our own, that *institutions,* not *human beings,* are of paramount consideration.

Indeed, people do seem to be experiencing a growing disenchantment with institutions. But if there is any "crisis" in this, it is only a threat to the power positions that institutions enjoy over people. Rather than joining with the voices of social control to lament this disillusionment, however, we would be better advised to regard the situation as an opportunity for us to reassert personal control over our own lives. If there is any potential tragedy here, it would lie *not* in a weakening of institutional control over people, but in our willingness to succumb—like well-trained children giving in to the guilt-manipulations of domineering parents—to the fear-peddling and moralizing of institutional leaders. *Of course* the institutional monopolists will decry the reluctance of people to put aside their own hopes and preferences to serve organizational interests; *of course* they will treat the refusal of people to give institutions a blank check over their lives and property as "self-indulgence." Every racketeer wants to keep his "conscript clientele" in line. But if our vicious, life-destroying practices are to end, we must begin to question whether the games others create for us are really worth our playing.

If our society is, indeed, experiencing a general weakening of institutional authority, ought we not take the opportunity to examine our own attitudes and our dependence upon organizational structures? Even if institutions were to suffer a decline and fall, we are in a position to arise and take back the control over and responsibility for our lives. The crumbling of prison walls—particularly those we have helped to construct—is the first step toward our own liberation.

Some might object that we cannot live well without institutions because they civilize us and make for social order. But is any of this true? Do we live well *with* institutions? Is organizational structuring truly consistent with our natures? If so, why are we not happier with what we have become? Why are we angry and ulcer-ridden; why do we suffer from high blood pressure and nervous breakdowns; why are we so filled with self-directed anger that we must either project the cause of our anger onto others, or escape from our own miseries in drugs, alcohol, or neurotic/psychotic delusions? Is our compulsively-organized and highly-structured style of living really mankind's "golden age" of social development?

Has the evolutionary march of the human species led us only to the battlefield, the altar, the jail-cell, the dunce stool, or the boardroom? Have the processes of natural selection dictated that we live on our knees, heads bowed in worship of constituted authorities? Has it all come to no more than this, that we "might sit in the gallery of a coal mine and operate the super-hyper-adding machine with the great toe of [our] right foot?"[3] Have we evolved a sophisticated intelligence only to abandon it in favor of organized irrationalities?

For centuries, we humans have sought peace and order in governments, only to experience wars and disorder; we have sought God in churches, only to discover confused priests; we have sought intelligence and understanding in schools, but emerge with only indoctrination and training; we have sought rationality and morality in philosophic systems, only to find rationalization and moralizing; we have sought well-being and the joy of work within business firms, only to be rewarded with money for our participation in monotonous routines. We were assured that institutions would provide the order and rationality that would permit us to experience the essence of being human. But where we thought we would find planned order, we have discovered only calculated chaos; where we expected sanity, we found a nearly universal commitment to sanctioned schizophrenia; where we had hoped for inner peace, we experienced only the normal neuroses of so-called "civilized" living; and where we looked for the essence of humanity, we discovered only twisted and mutilated humanoids.

It has often been said that people favor peace, but oppose the conditions that make for peace. The world is becoming saturated in the blood of wars and other forms of violence; it throbs with the pain of conflict. Such has always been the human condition, perhaps, but with more powerful technologies and institutional apparatuses available, the scope and intensity of human suffering have greatly increased. The machinery of conflict has become thoroughly democratized, redistributed downward such that the most vile barbarian now has the capacity to employ nuclear weapons in further- ance of his self-righteous delusions. Conflict and violence now threaten to make human life absolutely intolerable. Ignorance of the causes of these insane practices is a luxury whose costs mankind can no longer afford.

We will either put an end to conflict, or conflict will put an end to us. But for us to *end* conflict, we must first *understand* it. We have become so accustomed to confronting and treat- ing only the *symptoms* of conflict, that we fail to observe the underlying divisions and antagonisms that separate us from one another. We identify such problems as war, racism, crime, terrorism, rivalry, nationalism, rioting, bigotry, compulsion, slavery, class structures, or other manifestations of social discord, and appeal to institutions to resolve them. In so doing, we help to perpetuate the vicious circle of seeking institutional answers to institutionally-generated conflicts. Being unwilling to examine our own deeper involve- ment with conflict—particularly our institutional attach- ments—we content ourselves with efforts to *manage* conflict, to keep the turmoil within tolerable limits. Despite repeated failures, we continue our quest for some new and improved formula of organizational wizardry, hoping to find answers in some magical incantation, a catechism etched on a marble wall, or a glittering knight atop a white horse. Even as our highly-structured society erupts from internal pressures, we search for the new leaders or the new programs capable of restoring confidence in our bankrupt institutions.

Most readers will recall having seen the puzzle presented below. The problem consists of connecting all nine dots using

.   .   .

.   .   .

.   .   .

four straight lines and without lifting the pen from the paper. The problem is easily solved,[4] but only if one does not accept the mind-set of the square itself, and is able to go outside its boundaries. Our ability to resolve the problems of social conflict also depends upon our stepping outside our institutional confines. Institutions are too bound up in conflict and disorder—too much a part of and dependent upon conflict for their existences—to be able or willing to resolve it. Courts will not solve the problem of litigiousness in society; governments will not put an end to intergroup squabbles or the use of legalized coercion; police departments will not find a solution to crime problems; the military will not end wars; the business system will not deal with the problems of competitive strife or the technological domination of society; and religions will not end bigotry. Institutions will do no more than tinker with these problems, rearranging the battlefield alignments, designing new strategies for combat, modifying the rules under which our continuing social discord is played out, or changing the names and positions of the players. But institutions *cannot* and *will not* confront and resolve the fundamental problem of social conflict.

Only you and I can do that, by examining our own consciousness and our understanding, and by becoming completely aware of how we involve ourselves in conflict. As long as we endeavor to reduce or eliminate social conflict by changing *others* through institutional means, we are bound to be frustrated. Because we have no effective control and little influence over institutions—and no control over other people—we begin to experience feelings of impotence and despair that turn to pessimism about the future of mankind. But as soon as you and I begin to understand that the problem of conflict is within each of us—that *you* and *I are* conflict—a sense of optimism blossoms. Because I have control over the conflict that is within *me*—the conflict that *is* me—I have the capacity to confront and put an end to the conflict in my life; I have the power to create my own peace and end my conflict with others.

Perhaps in the rubble of social disintegration we humans will be able, one by one, to rediscover the basis for a peaceful and humane society. Such conditions cannot exist, however, in the absence of our acknowledging the fundamental wholeness and inviolability of each person. No matter how well-intended we may be, no matter how noble our purposes, we do not exhibit such respect as long as we have expectations of others, and are willing to manipulate or compel others to adhere to those expectations. In the words of Albert Schweitzer:

> Whenever I in any way sacrifice or injure life, I am not within the sphere of the ethical, but I become guilty, whether it be especially guilty for the sake of maintaining my own existence or welfare, or unegotistically guilty for the sake of maintaining a greater number of other existences or their welfare.[5]

Or, as Immanuel Kant has stated: "Act so that you treat humanity, whether in your own person or in that of another, always as an end and never as a means only."[6]

We are, as we have seen, social beings with needs which can often best be met by organizations. But even our social needs remain personal. We must be careful that we associate ourselves with only those forms that harmonize our *individual* and *social* natures, . . . not those institutional arrangements that sacrifice the former for the aggrandizement of the latter. A system that serves a few, or many, or even most people, but which does so at the expense of sacrificing any other persons, destroys the one essential element for a peaceful and civilized society: *respect for the autonomy and integrity of each human being.* Institutions, by setting their purposes against the interests of individuals, have destroyed this element of mutual respect and made of human society an organized system for mutual victimization. By fostering the pernicious utilitarian premise that it is good to sacrifice the few to the greater good of the many, institutions have helped to convert society into a respectable form of cannibalism. In the end, the social needs that brought us together end up being perverted by cynical and predatory agencies used by people to promote private and institutional interests under the most plausible of altruistic hypocrises.

In spite of all this, there remain those who continue to speak of the necessity for institutionalized forms of society. But then, the progress of more peaceful and rational living has always been resisted by those whose interests are identified with the established order and those who have been conditioned to acknowledge the propriety of their own institutional detention. There were those who believed in the economic and moral necessity of a system of slavery, just as there were those who could not conceive of the maintenance of a Christian society without constituted tribunals to ferret out witches, heretics, and freethinkers. Any revolution in human awareness will always be opposed by contemporary institutional Tories. Human understanding has never progressed uniformly or en masse: it has always been the product of individual inquiry.

Mankind's understanding of the universe has progressed in a manner that can, perhaps, be analogized to a set of Chinese boxes. We have sought to preserve our limited understanding and to confront our fears of uncertainty by structuring—and thus rigidifying—our knowledge. We have built ourselves into a small black box, projecting onto the interior walls of that box the images of our limited awareness of the universe. Not having seen beyond the walls, we have taken comfort in the certainty that the nature and extent of our universe is as it appears from our own projections. The black box, in other words, becomes our universe.

Because our knowledge is always limited by being incomplete and based upon the past, such structuring conflicts with our needs for present understanding. Men and women who have not allowed convention to restrict the scope of their inquiries have opened a few windows revealing glimpses of a reality beyond our own black box. This new knowledge is initially resisted by the high priests of the black box but, in time, the structure succumbs to reality and the new knowledge is accepted. The revolutionary theory and the startling discovery become the established and common knowledge and, themselves, are incorporated in the construction of a new and improved black box. In this manner, for example, the physics of Copernicus was modified by Newton, Newton's by Einstein, Einstein's by recent work in quantum mechanics, and so on.

Human understanding, in other words, has always depended upon our being able to transcend the limitations of our prior learning, and to overcome the inertia associated with any established body of knowledge. Mankind has been rather successful at this in developing a better understanding of the physical laws of nature. Perhaps this has been due to the demonstrably pragmatic benefits involved. The pre-Copernican view of a divinely-created and managed, earth-centered universe has long been abandoned. More recently, the Newtonian picture of a mechanistic, fragmented reality has given way to a view suggesting an organic, interdependent universe. The absolute and certain reality of Newton has become relative and probable in this modern age of quantum physics, but with the change—as paradoxical as it first appears—mankind has moved closer to an understanding of the fundamental nature of reality. Just as periods of "creative chaos" in our lives have often produced quantum leaps in our understanding, a collapse of institutionally-structured systems of order reveals to us—if we choose to be perceptive—the patterns of universal order within nature. Order and transformation, in other words, often emerge from turmoil. Perhaps we are discovering that uncertainty and doubt produce questions, and that *questions*—not answers—provide the key to understanding. If so, we may learn how to live on the exciting precipice of constant total awareness, and to be able to confront that deep, dark abyss of endless uncertainty *not* in abject *fear,* but with the sense of euphoria that comes with the unleashing of the human spirit.

Though we have overcome many of the restrictions inherent in black box epistemology, and greatly expanded our understanding of the physical universe, we have not advanced very far in comprehending the nature of man or social relationships. We are the most technologically sophisticated people known to human history and yet, socially and organizationally, we have hardly advanced beyond the basic premises extant during the life of Henry VIII. We live in a rapidly decentralizing universe, and yet we still cling to pre-Copernican doctrines about the central role of institutions in human affairs. The relative nature of space and time, of matter and energy, are familiar to every high school student, and yet we continue allowing political and religious institutions to impose their absolute authority upon mankind. Even though physicists acknowledge that subatomic life of the universe functions on principles that allow little more than a statement of the *probability* of consequences, institutions continue to insist upon moral and behavioral *certainty.*

While the physical universe demonstrates to us that opposites *attract* and can serve as a basis for *order,* the power of institutions reminds us that differences can be used to *separate* us and generate destructive *conflict.*

Is it possible for us to transcend all of this, to get outside that primordial black box upon whose walls continue to be projected the most depressing and dehumanized understanding of man's nature? If we are able to do so, we will discover that, contrary to the black box dogmas, every institution acts to control people. Whether the methods employed include coercion, fear, intimidation, or the threat of withdrawal of benefits, every institution seeks to create an environment in which the behavior of individuals can be redirected from personal pursuits to the accomplishment of organizational goals. Institutions have helped us to become externalized, alienated persons. They have insisted that we look outside ourselves for meaning and direction for our lives, and have helped us learn to regard other people or institutions or ideas as being more important to us than our own selves.

Institutions have also persuaded us to look beyond the present and regard the future as our focal point and to look upon the perpetual postponement of the enjoyment of life as the mark of responsibility. As children, for example, we are taught to prepare ourselves for adulthood. School children are told that their learning is designed to prepare them for college, while college students are told that they are preparing themselves for careers. Young adults are taught to prepare themselves for parenthood so that they, in turn, can prepare *their* children for the same cycle. Middle-aged people are taught to prepare for their retirement, while retired persons are told to prepare themselves for an alleged life after death.

How sad all of this is, that we should not only have learned to live by the palpably absurd proposition that we could abandon the control of our lives to others, but that we should regard our own lives as so generally worthless that we could subject them to even the most arbitrary exercise of institutional preemption and sacrifice. Can a more debased, dehumanizing, and anti-life premise be hypothecated than that underlying the world's institutions? Is it any wonder that those who have made themselves aware of the nature of our institutionalized life-styles would, in increasing numbers, be seeking pro-life alternatives? What such persons may be on the verge of discovering, perhaps in time to avoid the implicit consequences, is that our institutional black box is, in reality, a black hole. Perhaps, due to the weight and the centripetal pressures inherent in its institutional superstructure, mankind is collapsing back upon itself. While the rest of the universe continues its fulfillment in centrifugation, it may be the destiny of mankind to consume itself in a centralizing self-destructiveness of such enormous intensity that nothing will be able to escape its inward collapse, its relentless plunge into eternal darkness. Such, at any rate, is the dreary future as envisioned in Orwell's *1984*, Huxley's *Brave New World*, and David Karp's *One*.

I remember how, as a child, I would listen to adults express the orthodox social dream of peace and freedom that would be realized as a result of the wartime sacrifices of young men. But as one war ended, and our political leaders prepared us for yet another war and more human sacrifices, I began to realize that we were to enjoy neither peace nor freedom. In time, I began to understand how, throughout history, kings, queens, presidents, czars, prime ministers, emperors, dictators, and other confidence men had used this same wicked bunco scheme to swindle men and women out of the very essence of their lives and degrade the quality of human life. I became aware of how institutions have suppressed our most peaceful, cooperative, loving, and responsible impulses—the best of what it means to be human—and released the unthinking, noncaring, greedy, and conflict-ridden behavior that is the substance of institutionalism. In order to induce their participation in this hallowed butchery, men have been taught that the willingness to fight and kill and die without hesitation was a virtue that represented the strength of the species, while pacifism and respect for life were synonymous with weakness—the attributes of sniveling wimps, cowards, and sissies. It also became evident to me that such vicious practices would cease *only* if the victims refused to participate in them, and that this would occur only if there was a profound change in human thinking.

We can, of course, continue playing our traditional games—deluding ourselves that the universe can be tricked, and sacrificing the values upon which a peaceful society depends—in order to further institutional interests. We cannot, however, avoid the consequences of our so doing. But if we *are* to change—if society is to become peaceful, sane, and mutually supportive instead of coercive, irrational, and predatory—there must be a *revolution*. Not the organized, violent type of political revolution through which only leadership changes in the power structure are effected, but a psychological and spiritual revolution on the same order as the scientific and industrial revolutions. Such profound changes will occur *not* through our attempting to reorder the lives and personalities of *others*, but through a revolution within *ourselves*. "They" do not represent the establishment: you and I do.

We must begin by questioning our self-induced subservience to, and dependencies upon, established authorities. We must be willing to assert our self-controlling claims to the ownership of our own selves by declaring that life belongs to the living, *not* to institutional entities or other fictions. Above all else, we need to develop a *passion* for life itself. We must understand that institutionalism is not compatible with life, for it takes from life its individuality, its spontaneity, and its autonomous nature. We must abandon not only our cannibalistic appetites for human sacrifice, but the Old Testament mentality that tells us life is tainted by original sin and must be brought under the superintending direction of sanctified authorities. As men and women who love life, we need to declare our determination that life is going to survive on this planet, and that those who insist upon their destructive practices must stand aside. A popular bumper sticker suggests that we "question authority." But that is not enough. If human life is to continue, we must learn to live *without* authorities; to live *not* by *rules*, but by a shared understanding of what behavior is appropriate for life.

As we continue our prelude to the twenty-first century, one of the fundamental social questions we must confront is whether human life shall be allowed its autonomous spontaneity, or is it to be subjected to supervised planning; whether we shall live by our own decision-making, or under the direction of institutional people pushers; whether we shall enjoy the benefits of mutual cooperation, or continue to suffer from sacrificial compulsion? Such a question has implications that go much deeper than the superficial rhetoric of narrow, neo-romantic ideologies. Because this question goes to the essence of what it means to be a human being, and because the fate of mankind depends upon how we answer it, we must explore its length and breadth with the full use of our conscious and unconscious energies. If we are unwilling to generate such an intensive inquiry, we are unlikely to produce the kinds of changes necessary to overcome our self-destructive habits.

It is, no doubt, our materialistic and pragmatic conditioning that causes us to be so impatient for change. Business and political institutions have helped train us to seek instant fulfillment, to "want what we want when we want it." Things get done, we believe, by the movers and shakers of the world, and we have learned to regard progress and development and self-actualization (and all our other desired consequences of change) as the products of goal-directed activism. We do not understand that the only real change comes quietly from within ourselves. But then, our culture does not place a high value upon quiet observation. Indeed, we tend to equate such contemplative qualities with apathy, or as being symptomatic of social malaise. Nevertheless, the only meaningful change is that which comes about through *understanding*, for only in understanding can we hope to transcend the limitations of our past. When we act purposefully, in anticipation of *getting* something or *accomplishing* something, we are not *understanding*. To understand requires purpose*less*, unmotivated, uninvolved, quiet watching. To be totally *aware* of the present, without *wanting*, and without allowing our conscious mind to chatter endlessly about the past, therein lies the basis for a truly significant social revolution.

Many so-called revolutions have been recorded in history, but none of them have challenged the premise of the dominance of institutions in human society. They may have modified institutional forms, or effected a change in institutional leadership, but none have advanced the proposition that human life should be free of structured management and control. Though partisans of the political left, right, and middle insist upon their alleged irreconcilable differences with one another, they share a consensus about the need for structured social control. Institutionalism itself is "a grand cultural imperative which is beyond question, beyond discussion."[7] Far from effecting any truly significant change, such endeavors only end up "redesigning the turrets and towers of the technocratic citadel."[8]

These assumptions are beginning to be challenged by the silent revolution that has begun within the minds of many people. A number of men and women, peering beyond the black box, are seeing glimpses of a world without the contrived chaos, misery, and human sacrifice inherent in all systems of synthetic order. Unlike previous revolutions that sought only to continue playing institutional games under new rules, the silent revolution should prove itself immune to any counteraction by the established order. The revolt, after all, will not be in the streets, but in the only place where no earthly authority can go except by permission of the possessor: the conscious mind. There will be no barricades to defend, no riots in the streets, no bloody confrontations with police. The revolutionaries will not be found *attacking* institutions, but *walking away* from them.

If we are able to experience a revolution in human understanding, we may be able to avoid so repressive and spiritless a fate as is implicit in dominant institutionalism. Such a revolution must, however, consist of something more than continuing to accommodate our prior learning with our present understanding by enlarging the outer walls of our black box. We must learn how to break out of the suffocating confines of that box altogether, and to experience the peace and order that comes from our total integration with all of nature. To do so, we need only stand back from the petty and vexatious organizational pursuits we have considered of such vital concern, and observe our thought processes. If we only *watch* ourselves—without analysis, without passing judgment, without plan or purpose—we will become aware of what we have been doing to ourselves with our belief systems and attachments. If we can become totally conscious of our behavior and the functioning of our mind, we shall start to unshackle the chains with which we have restrained ourselves and begin to move out of our artificial darkness. In doing so, we will shed our dependency upon the agencies of chaos and violence that have dominated our lives. We will then begin to experience the reality of being one with the universe, an integral part of a total process, rather than just an interested observer of something that is "out there" beyond us. But in order to shed our dependency, there must first be a realization on our part that we *are* dependent.

We have a good deal of technical and structural knowledge of our universe. We have microscopes that can take us as far *within* as our telescopes do *beyond*. We have technologies that can pinpoint rocket landings on other planets, or record the seemingly aimless meanderings of subatomic particles. So confident are we in our knowledge and skills, that we deem it unthinkable not to have a fix-it remedy for every problem we encounter. And yet, in spite of our knowledge— or, perhaps, *because* of it—we have very little *understanding* of the universe. This is due, in large part, to our insistence upon the supremacy of linear, verbal, "left-brain" thinking over spatial, intuitive, "right-brain" thinking. In matters of importance, we have favored information that comes to us as hard, raw, verifiable facts, and discredited that which we have experienced through our sentiments, emotions, and insights. We prefer the advice of scientists and engineers to that of poets and philosophers. Having been unable to integrate our knowledge and experiences, we have convinced ourselves that nature is simply too *complex* to understand. Our problem, however, lies not within nature, but with the inherent deficiencies of knowledge itself, as well as with the fragmented, structured nature of our minds. If we can get beyond the data-collection-and-analysis approach to learning, and can end the division and confusion in our thinking, we will be able to discover a complexity to the universe that is nevertheless capable of being understood. It has been our effort to subject the world to our conscious, rational control—an undertaking born of the structured nature of our intellect—that makes our world appear more complicated than it is. Our conscious minds have been able to fabricate not only such make-believe realities as tax codes, religious liturgies, and insurance claim forms, but more elaborate depictions of a confounding and unknowable universe. Only an uncomplicated mind is capable of understanding a complex world.

In a sense, we continue to be like children on a field trip who stand outside a factory and gaze, in wondrous awe, at the gigantic structure that belches smoke, screeches, and, somehow or other, produces something or other. We marvel that this industrial leviathan can bring in people and train-loads of "stuff" at one end, and turn out automobiles or dishwashers at the other. But once we go into the building and become a part of all that noise and activity, we not only understand what goes on there, but the entire manufacturing process becomes unbelievably simple to us. Our understanding takes away the veil of mystery.

Is it possible for us to take a field trip into the universe itself, in order to understand its workings and processes? Can we step totally outside our institutional black box and experience a reality beyond what we have been led to believe could exist? Imagine, if you will, getting away from committee meetings and managed news stories and tax auditors and television commercials and memos and traffic jams and telephone calls and moral dilemmas and all the other trappings of our carefully organized disorder, and discovering the quiet beauty and order of a relentless universe. Imagine experiencing, once again, that childhood excitement of discovering how something really works!

Where would such a trip take us? That depends, I suppose, on where each of us thinks we can best begin to understand nature. Whether we begin with ourselves, or a flower, or a crystal, or peer through telescopes or microscopes, we shall all be taking the same route. The universe is not something apart from us, millions of light years out into space: it is to be found in all that surrounds us, *including us*. Indeed, if the universe is holographic in nature, it can be said that each part of the universe reflects the whole, and the whole is to be found in each part. Perhaps John Cage's efforts to set to music the random patterns in nature could provide us with some accompanying theme music. Classical music is already being used in some consciousness alteration programs. My own preferences, in this regard, run more to the unstructured, spirited tones of jazz (perhaps Count Basie, or maybe Dave Brubeck's and Paul Desmond's "Take Five"), than to highly-structured, church-commissioned baroque fugues.

What would we experience on our trips? I cannot be certain, but I seriously doubt that we will be asked to display our passports, or swear any allegiances, or forced into servitude, or taxed for the privilege of taking the trip, or lectured to, or locked up, or told to remain on our knees in order that we not see too much along the way. I doubt that any statute books or warning notices or Bibles or even hymnals will be passed out to us, and I strongly suspect we will be able to complete our journeys without having to call in a priest, a lawyer, a consul officer, an ombudsman, or a consumer advocate to assist us.

I do have doubts, though, about our willingness to ever return from whence we had started. Who, having once experienced the spirit that pervades the universe, would thereafter be content to kiss the feet of priests or the derrieres of politicians? Who, having discovered *nature's* laws, could thereafter find any meaning in man's *artificial* ones? Who, having rediscovered the joy of learning and the significance of understanding, could ever again be satisfied with the dulled contentment of formalized and certified ignorance? Who, having visited paradise, would be prepared to crowd onto the bus for the return trip into hell?

Once we begin observing the chaos concealed behind the facade of institutional order, and begin experiencing something of the order inherent throughout nature, many of us are likely to undertake a critical examination of our institutionalized commitments. Our expanded awareness will permit us to see the exploitive and dehumanizing nature of these revered agencies; to understand that our weakness alone has kept us groveling at the feet of established authorities, that our ignorance and fear has kept us trembling in the shadows of sacrosanct temples, palaces, and citadels. Such a realization fosters a liberation of the spirit which, in turn, generates within us the power to break our chains of dependency. In discovering the truth of what it really means to live together in society as human beings, we can abandon the patterns of agreed-upon lies and sanctified deceptions that have kept us at war with ourselves and our neighbors. While others continue to tear out their own souls upon organizational altars, and deliver their own children into sanctioned servitude, we will be able to walk away from our self-imposed bondage. For us, the power of institutions over our lives will have ended. Their antiquated forms—built upon the sacrifice of those values that represent the very best of mankind—will doubtless remain, but their authority over our minds and souls will have faded. For us, the power and the majesty of these agencies will be no more than was the archaic sovereign "Ozymandias" to the lyric archeologist Shelley:

> I met a traveller from an antique land
> Who said: "Two vast and trunkless legs of stone
> Stand in the desert. Near them, on the sand,
> Half sunk, a shattered visage lies, whose frown,
> And wrinkled lip, and sneer of cold command,
> Tell that its sculptor well those passions read
> Which yet survive, stamped on these lifeless things,
> The hand that mocked them, and the heart that fed;
> And on the pedestal these words appear:
> *My name is Ozymandias, King of Kings:*
> *Look on my works, ye Mighty, and despair!*
> Nothing beside remains. Round the decay
> Of that colossal wreck, boundless and bare
> The lone and level sands stretch far away."[9]

FOOTNOTES

Chapter 1.

1. Jean Jacques Rousseau, *The Social Contract* (1762); reprinted in William Ebenstein, *Great Political Thinkers* (New York: Rinehart and Company, 2nd ed., 1956), at 419.

2. Borrowed from Herbert Spencer's *The Man Versus the State* (1884); reprinted in Ebenstein, ibid, at 632.

3. From Webster's *Third New International Dictionary* (Springfield, Mass.: Merriam-Webster Inc., publishers of the Merriam-Webster Dictionaries, copyright 1981), at 1172.

4. Frank Chodorov's statement was made in a talk to a group of students at Rampart College (Colorado) in the early 1960's.

Chapter 2.

1. William Shakespeare, *Julius Caesar* (1599), Act I, Scene 2, Line 134.

2. Marshall McLuhan, *Understanding Media* (New York: The New American Library, 1964), at 55.

3. David Riesman, with Nathan Glazer and Reuel Denney, *The Lonely Crowd* (New Haven: Yale University Press, 1950).

4. A.E. Housman, *Last Poems, xii* (1922).

Chapter 3.

1. Stephen Crane, *The Black Riders* (1895).

2. Frederick Perls, *Gestalt Therapy Verbatim* (New York: Bantam

Press, 1971), at 7ff.; originally published Moab, Utah: Real People Press, 1969.

3. Ludwig von Bertalanffy, *Robots, Men and Minds* (New York: George Braziller, 1967).

4. James N. Powell, *The Tao of Symbols* (New York: Quill, 1982), at 15.

5. Perls, supra, at 13.

6. David Bohm, *Wholeness and the Implicate Order* (London: Routledge & Kegan Paul, 1981), at 15-16.

7. Herbert Spencer, supra, at 621.

Chapter 4.

1. Mrs. Edward Craster, in *Pinafore Poems* (1871).

2. Harold J. Laski, "The Dangers of Obedience," in 159 *Harper's Magazine,* June, 1929, at 3.

3. Snell and Gail Putney, *The Adjusted American: Normal Neuroses in the Individual and Society* (New York: Harper & Row, 1964), at 38.

4. Rollo May, *Power and Innocence* (New York: W.W. Norton & Co., 1972), at 21.

5. This statement was made in the course of a television news interview by a Los Angeles television station.

Chapter 5.

1. Abraham Maslow, "A Theory of Human Motivation," in 50 *Psychological Review* (1943), at 370ff.

2. This phrase is borrowed from Edgar Z. Friedenberg, *The Disposal of Liberty and Other Industrial Wastes* (Garden City: Doubleday & Co., 1975), at lff.

3. Albert Jay Nock, *Our Enemy the State* (Caldwell, Ida.: Caxton Printers, 1959), at 25.

4. Robert S. McNamara, *The Essence of Security* (New York: Harper & Row, 1968), at 109-110.

5. Fritjof Capra, after contrasting the "mechanistic" view of nature—premised on Descartes' division into "mind" and "matter"—and the "organic" view of modern physicists, declares, in words appropriate to the general inquiry herein: "The fragmented view is further extended to society, which is split into different nations, races, religious and political groups. The belief that all these fragments—in ourselves, in our environment, and in our society—are really separate can be seen as the essential reason for the present series of social, ecological, and cultural crises." Capra, *The Tao of Physics* (New York: Bantam Books, 1975), at 9.

6. Eric Kraus, "The Unpredictable Environment," which first appeared in 63 *New Scientist* (London: 1974), the weekly review of science and technology, at 649-652.

7. David Ehrenfeld, *The Arrogance of Humanism* (New York: Oxford University Press, 1978), at 126.

8. See, e.g., Capra, Ehrenfeld, Bohm, supra; Gary Zukav, *The Dancing Wu Li Masters: An Overview of the New Physics* (New York: William Morrow & Co., 1979); Karl Pribram, *Languages of the Brain* (Englewood Cliffs: Prentice Hall, 1971); Fred A. Wolf, *Taking the Quantum Leap* (New York: Harper & Row, 1981); Robert March, *Physics for Poets* (Chicago: Contemporary Books, Inc., 1978); Rupert Sheldrake, *A New Science of Life* (Los Angeles: J.P. Tarcher, Inc., 1981); Erich Jantsch, *The Self-Organizing Universe* (New York: Pergamon Press, 1980); Ilya Prigogine and Isabelle Stengers, *Order Out of Chaos* (New York: Bantam Books, 1984). Other related inquiries can be found in Lewis Thomas, *The Lives of a Cell* (New York: Bantam Books, 1974); Ken Wilber, ed., *The Holographic Paradigm and Other Paradoxes* (Boulder, Colo.: Shambhala, 1982);

Arthur Koestler, *The Ghost in the Machine* (New York: The Macmillan Company, 1967); and Michael Talbot, *Mysticism and the New Physics* (New York: Bantam Books, 1980).

9. Zukav, ibid, at 57.

10. Quoted in film, *Continents Adrift,* produced by American Educational Films (1979).

11. Snell Putney, *The Conquest of Society* (Belmont, Calif.: Wadsworth Publishing, 1972), at 37, 41.

12. Theodore Roszak, *Person/Planet* (Garden City: Anchor Press/ Doubleday, 1979), at 106.

13. R.D. Laing, *The Politics of Experience* (New York: Ballantine Books, 1967), at 95.

14. Roszak, supra, at 117.

15. Laski, supra, at 2.

16. For an interesting demonstration of how "hyperactivity" has been used to enforce institutionally-serving behavior upon children, see Peter Schrag and Diane Divoky, *The Myth of the Hyperactive Child* (New York: Pantheon Books, 1975).

17. Thomas Szasz, *The Manufacture of Madness* (New York: Harper & Row, 1970).

18. Wilhelm Reich's experiences have been presented in Colin Wilson's *The Quest for Wilhelm Reich* (Garden City: Anchor Press/ Doubleday, 1981).

19. Thomas H. Huxley, "The Coming of Age of 'The Origin of Species'," (essay written in 1880), in Huxley's *Darwiniana* (New York: D. Appleton & Co., 1896), at 229.

20. From Alice B. Toklas, *What Is Remembered* (New York: Holt, Rinehart & Winston, 1963), at 173.

21. Hal Holbrook, *Mark Twain Tonight* (New York: Ives Washburn, Inc., 1959), at 140. This portion of Holbrook's stage presentation was adapted from Mark Twain's *Roughing It.*

Chapter 6.

1. John Steinbeck, *The Grapes of Wrath* (New York: The Viking Press, 1958; originally published in 1939), at 42.

2. *Webster's New World Dictionary: College Edition* (New York: The World Publishing Company, 1962), at 1146.

3. See 36 *Machine Design* (January 2, 1964), at 164; reprinted in William J. Colson, "To Neutralize the Pragmatist," in 3 *Rampart Journal of Individualist Thought* (1967), at 19-20.

4. See, e.g., Joseph Borkin, *The Crime and Punishment of I.G. Farben* (New York: The Free Press, 1978).

5. Roszak, supra, at 105, 107.

6. William G. Scott and David K. Hart, *Organizational America* (Boston: Houghton Mifflin Company, 1979), at 30 (emphasis in original).

7. Viktor Frankl, *Man's Search for Meaning* (New York: Washington Square Press, 1963), at 78-79.

8. Douglas McGregor, *The Human Side of Enterprise* (New York: McGraw-Hill Book Company, 1960), at 33-34.

9. Ibid, at 47-48.

10. Mancur Olson, *The Logic of Collective Action* (Cambridge: Harvard University Press, 1965), at 2 (emphasis in original).

11. Ibid, at 36.

12. E.F. Schumacher, *Small Is Beautiful: Economics As If People Mattered* (New York: Harper & Row, 1973), at 38.

Chapter 7.

1. H.L. Mencken, *Minority Report: H.L. Mencken's Notebooks* (New York: Alfred A. Knopf, Inc., 1956), at 57.

2. For an interesting examination of primitive man's distrust of political power, see Pierre Clastres, *Society Against the State* (New York: Urizen Books, 1977).

3. From Thomas Hobbes, *Leviathan* (1651), reprinted in Ebenstein, supra, at 346.

4. Nock, supra, at 5.

5. The effect that minimum wage laws have had in producing unemployment—particularly among the young, the poor, and the unskilled—has been amply demonstrated. See, e.g., Brozen, "The Effect of Statutory Minimum Wage Increases on Teen-Age Unemployment," in 12 *The Journal of Law and Economics* (1969), at 109ff.; Benewitz and Weintraub, "Employment Effects of a Local Minimum Wage," in 17 *Industrial and Labor Relations Review* (1964), at 276ff.; Douty, "Some Effects of the $1.00 Minimum Wage in the United States," in 27 *Economica* (New Series, 1960), at 137ff.; Peterson, "Employment Effects of State Minimum Wages for Women: Three Historical Cases Re-Examined," in 12 *Industrial and Labor Relations Review* (1959), at 406ff.; Peterson, "Employment Effects of Minimum Wages: 1938-1950," in 65 *Journal of Political Economy* (1957), at 412ff.; and Stigler, "The Economics of Minimum Wage Legislation," in 36 *American Economic Review* (1946), at 358ff.

Chapter 8.

1. Nicolo Machiavelli, *The Prince* (1513), reprinted in Ebenstein, supra, at 286.

2. Randolph Bourne, *War and the Intellectuals* (New York: Harper & Row, 1964), at 71.

3. The quote is from the late Lane W. Lancaster, a former Professor of Political Science at the University of Nebraska.

4. *Report From Iron Mountain on the Possibility and Desirability of Peace* (New York: The Dial Press, 1967).

5. Ibid, at 29, 34, 44, 64.

6. Ibid, at 30, 57ff.

7. Ibid, at 57ff., 67.

8. From the movie *Holocaust,* written by Gerald Green, produced by Robert Berger, directed by Marvin Chomsky; a Herbert Brodkin Production.

9. Stanley Milgram, *Obedience to Authority* (New York: Harper & Row, 1974), at 188-189 (emphasis added).

10. There is irony in the fact that, after having finished the writing of this book—including my references to "the cookie cutter people"—I discovered that the Defense Department refers to the neutron bomb as "the cookie cutter."

11. For an extended treatment of human beings as servomechanisms, see Bertalanffy, supra.

12. Roszak, in Paul Goodman, ed., *Seeds of Liberation* (New York: George Braziller, 1964), at 450.

Chapter 9.

1. Henry James, ed., *The Letters of William James* (Boston: Little, Brown & Co., 1926), vol. II, at 90.

2. The costs to consumers of government regulation have been examined in Murray Weidenbaum's excellent study, *Government Mandated Price Increases: A Neglected Aspect of Inflation* (Washington: American Enterprise Institute for Public Policy Research, 1975).

3. Clair Wilcox, *Public Policies Toward Business* (Homewood, Ill.: Richard D. Irwin, Inc., 4th ed., 1971), at 8.

4. The economic self-serving nature of regulatory legislation has been developed in such works as Gabriel Kolko, *The Triumph of Conservatism* (New York: The Free Press, 1963); Gabriel Kolko, *Railroads and Regulation: 1877-1916* (Princeton: Princeton University Press, 1963); James Weinstein, *The Corporate Ideal in the Liberal State: 1900-1918* (Boston: Beacon Press, 1968); William Domhoff, *The Higher Circles* (New York: Random House, 1970); Michael Parrish, *Securities Regulation and the New Deal* (New Haven: Yale University Press, 1970); Robert Cuff, *The War Industries Board:Business-Government Relations During World War I* (Baltimore: The Johns Hopkins University Press, 1973); Murray Rothbard, *America's Great Depression* (Princeton: Van Nostrand, 1963); Ron Radosh and Murray Rothbard, eds., *A New History of Leviathan* (New York: E.P. Dutton & Co., 1972); Melvin Urofsky, *Big Steel and the Wilson Administration: A Study in Business-Government Relations* (Columbus: Ohio State University Press, 1969); James Gilbert, *Designing the Industrial State: The Intellectual Pursuit of Collectivism in America, 1880-1940* (Chicago: Quadrangle Books, 1972); Ellis Hawley, *The New Deal and the Problem of Monopoly* (Princeton: Princeton University Press, 1966); Robert Himmelberg, *The Origins of the National Recovery Administration* (New York: Fordham University Press, 1976); and my own soon-to-be-published manuscript, *In Restraint of Trade: Business Attitudes Toward Competition and Regulation, 1918-1938.*

5. Walter Adams, "The Military-Industrial Complex and the New Industrial State," in 58 *American Economic Review (Papers & Proceedings)*, May, 1968, at 652-65; reprinted in Ralph Andreano, ed., *Superconcentration/Supercorporation* (Andover, Mass.: Warner Modular Publications, Inc., 1973), at R337-2-3.

6. Gabriel Kolko, for example, has concluded:

> The dominant fact of American political life at the beginning of this century was that big business led the struggle for the federal regulation of the economy. If economic regulation could not be attained by mergers and voluntary economic methods, a growing number of important businessmen reasoned, perhaps political means might succeed. (Kolko, *Triumph of Conservatism*, supra, at 57-58.)

Or, as Myron Watkins has observed:

> From the time of President Theodore Roosevelt's second admin-
> istration there had been an insistent movement among certain
> industrial leaders for either a legislative or administrative defi-
> nition of an exact standard of competitive conduct. (Myron
> Watkins, *Public Regulation of Competitive Practices in Business Enter-
> prise* (New York: National Industrial Conference Board, 3rd
> ed., 1940), at 38.)

7. Quoted in *Nation's Business* (November, 1928), at 15.

8. For an interesting examination of government funding of industrial research and development, see H.L. Nieburg, *In the Name of
Science* (Chicago: Quadrangle Books, rev. ed., 1970), at 74ff.

9. Eighteenth and nineteenth century regulatory practices have
been examined in such works as Kolko, *Railroads and Regulation,*
supra; Charles A. Beard, *An Economic Interpretation of the Constitution
of the United States* (New York: The Free Press, 1965); F.W. Taussig,
The Tariff History of the United States (New York: G.P. Putnam's
Sons, 1892); Louis Hartz, *Economic Policy and Democratic Thought:
Pennsylvania, 1776-1860* (Chicago: Quadrangle Books, 1968).

10. See, e.g., Kolko, *Triumph of Conservatism,* supra; Arthur S.
Dewing, *Corporate Promotions and Reorganizations* (Cambridge: Harvard University Press, 1914); but cf., Alfred D. Chandler, *Strategy
and Structure: Chapters in the History of the Individual Enterprise* (Cambridge: Harvard University Press, 1977).

11. Dewing, ibid, at 546-547, 558.

12. Kolko, *Triumph of Conservatism,* supra, at 37-38, 46.

13. Laski, supra, at 9.

14. Ibid.

Chapter 10.

1. Robert G. Ingersoll, *The Ghosts and Other Lectures* (Washington: C.P. Farrell, Publisher, 1879), at 14-15; reprinted in *The Works of Robert Ingersoll* (New York: The Dresden Publishing Co., and C.P. Farrell, 1901), vol. I, at 270-271.

2. The Maryland legislation is referred to, ibid, vol. I, at 147.

3. H.L. Mencken, *Treatise on the Gods* (New York: Alfred A. Knopf, Inc., 1930), at 324.

4. Blaise Pascal, *Pensees,* sect. 14, no. 894 (1670).

5. From *Webster's Ninth New Collegiate Dictionary* (Springfield, Mass.: Merriam-Webster Inc., publishers of the Merriam-Webster Dictionaries, 1983), at 613.

6. Mark Twain, *Pudd'nhead Wilson*: *Pudd'nhead Wilson's Calendar* (1894), chap. 15.

7. Eric Hoffer, *The True Believer* (New York: North American Library, 1958; originally published New York: Harper & Bros., 1951).

8. Ibid, at 24.

Chapter 11.

1. Mencken, *Minority Report,* supra, at 282.

2. Socrates, *Apology,* 38.

3. Jacob Bronowski, *The Ascent of Man* (Boston: Little, Brown and Company, 1973), at 365.

4. Quoted in W.I.B. Beveridge, *The Art of Scientific Investigation* (New York: W.W. Norton & Company, rev. ed., 1957), at 34.

5. Story related in Kenneth Walker, *A Study of Gurdjieff's Teaching* (New York: Award Books, 1957), at 20.

6. Kenneth Boulding, *The Meaning of the Twentieth Century* (New York: Harper & Row, 1964), at 164.

7. Bernard de Mandeville, *The Fable of the Bees* (1714); reprinted, (New York: Capricorn Books, 1962), at 44-45.

8. Friedrich Nietzsche, "The Antichrist," sect. 44 (1888), in Walter Kaufmann, ed., *The Portable Nietzsche* (New York: Penguin Books, 1976), at 621 (emphasis in original).

9. Roszak, *Person/Planet,* supra, at 92.

10. H.L. Mencken, *A Mencken Chrestomathy* (New York: Alfred A. Knopf, Inc., 1967), at 624.

11. Friedenberg, supra, at 107.

12. David Paletz and William Harris, "Four-Letter Threats to Authority," in 37 *The Journal of Politics* (1975), at 965.

Chapter 12.

1. Roald Dahl, *Charlie and the Chocolate Factory* (New York: Alfred A. Knopf, Inc., 1964), at 85.

2. Mencken, *Chrestomathy,* supra, at 316.

3. Ivan Illich, in Alan Gartner, Colin Greer, and Frank Riessman, eds., *After Deschooling, What?* (New York: Harper & Row, 1973), at 8-9.

4. Ivan Illich, *Deschooling Society* (New York: Harper & Row, 1972), at 56.

5. See, e.g., Lysander Spooner, *The Constitution of No Authority* (Larkspur, Colo.: Pine Tree Press, 1966); originally published in

1870. For an excellent discussion of the intellectual structuring that occurs in law schools, see Duncan Kennedy, "Legal Education as Training for Hierarchy," in David Kairys, ed., *The Politics of Law: A Progressive Critique* (New York: Pantheon Books, 1982), at 40ff.

6. Illich, *Deschooling Society,* supra, at 163.

7. From a pamphlet "Laws for Youth," published by the County of Los Angeles, California (December, 1977), at 40.

8. From a pamphlet "Discipline and the Law," published by the Burbank (Calif.) Unified School District (1971, revised, July, 1980).

9. Laing, supra, at 58.

Chapter 13.

1. From Brooks Atkinson, ed., *The Selected Writings of Ralph Waldo Emerson* (New York: The Modern Library, 1950), at 434.

2. Lewis Carroll, *Alice Through the Looking-Glass* (1872), chap. 6.

3. For an interesting consideration of the relationship between equality and social structuring, see Elias Canetti, *Crowds and Power* (Hamburg: Claasen Verlag Hamburg, 1960; English translation copyrighted 1962, 1973, by Victor Gollancz, Ltd.), reprinted, (New York: Seabury Press, 1978).

4. E.E. Cummings, "Jottings," originally published in *The Harvard Wake* (1951), reprinted in E.E. Cummings, *Six Nonlectures* (Cambridge: Harvard University Press, 1962), at 70.

5. The "Handicapper-General" is found in Kurt Vonnegut, "Harrison Bergeron," in 21 *Magazine of Fantasy and Science Fiction* (October, 1961), at 5ff.

6. Rousseau, in Ebenstein, supra, at 425.

7. Roszak, *Person/Planet,* supra, at 14.

8. Epictetus, *The Discourses and the Manual,* (trans. by P.E. Matheson, Oxford: Oxford University Press, 1916), reprinted in Ebenstein, supra, at 148.

9. Frankl, supra, at 104, 106.

10. Laski, supra, at 10.

11. This quotation has been attributed to the late F.A. Harper.

12. Albert Schweitzer, *The Philosophy of Civilization* (New York: The Macmillan Company, 1957), at 292.

Chapter 14.

1. Robert Ingersoll, "Some Reasons Why" (written in 1881), reprinted in *The Works of Robert Ingersoll,* supra, vol. II, at 315.

2. Lewis Thomas, "Notes of a Biology Watcher: Germs," in 287 *The New England Journal of Medicine* (September 14, 1972), 553, at 554.

3. Bohm, Pribram, supra.

Chapter 15.

1. Anatole France, *The Crime of Sylvester Bonnard* (1881), chap. 4.

2. See, e.g., Edward S. Herman, *The Real Terror Network: Terrorism in Fact and Propaganda* (Boston: South End Press, 1982); Jonathan Kwitny, *Endless Enemies: The Making of an Unfriendly World* (New York: Congdon & Weed, Inc., 1984).

3. *United States v. Holmes,* 26 Fed. Cases 360 (No. 15383, C.C.E.D.Pa., 1842).

Chapter 16.

1. Epictetus, first quotation from *The Discourses and the Manual,* supra, reprinted in Ebenstein, supra, at 147; second quotation from John Bonforte, *The Philosophy of Epictetus,* tr. by Thomas W. Higginson (1865) (New York: Philosophical Library, 1955), at 92.

Chapter 17.

1. Rousseau, in Ebenstein, supra, at 423.

2. The phrase "perpetual war for perpetual peace" is taken from a book of that title, written by Harry Elmer Barnes (Caldwell, Ida.: Caxton Printers, 1953), a phrase Barnes attributed to the late historian Charles A. Beard.

3. E.E. Cummings, *Complete Poems: 1913-1962* (New York: Harcourt Brace Jovanovich, Inc., 1972; original copyright 1950), at 620.

4. Illich, *Deschooling Society,* supra, at 76.

5. Jantsch, supra, at 27-28, 40.

Chapter 18.

1. Mary Chase, *Harvey* (New York: Oxford University Press, 1953), Act 2, Scene 2; play originally copyrighted in 1943, under title *The White Rabbit; Harvey* copyrighted 1944, 1953, and renewed in 1971, 1972, 1981, by Mary Chase.

2. For an excellent account of this development, see Marilyn Ferguson, *The Aquarian Conspiracy* (Los Angeles: Tarcher Publishing, 1980).

3. See the continuing study conducted by the Center for Political Studies at the University of Michigan, in Arthur Miller, Thad

Brown, and Alden Raine, *Social Conflict and Political Estrangement*: *1958-1972* (Ann Arbor: University of Michigan Center for Political Studies).

4. Schumacher, Scott and Hart, supra; Alvin Toffler, *The Third Wave* (New York: William Morrow, 1980); Kirkpatrick Sale, *Human Scale* (New York: Coward, McCann & Geohegan, 1980). See, as well, Karl Hess, *Dear America* (New York: William Morrow, 1975); Richard Cornuelle, *De-Managing America* (New York: Random House, 1975); Richard Cornuelle, *Reclaiming the American Dream* (New York: Random House, 1965); and Harry Browne, *How I Found Freedom in an Unfree World* (New York: The Macmillan Co., 1973).

5. Regarding alternative home designs, see Farallones Institute, *The Integral Urban House*: *Self-Reliant Living in the City* (San Francisco: Sierra Club Books, 1979).

6. A poster attributes this quotation to Maria Montessori.

7. Abraham H. Maslow, *Toward a Psychology of Being* (Princeton: D. Van Nostrand Co., 1962).

8. Ferguson, supra, at 347-348.

Chapter 19.

1. Kenneth E. Boulding, "Post-Civilization," in Goodman, supra, at 23.

2. *Los Angeles Times,* July 16, 1979, part I, pages 1 (col. 6) and 14 (col. 1).

3. Elmer Rice, *The Adding Machine* (copyright by Elmer Rice, 1922, 1949), in *Seven Plays by Elmer Rice* (New York: The Viking Press, 1950), at 107.

4. The solution to this puzzle is:

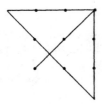

5. Schweitzer, supra, at 325.

6. Immanuel Kant, *Critique of Practical Reason and Other Writings in Moral Philosophy,* tr. and ed. by Lewis White Beck (Chicago: University of Chicago Press, 1949), at 87.

7. Theodore Roszak, *The Making of a Counter Culture* (Garden City: Anchor Books/Doubleday & Co., 1969), at 9.

8. Ibid, at 55.

9. Percy Bysse Shelley, *Ozymandias* (1817).

Printed in the United Kingdom
by Lightning Source UK Ltd.
105769UKS00001B/77